Gender, State and Society in Soviet and Post-Soviet Russia

Edited by Sarah Ashwin

London and New York

First published 2000
by Routledge
11 New Fetter Lane, London EC4P 4EE

Simultaneously published in the USA and Canada
by Routledge
29 West 35th Street, New York, NY 10001

Routledge is an imprint of the Taylor & Francis Group

Typeset in Sabon by Taylor & Francis Books Ltd
Printed and bound in Great Britain by TJ International Ltd, Padstow,
Cornwall

British Library Cataloguing in Publication Data
A catalogue record for this book is available from the British Library

Library of Congress Cataloging in Publication Data
Gender, state and society in Soviet and post-Soviet Russia/edited by
Sarah Ashwin.
Includes bibliographical references and index.
1. Sex role–Soviet Union. 2. Sex role–Russia (Federation). 3.
Communism and society–Soviet Union. 4. Communism and society–
Russia (Federation). 5. Soviet Union–Social conditions. 6. Russia
(Federation)–Social conditions–1991–. I. Ashwin, Sarah.
HQ1075.5.S65 G46 2000
305.3'0947–dc21   99-088907

ISBN 0–415–21488–2 (hbk)
ISBN 0–415–23883–8 (pbk)

Contents

Contributors

Sarah Ashwin is a lecturer in industrial relations at the London School of Economics. She has been conducting research on gender and employment in Russia since 1996, and is currently co-ordinating a project on male and female employment strategies during the transition. She is the author of *Russian Workers: The Anatomy of Patience* (Manchester University Press, 1999).

Olga Issoupova is a researcher at the Department of Methodology of the Institute of Sociology of the Russian Academy of Sciences, and a Ph.D. student at the Department of Sociology of the University of Manchester. Her thesis is an analysis of the social construction of motherhood in Soviet and post-Soviet Russia.

Marina Kiblitskaya is a researcher at the Moscow branch of the Institute for Comparative Labour Relations Research (ISITO). She recently obtained a Ph.D. from the Department of Sociology at the University of Warwick, which was based on a comparative analysis of the formal and informal relations of two enterprises, one British, one Russian, undergoing the process of privatisation. She is an experienced ethnographer and is currently working on a book on the experiences of single mothers during the economic transition in Russia.

Sergei Kukhterin is director of the Centre for Sociological Education at the Institute of Sociology of the Russian Academy of Sciences. He trained as a social psychologist and is an experienced researcher.

Elena Meshcherkina works at the Institute of Sociology of the Russian Academy of Sciences. She has been conducting life-history research for several years, initially within the framework of a Franco-Russian project directed by Professor Daniel Bertaux. She has published widely in Russian.

Elena Omel'chenko is vice-president of the Department of Advertising and Marketing at Ul'yanovsk State University. She has been conducting research on Russian youth culture for several years and has published widely in English and Russian. She has a candidate's degree in philosophy.

Irina Tartakovskaya is a researcher at the Sociological Laboratory of Samara Pedagogical Institute. Her candidate's dissertation for the Institute of Culture, Russian Academy of Sciences, was based on a qualitative analysis of cultural representations. She has researched and published articles about gender relations in the Russian workplace.

Acknowledgements

This volume is the product of a very enjoyable period of collaboration on the part of the contributors, which was facilitated by an INTAS grant (grant no. INTAS 95–0290). To use Soviet terminology, we were a very close 'collective', and our meetings always involved lots of laughter amid the discussion of hypotheses and papers.

The project would not have happened without Simon Clarke, who gathered the research team together and applied for the research grant. He has provided invaluable support throughout. Elain Bowers and Irina Aristarkhova, meanwhile, played an important role in initiating the project. As editor, I am also indebted to Anne White, Carol Wolkowitz, and the anonymous reviewer of the book proposal for his/her helpful comments, as well as to Caroline Wintersgill, formerly of UCL Press, for her support for the book.

On behalf of the Russian contributors, I would like to thank all the respondents who agreed to be interviewed as part of this project and were so open about their lives. I would also like to express gratitude to members and associates of the Institute for Comparative Labour Relations Research (ISITO) in Russia for allowing us access to their interview transcripts from other research projects.

A final note: all the chapters have been translated from Russian and edited by Sarah Ashwin, except for Chapter 7 which has been translated by John Andrew. Additional comments by the editor within chapters are marked '[SA]'.

Sarah Ashwin
August 1999

Introduction

Gender, state and society in Soviet and post-Soviet Russia

Sarah Ashwin

This is a book about gender relations and gender identities; it is not an analysis of the changing contours of women's oppression in communist and post-communist Russia. Its starting point is the premise that the Soviet state promoted and institutionalised a distinctive 'gender order'[1] which is now being reformulated in the present period of rapid change. The individual chapters within this book explore the nature of this Soviet gender order, and examine the implications of the collapse of communism for gender relations and gender identities in contemporary Russia.

Gender was always a key organising principle of the Soviet system. In the immediate post-revolutionary period, the Communist Party attempted to transform traditional patterns of gender relations in order to consolidate its rule. The disruption of the existing gender system was both a potent symbol of the triumph of the new regime and a means of undermining the social foundations of the old order. Later, as the regime strengthened its position, gender became the basis on which the duties of citizens to the new polity were defined: men and women had distinctive roles to play in the building of communism. In the case of women, their role was defined as worker-mothers who had a duty to work, to produce future generations of workers, as well as to oversee the running of the household. In return, they were to receive 'protection' from the state in their capacity as mothers, as well as independence through their access to paid work. Men, meanwhile, had an at once more limited and higher-status role to play. They were to serve as leaders, managers, soldiers, workers – in effect, they were to manage and build the communist system – while the state assumed responsibility for the fulfilment of the traditional masculine roles of father and provider, becoming, in effect, a universal patriarch to which both men and women were subject.[2] In this way, masculinity became socialised and embodied in the Soviet state, the masculinity of individual men being officially defined by their position in the service of that state.

As far as the Soviet era is concerned, this book aims to highlight the attempts of the communist authorities to construct a particular set of gender relations – a triangular set of relations in which the primary relationship of individual men and women was to the state rather than to each other. (The state was in effect the body to which the primary loyalty of citizens was due, even though this was generally expressed in other terms. It was more usual, and more palatable, to say that what should be given priority were the interests of the Communist Party, the communist cause, 'society', 'the collective', or the motherland.) The contributors to this volume also look at the men and women who were the subjects of the state's attention, analysing their active role in defining gender identities within the macro-parameters laid down by the state. Since it is clear that gender distinctions are developed, reproduced and modified *by both men and women*, this collection does not focus exclusively on the experience of women.

The same approach is used with regard to the post-Soviet era. The analysis of gender relations during the political transition proceeds from the idea that the collapse of the Soviet state has removed the institutional underpinning of the gender order forged in the Soviet era. Women are no longer guaranteed work outside the home and, at the same time, social benefits are being eroded and motherhood is being redefined as a private institution and responsibility. The corollary of this is that men are expected to reassume the traditional 'male' responsibilities which have now been abandoned by the state, but in a context in which real wages are falling and traditionally high-status male industries, such as mining, metallurgy and the military-industrial complex, have been particularly badly hit by the economic crisis. Meanwhile, the erosion of the material and institutional basis of old norms has been combined with a dramatic limitation of the prescriptive capacities and ambitions of the state in the post-communist era. This has enshrined a new pluralism in which competing visions of the desirable form of gender relations can be expressed. The implications of this are far from clear-cut, however. This book aims to identify and analyse the key dynamics amid this diversity.

Although the chapters of this book are written by individual researchers, all the papers have as a starting point the jointly elaborated conception of the Soviet gender order laid out above. This was initially developed in discussions between Elain Bowers, Simon Clarke, Irina Aristarkhova, Marina Kiblitskaya and myself at the University of Warwick, and Galina Monousova, Irina Tartakovskaya and Sergei Kukhterin in Moscow, and further elaborated in seminars including all the contributors to this book. The first stage of the research in Russia was made possible by a grant to Elain Bowers from the Nuffield Foundation, and the second stage, which has resulted in the articles presented here, was made possible by a grant from INTAS involving the collaboration of researchers from the University of Warwick, University of Bielefeld in Germany and various institutions in Russia. I co-ordinated this phase of the research. All the chapters are based on qualitative studies, each of which focuses on a different dimension of gender relations and identity.

Gender in the service of Soviet state power

The importance of gender relations and gender identity to the establishment of state authority and the exercise of state power has been recognised
in literature pertaining to other societies, but has not been sufficiently
appreciated with regard to the communist regimes of Eastern Europe and
the USSR.[3] State approaches to gender are usually defined with regard to
women, who are, as Floya Anthias and Nira Yuval-Davis have argued, 'a
special focus of state concerns as a social category with a specific role
(particularly human reproduction)' (Anthias and Yuval-Davis, 1989). In
their analysis of ethnicity and nationalism they identify five central ways in
which women act as the objects and agents of state practices: as biological
reproducers of members of ethnic collectivities; as reproducers of the
boundaries of ethnic/national groups; as central participants in the
ideological reproduction of the collectivity and as transmitters of its
culture; as signifiers of ethnic/national differences; and as participants in
national, economic, political and military struggles (ibid.: 7). This analysis
of the role of women in the formation and reproduction of nations (and, in
this case, polities) is very helpful with regard to understanding the Soviet
approach to gender. The communist authorities devoted noticeably more
attention to the role of women than they did to the role of men *as men* (as
opposed to as communists, workers or peasants). Anthias' and Yuval-
Davis' analysis would suggest that they did so not so much out of an
altruistic concern for women's welfare, but because the production of
future generations of communists was in women's hands and because
women played an important role in the Soviet symbolic system.

In the initial post-revolutionary period, however, the main role of
women was as *levers* through which the regime could gain increased
control over society. A similar idea has already been convincingly
expounded with regard to Soviet Central Asia by Gregory Massell in his
classic study, *The Surrogate Proletariat* (1974). He argued that here the
Bolsheviks sought to consolidate their rule through the use of women in
their capacity as

> a weak link in society, a relatively deprived and hence potentially
> deviant and subversive substratum susceptible to militant appeal, a
> *surrogate proletariat* where no proletariat in a Marxist sense existed.
> Given such a stratum it was conceivable that reliable native cadres
> could be recruited from it and used, first to loosen and disintegrate
> traditional social relationships, then to rebuild society when its very
> dissolution compelled reconstitution.
>
> (Massell, 1974: 76, emphasis in original)

Clearly, in Russia some sort of proletariat already existed, if a small
one. And women were not the only 'levers' exploited by the communist
regime – for example, the poor peasants were a good stick with which to

beat the Kulaks (rich peasants), and the means through which the Bolsheviks could extend their influence in rural areas. But attaining political control did not guarantee social and cultural control. Massell argues that in Soviet Central Asia the key to *cultural revolution* was the destruction of the pre-existing family and kinship system through the mobilisation of women (ibid.: 86). A comparable argument can be made with regard to Russia, in particular peasant Russia. Here, the only way to storm what Bukharin called 'the most conservative stronghold of the old regime' – the peasant household (Lapidus, 1978: 83) – was to exploit the status of women as the weak link.

Certainly, the most brutal example of the use of women as a means to further the cause of the revolution occurred in Soviet Central Asia. The campaign to promote the mass unveiling of Central Asian women, launched in autumn 1926, was dubbed by the authorities the *khudzhum* – a word which denoted 'all-out attack, sweeping advance, assault, storm' in all of the three main languages of Central Asia's cultural heritage, Turkish, Arabic and Persian (Massell, 1974: 229). The name of the policy reveals its main intention: it was conceived not in order to eradicate oppression and injustice, but as a means forcibly to enshrine a new culture and proclaim the triumph of Bolshevism over indigenous culture and religion. Nor was the policy formed with regard to the opinions of Central Asian women. Indeed, it was the local, predominantly male, communist elite who were to take the lead in the campaign, by ensuring that their female relatives were unveiled: this would show that their loyalty lay with the communists rather than with the traditional order (ibid.: 234–5). The extent to which women's wishes were taken into account can be gauged by the fact that in 1928 it was allowed that criminal charges could be brought against men perpetrating 'traditional' offences such as polygamy and underage marriage *regardless of the desires of the woman concerned* (ibid.: 313). Such compulsion threatened to put women's very lives at risk: Massell estimates that thousands of men and women died as a result of revenge attacks associated with the unveiling (ibid.: 282–3). It is therefore not surprising that the Central Asians experienced the campaign as a 'defeat and a brutal rape' (Akiner, 1997: 270). As Akiner reports, no other measure of Soviet policy in Central Asia – the closure of the mosques, the sedentarisation of the nomads, collectivisation or the purges – provoked such violent and outspoken resistance (ibid.: 271). This underlines Anthias' and Yuval-Davis' point about the crucial role of women in the ideological definition and reproduction of collectivities: both the perpetrators and the opponents of the campaign were well aware that the future of Central Asian society was at stake in the *khudzhum*.

The assault on tradition in Russia was not quite so brutal, but it was equally determined. Following Massell, this can be seen as taking the form of a concerted attack, followed by a period of reconstitution on communist-approved lines. Seeing Bolshevik gender politics in this way implies a break with what until recently have been the dominant approaches in the Soviet and Western literature. As Elizabeth Wood has argued, Soviet accounts tended to ask whether or not the Bolsheviks successfully 'solved' the woman question, while Western commentators have asked 'whether the Bolshevik motives were more "emancipatory" or "instrumental" ' (Wood, 1997: 3).[4] As she implies, this analytical framework fails to capture the way in which the Bolsheviks mobilised conceptions of gender to achieve the transformation of society. Once looked at from this point of view, it becomes clear that the policy of the Bolshevik state was never directed at the liberation of women from men, it was directed at breaking the subordination of women to the patriarchal family in order to 'free' both men and women to serve the communist cause. It may be that many communists believed that eventually this would result in liberation of the whole of the proletariat (and possibly the poorer peasants), but in the meantime the watchword of the new society was not liberation, but discipline.

What forms did the Bolshevik 'cultural revolution' take in Russia? The first step, as both Irina Aristarkhova and Elizabeth Wood have pointed out, was to highlight the necessity of action at a discursive level. Aristarkhova sees 'governmental problematization' of the family as a means of legitimising intervention in the private sphere. She argues that 'the Bolsheviks problematized women's position within the family, labour and society in order to subject them to the fulfilment of the communist order' (Aristarkhova, 1995: 22). Similarly, Wood argues that 'the perceived backwardness of the female population ... gave the Bolsheviks entrée into the most private of relationships, those between husband and wife, parent and child' (1997: 3). The backwardness of the family and of women was a subject on which all Bolshevik leaders could agree. Aleksandra Kollontai, the head of the Party's women's division until early 1922, argued that in the period of the dictatorship of the proletariat the family economic unit was 'not only useless but harmful' because its existence necessitated uneconomic 'expenditure on products and fuel' and 'unproductive labour, especially by women'. Moreover, the family was the site of women's oppression, and 'teaches and instills egotism' (Kollontai, [1921a] 1977: 226). Given these assumptions it is not surprising that she argued that, along with its twin evil of prostitution, 'under communism ... the contemporary family will disappear. Healthy, joyful and free relationships between the sexes will develop. A new generation will come into being ... a generation which places the good of the collective above all else' (Kollontai, [1921b] 1977: 275). Lenin, meanwhile, frequently worried about the effect of what he referred to as the 'most petty, most menial, most arduous, and most stultifying work of the kitchen and ... isolated domestic, family economy' (Lenin, [1921] 1937: 500) on women's political consciousness, claiming that in their backward state they were 'little worms which, unseen, slowly but surely rot and corrode' (Zetkin, 1934:

56–7, quoted in Lapidus, 1978: 74). Those who argue that Stalin sought to restore the traditional family should note the essential similarity of his sentiments regarding women and the family:[5]

> Working and peasant women are mothers who raise our youth – the future of our country. They can cripple the soul of youth. The healthy soul of our youth and the advancement of our country depends on whether the mother sympathises with the Soviet order or trails along behind the priest, kulak and bourgeois.
>
> (Quoted in Lapidus, 1978: 76)

While women were viewed as a potential brake on development, however, the revolutionary potential of transforming their status was also acutely perceived. It was addressing the 'woman question' which would give the Bolsheviks access to the private sphere and the chance to form 'a generation which places the good of the collective above all else'.

Another feature of gender relations which was subjected to 'governmental problematization' was the love and sexual attraction felt by couples. This was seen as detracting from the revolutionary struggle, as can be seen by the comments of Kollontai on the subject:

> In view of the need to encourage the development and growth of feelings of solidarity, it should above all be established that the isolation of the 'couple' as a special unit does not answer the interests of communism. ... The interests of the individual must be subordinated to the collective.
>
> (Kollontai, [1921a] 1977: 230)

> Modern love always sins because it absorbs the thoughts and feelings of the 'loving hearts' and isolates the loving pair from the collective.
>
> (Kollontai, [1923] 1977: 290)

Eric Naiman in his book *Sex in Public* has provided a brilliant analysis of the anxiety of the Bolsheviks regarding issues of sexuality in the 1920s. The relatively liberal New Economic Policy was a compromise which was hard for many Bolsheviks to swallow – they were, after all, members of a party defined by revolutionary impatience. Their anguish about the postponement of utopia, Naiman argues, expressed itself in 'a particular dread of erotic urges' (1997: 15), which became a 'symbolic shorthand for all forms of contamination' (ibid.: 16) feared by the regime. Thus, nearly all commentators in the early and mid-1920s (including Lenin) spoke about sex in a language dominated by images of dissolution: words beginning with the prefix indicating this in Russian (*raz/ras*) were repeatedly intoned. The polity was threatened by *razvrat* (depravity), *raspushchennost'* (dissipation), *razlozhenie* (decay/decomposition) (ibid.:

116). Naiman's argument regarding the function of this obsessive discussion of sex is very similar to that laid out above with regard to women and the family. He contends that the 'infiltration of private life' was achieved 'by means of a "debate" on sexuality, the conquest of Eros by his own arrows' (ibid.: 123).[6]

The 1920s thus saw a thoroughgoing incursion into private life at a discursive level. How was this translated into action? Early Bolshevik legislation can be seen as a key mechanism through which such intrusion was facilitated. The 1918 Code of Laws concerning the Civil Registration of Deaths, Births and Marriages is a prime example of this. The Code, among other things, abolished the inferior position of women under the law; set up local bureaux of statistics for the civil registration of marriage, divorce, birth and death; gave legal status to civil marriage only; permitted divorce; abolished illegitimacy and gave all children equal rights, and allowed women to retain full control over their property and earnings after marriage. Both Buckley and Goldman see these provisions as evidence of the regime's initial commitment to women's liberation: indeed, Goldman proclaims the Code as 'the most progressive family and gender legislation the world had ever seen', through which 'centuries of property law and male privilege were swept away' (Goldman, 1989: 62). In contrast, Aristarkhova perceives it as a key plank of the Bolshevik drive to establish their control over society. The Code, she argues, was explicitly designed to undermine the competing authority of the church – marriages registered in church became illegal – and to assert the position of the Bolsheviks as the 'REAL power ... because now people, in order to be registered and, thus, get personal documents, had to go to the Bolshevik official civil authorities' (Aristarkhova, 1995: 16). The Code proclaimed a break with past institutions at the same time as permitting the new regime to exercise 'positive control over the population through the introduction of registration/inventory' (ibid.: 16).

It also had enormous implications for the 80 per cent of the population who were peasants: the Code's provisions were 'strikingly at odds with the economy and social customs of the village' (Goldman, 1989: 63), presenting a deliberate challenge to the collective principle of the peasant household and the patrilocal focus of social relations in the countryside. As Goldman herself notes, the Code generated a good deal of conflict and resistance: 'Peasant men and women frequently resented the imposition of a "foreign" morality, and opposed the laws on divorce and alimony for clear economic reasons' (ibid.: 75–6). While Goldman stresses that 'a small but significant minority' of peasant women 'eagerly embraced' the changes (ibid.: 67), the family code and the subsequent 1926 Code of Laws on Marriage, the Family and Guardianship[7] cannot be seen as a response to the expressed needs of women: indeed, Goldman's own evidence belies her assertion that these codes were developed 'in dynamic relation to material conditions, local interests, and the activities and opinions of working-class and peasant women' (ibid.: 61). Rather, these changes were imposed on a peasantry with good reasons for recalcitrance: the laws were designed to undermine the existing form of the peasant household which was regarded by Bolsheviks as the epitome of backwardness, a cradle of subversion, a remnant of the past which had to be transformed. The struggle for the all-important allegiance of peasant women was strikingly reflected in the lyrics of a popular village song of the 1920s: 'Now that we have Soviet Power/My husband I don't fear' (Stites, 1978: 366). Evidently, the Bolshevik attempts to embolden women and thereby subvert the traditional family had an impact, for village studies of the 1920s highlighted the incidence of generational struggles, fragmentation of families and insurrection of wives and daughters. Whatever may have been the personal gains made by individuals during this period, it is clear that the 'liberation' of peasant women, like the unveiling of Muslim women, had as its wider aim the subjection of the peasantry to the Bolshevik will.[8]

The Zhenotdel, the women's department which was created in 1919 with the aim of spreading the message of the Communist Party to women, can be analysed in similar terms. The Zhenotdel had local branches attached to Party committees at every level of the hierarchy which were charged with organising and propagandising among women through meetings, distribution of Party publications, the establishment of reading rooms and literacy programmes, and the election of representatives to take part in 'delegate meetings' which served as 'a continuous school in politics and liberation' (ibid.: 337). The local branches of the Zhenotdel also performed a number of other functions such as child and orphan care, food distribution, housing supervision and public health promotion. Wendy Goldman has argued that, 'Historians searching for the precise historical moment when the Party officially and explicitly jettisoned its commitment to a revolutionary vision of women's liberation need look no further than 5 January 1930' – the day the politburo eliminated the Zhenotdel (Goldman, 1996: 77). Goldman bases her case for seeing the Zhenotdel as feminist on its members' dogged advocacy of a transformation of *byt* (everyday life) through the socialisation of domestic drudgery. But other historians have viewed the same evidence in a different light. Michelle Fuqua sees the Zhenotdel's quest for a '*novyi byt*' (new domestic life) as a means of extending the scope of the public sphere at the expense of the private, by bringing women's domestic role under the control of the state (Fuqua, 1996: 9–10).[9] If Lenin is to be believed, Fuqua's interpretation gets closer to the truth. He insisted that the women's department was *not* inspired by 'bourgeois "feminism" ' but by 'practical revolutionary expediency': the Zhenotdel was under the strict control of the Party and had the aim of 'rousing the broad masses of women, bringing them into contact with the Party and keeping them under its influence' (Lenin, n. d.: 106, quoted in Stites, 1978: 341).[10] Self-emancipation was clearly not on the Bolsheviks' agenda. Rather, as Fuqua shows, the significance of the

Zhenotdel lay in the use of gender politics as a means of spreading the Bolshevik word, of gaining access to and mobilising a key section of the population in the service of the new state,[11] and of extending the sphere of state control into the private household.[12]

What the above examples all highlight is that, while the greater or lesser liberation of women in different spheres of their lives may or may not have been the outcome of Bolshevik policies, at no time was this the direct focus of Soviet social policy, nor was it the focus of debate within the Party. As already mentioned, the undermining of tradition was to be followed by a period of transformation, in which institutions such as the family would be reconstituted along communist lines. In reality, it is hard to separate out these two phases – partly because the traditional family was never fully destroyed – but provisionally the reconstruction of society in the desired image of the Bolsheviks can be seen as taking place in the second half of the 1930s. This means that the supposed 'resurrection' of the family in the Stalin era should not be viewed as a conservative retreat which curtailed the revolutionary potential of the 1920s.[13] Rather, what occurred was an attempt to recreate the family as a specifically *Soviet* family, which, instead of serving as a 'conservative stronghold of the old regime', would become a functional unit in the new polity. Seeing the Stalinist attitude to the family in this way resolves the apparent contradiction identified by Robert Thurston (1991) – that is, the fact that the regime seemed simultaneously determined to undermine family loyalties in pursuit of the goal of 'atomisation', while at the same time strengthening the family through the restrictions on divorce and abortion introduced in 1935 and 1936. The way of solving this paradox is to understand that the regime accepted the family, but only in its reconstituted form as the primary cell of Soviet society. This implied that citizens – while allowed to remain in families – had to be constantly reminded that their primary duty was to the state. The cult of the arch-betrayer of blood-ties, Pavlik Morozov, was the most visible example of the latter tendency.[14]

As will be seen below, the official vision of the reconstituted Soviet man, woman and family contained many contradictions. It is these contradictions at the heart of the Soviet approach to gender, and not fluctuations in the level of commitment to the principles of equality and liberation, which underlie the later twists and turns in policy. The following two sections consider the roles prescribed for women and men within the new Soviet family and polity.

Worker-mothers: women's role in the new order

The two main implications of the Bolshevik project for women concerned work and motherhood. Women's labour participation was integral to the Bolshevik political project in a number of ways. It was one thing to undermine the traditional family and the private subordination of women, but this would only have the desired effect if women could be found a new role and a new arena of social integration. Establishing a direct link between the state and women was highly problematic: the Zhenotdel can be seen as an attempt to do this, but as such it proved relatively ineffective and, in addition, provoked serious social conflict. The answer, already at the heart of Marxist orthodoxy, was the integration of women into society through their participation in social labour. Thus, women would be liberated from the patriarchal family and transferred from private dependence on men to the 'protection' of the Soviet state. This would moreover serve to remove children from the potentially 'backward' influence of their parents: women would henceforth bring up the children not of the private man but of the socialist state. This logic is quite clear in the work of Kollontai: 'The woman in Communist society no longer depends upon her husband, but on her work. It is not in her husband but in her capacity for work that she will find support. She need have no anxiety about her children. The workers' state will assume responsibility for them' (Kollontai, [1919] 1977: 258–9). Thus, participation in work outside the home would transform women's consciousness and render them more amenable to control by the state. Work was seen as a vital form of socialisation and over time the labour collective[15] became the primary locus of social integration within Soviet society for both women and men (Ashwin, 1999a). In addition, the labour power of women was obviously crucial to the project of industrialisation and 'catching up with and overtaking' the West. During the economic dislocation of the NEP (New Economic Policy) period, female unemployment was a major problem, and the Zhenotdel faced the question of how to ensure that women did not fall out of the Party's sphere of influence (Fuqua, 1996: 24). But in the 1930s women became a key source of new labour during the industrialisation drive, and thereafter their role in social production only increased.[16] In this sense, the problem of female integration into the Soviet polity – the essence of the 'woman question' from a communist perspective – was certainly 'solved' by Stalin.

The redefinition of motherhood was also integral to the Bolshevik project. Initially, this was linked to the plan of wrenching open the despised privacy of the family through the transfer of domestic functions from the private to the public sphere. Alongside plans for public canteens, laundries and 'special clothes-mending centres' (Kollontai, [1919] 1977: 255), the idea of 'child colonies' was also mooted. Kollontai, for example, looked forward to the day when 'children will grow up in the kindergarten, the children's colony, the crèche and the school under the care of experienced nurses. When the mother wants to see her child she only has to say the word; and when she has no time, she knows they are in good hands' (Kollontai, [1914] 1977: 134). During the 1920s, revolutionary plans for the complete socialisation of childcare were gradually abandoned for practical reasons, but the maternal role remained a central political issue. In place of full communal childcare, mothers were to act as mediators between the state and the child, with fathers, their role symbolically and materially appropriated by the state, banished to the margins of the new Soviet family. Thus, the endorsement of the family in the Stalin era should not be understood as a conservative reaction, but rather, within the limits imposed by material circumstances, as defining a *new* form of family relations. The politicisation of motherhood and childhood in the 1920s and 1930s is analysed in Olga Issoupova's chapter in this book (see Chapter 1), which highlights the way in which the authorities sought to forge an alliance with mothers through their definition of motherhood as a noble and rewarded service to the state, rather than as a private matter proceeding from the relationship between husbands and wives. Through her analysis of the Stalinist vision of the new Soviet family Issoupova reveals the continuity in policy between the 1920s and 1930s.

The Bolshevik emphasis on motherhood also reveals one of the central contradictions of Bolshevik gender politics: although it was a politics of social transformation it was premised on an entirely traditional view of 'natural' sexual difference. This shows how far the Bolshevik conception of gender was from any kind of feminism: all that interested the regime was that men and women serve the state in the way implied by their assumed 'natural' characteristics. Thus, it was taken for granted that mothers had a distinct biologically defined role which extended beyond birth and breast-feeding. The assumption of natural sexual difference persisted throughout the Soviet era, and informed both the terms on which women were integrated into the labour force (as second-class workers),[17] and what was expected of them as mothers. Correspondingly, while the Bolsheviks initially intended to transfer domestic functions from the private to the public sphere, the domestic realm was still very much seen as women's 'natural' responsibility. This is strikingly illustrated by Lenin's comments on the liberation of women from what he called their 'domestic slavery': 'We are establishing model institutions, dining rooms and crèches, which will liberate women from housework. And it is precisely the women who must undertake the work of building these institutions ... women workers themselves should see to the development of such institutions' (Lenin, [1919] 1937: 496–7). Even Kollontai shared the idea that the sexes should be assigned to 'different spheres of work' on account of 'their distinctive characteristics and qualities' (quoted in Naiman, 1997: 83). Clearly, whether it was conducted privately or publicly, domestic work was perceived as inalienably feminine by the Bolshevik elite. Thus, given that outside the realm of childcare the network of public domestic services remained woefully inadequate throughout the Soviet era, women were left with a substantial domestic burden to contend with in addition to their paid work. As the essays in this collection reveal, this combination of radicalism and tradition in the Bolshevik conception of gender roles found its echo in the lives of Soviet men and women, who were confronted with the conflicting imperatives of established and revolutionary norms (the latter of which were themselves contradictory).

Masculinity in the service of the state

Bolshevik policy with regard to women implied stripping men of their traditional role and authority, which was in turn assumed by the state. But, since traditional gender roles were not questioned, male dominance was still regarded as the norm – its legitimate expression was simply confined to the public sphere. Thus, men were encouraged to realise themselves in their work – that is, their self-realisation was to have a public character which coincided with the purposes of the regime; they were to serve the state as workers or soldiers. And, notwithstanding the encouragement of female labour participation, they were provided with abundant opportunities to realise themselves in this way: throughout the Soviet era they dominated in the most powerful, highest status and best remunerated positions in all spheres of society, while the more unpleasant male occupations, such as mining, were generally accorded a heroic status in compensation for hardships endured. (The same cannot be said for comparable female occupations.) The importance of this public recognition to Soviet masculine identity is highlighted in the chapters of Marina Kiblitskaya and Elena Meshcherkina.

While the state gave unambiguous tacit support to male dominance in the public sphere, the instrumental use of women as agents of social transformation in the 1920s implied a direct challenge to male authority. Moreover, as Sergei Kukhterin's chapter illustrates (see Chapter 3), it was experienced as such. Meanwhile, what was eventually defined as the approved role of women within the Soviet polity also posed a threat to the private power of men. First, the fact that women were drawn into social production *en masse* influenced private gender relations by giving women greater economic and social independence from men. Second, the politicisation of motherhood, and relative neglect of fatherhood, legitimised women's control over their children and undermined the position of men within the family. Third, in a number of ways the state added its authority to female attempts to control male behaviour: even after the 1920s it continued to use women as disciplining agents in its struggle for cultural transformation. In the endless war against drunkenness, for example, women were often portrayed and deployed as allies of the state in the struggle for sobriety. As Trotsky argued, 'the first place must be taken by women' in the struggle against drunkenness, 'for nothing bears so hard upon the working woman, and especially upon the working mother, as drunkenness' (Trotsky, [1926] 1973: 187–8).[18] Similarly, women were the key actors in the campaign for *kul'turnost'* (a raised cultural level) during the Stalin era. For example, the *obshchestvennitsy* (women activists, most of whom were members of the 'movement of wives'), a group who came to prominence in the late 1930s, were supposed, among other things, to do battle against 'uncultured behaviour' in their husbands' workplaces and at home. An *obshchestvennitsa* had to regulate her husband's behaviour: 'good workers were not absent or late and wives had to check this bad practice' (Buckley, 1996: 573).[19] Meanwhile, during the same period the Party and press would frequently expose instances of male abuse of women and castigate the men concerned (Kotkin, 1995: 189).[20] Thus, the role accorded to women as transmitters of the new ideology and culture, along with hostility to the privacy of the family, served to enhance the private position of women, albeit within a framework in which a 'natural' division of labour was assumed and endorsed. This contrasts with the practice of many conservative regimes, in particular theocracies, where men's private control over women is seen as a crucial buttress of the existing order: gender is likewise used as an organising principle of state power but the state's alliance is with men rather than with women.[21]

The second component of the communist challenge to traditional male authority was its attempt to define a new form of masculine identity based on work rather than on private patriarchal power. This shift sought to reconcile Soviet power with supposedly natural male dominance and was manifested in a noticeable ambivalence on the part of the regime concerning the traditional role of men as husbands and fathers. As the chapters in this volume by Issoupova and Kukhterin illustrate, the state was a somewhat jealous guardian of its patriarchal role. The regime's ambivalence about the traditional roles of men as husbands and fathers can be briefly illustrated here by reference to visual media not dealt with in this collection. As regards relations between individual men and women, what emerges from Aristarkhova's analysis of Soviet photography from the revolution to the late 1930s is the strict separation of women and men: women are portrayed at work or with children, men are shown at work, but the two sexes are rarely shown together in the private sphere (Aristarkhova, 1995: 9–14). This underlines the fact that fundamental to the Soviet approach to gender was that the relationship of women and men to the state was to take priority over their private relations with each other. Meanwhile, there are many examples of Stalin's symbolic appropriation of the role of husband and father. Susan Reid, for instance, provides a very interesting analysis of Vasilii Efanov's famous painting 'An unforgettable meeting' (1937), which depicts an *obshchestvennitsa* being congratulated by Stalin. The *obshchestvennitsa* 'is characterised in relation to Stalin the patriarch in two subordinate roles at once: child and blushing bride' (Reid, 1998: 157), while Molotov is positioned in such a way that he can be seen as presiding over the 'symbolic marriage between the party leadership and feminized masses' (ibid.: 158). Katerina Clark provides a similar analysis of Soviet literature, arguing that between 1928 and 1931 the 'kinship model' portrayed by Soviet literature was of a fraternal community, with Stalin as prophet. By late 1935 this model had been transformed into that of a hierarchy of fathers and sons, with Stalin as the ultimate father (Clark, 1977: 182). The heroes of the Soviet Union, such as the Stakhanovites, could sometimes attain the status of honorary father but most 'sons would not grow into fathers: rather they should be perfected as model sons. The burden of paternity was to fall on the very few' (ibid.: 93). Clark's analysis has been extended into the realm of cinema by Haynes, who illustrates it with his commentary on Dziga Vertov's 1937 film *Lullaby* (*Kolybel'naya*), which features contented Soviet women at work, rest and play with their infant children. Fathers are notable for their absence until, at the end of the film, the one true father, Stalin, appears (Haynes, 1996: 37).

This symbolic sidelining of men within the private sphere was not, of course, without consequences. As will be explored in the chapters by Kiblitskaya and Kukhterin, individual Soviet men certainly experienced anxiety and uncertainty about their role which expressed itself in a number of ways.

Contradictions of the Bolshevik legacy

After the Second World War, the contradictions at the heart of the Soviet approach to gender were thrown into relief. The abandonment of mass terror as a routine tool of government meant that the voluntary compliance of citizens became increasingly important to the functioning of Soviet society. One of the ways in which such compliance was to be secured was through the inculcation of 'communist morality', according to which citizens would subordinate their own interests to those of the state – which in practical terms meant that they would work hard and lead orderly personal lives within stable family units. But Soviet citizens showed a worrying unwillingness or inability to harmonise personal and social interests, something which, according to Soviet moralists, they should have been able to do 'without special difficulty' (Field, 1998: 603). The contradictions of the gender order put in place during the Stalin era can be seen as a key reason for this failure.

First, women had been sent out to work, and constituted over half the labour force in 1945. But after the enormous losses of the war the regime faced the task of re-population.[22] The ongoing campaign to induce women to produce more children while working full-time thus continued, but with less recourse to coercion (the 1936 ban on abortion was lifted in 1955). This tension between the demographic and economic priorities of the state was never resolved. Meanwhile, there was also a problem with men. They were supposed to realise themselves in the public sphere, success at work being the key to their social status. But, the regime belatedly decided, the disruption of the patriarchal order through women's independence and engagement in work was having a disastrous impact on the morale and motivation of the male worker. The authorities were not going to release women from their duty to work, however, and they could therefore do little to remedy the situation aside from encouraging female sensitivity to the male plight. This, it seemed, had little impact, for what also became increasingly apparent in the post-Second World War era was that the roles laid down for women and men did not make for happy families – the prevalence of divorce revealed that a cancer was spreading through the 'primary cells' of Soviet society.

The nature of the post-Second World War attempt to reconcile the roles of Soviet men and women is captured excellently in Vera Dunham's study of middle-class values in Soviet fiction. After the war, she argues:

> Woman ... was halted. Contradictory demands were now made of her. She was to continue to work and hymn the glory of her fulfilment in the public arena, but not excessively and not as much as previously. The proper balance was tricky. She was to hold the family together, to comfort her shellshocked husband and to support his aspirations.
>
> (ibid.: 214)

Thus, the fiction of this era presented the public success of a woman as problematic if it served to undermine the masculinity of the man with whom she was involved.[23] The musings of the husband about the eponymous protagonist in the novel of *kolkhoz* life, *Marya*, exemplify this dilemma. He has returned from the war, and in his absence his wife has become chair of the *kolkhoz*:

> Marya, she moves about, gives orders. And the more she gives orders, the more she grows, even in his eyes. And the more she grows, the smaller he gets. And she, she does not care. She wants to fly on the wings of her thoughts through the whole world. And she flies. She wants to read and she sits there burning the midnight oil. And it seems she needs her husband and then again it seems she does not.
>
> (ibid.: 216)

Marya is taken to task by the Party secretary who discovers that, sensitive to the charge of nepotism, she has given her husband a job trucking manure. Marya is effectively ordered by the secretary to restore her husband's public power: 'He needs work! Work that will engage all of his soul!' (ibid.: 217). As Dunham notes, in an earlier era a 'lagging' spouse would have been urged to catch up (ibid.: 200); in contrast, the literature of the post-war era is informed by a recognition that it is difficult for men to perform publicly if they are privately undermined. The means of resolving the dilemma is neatly identified in the tale *Agricultural Workers*, which is based on a true story. Shura, an enthusiastic and successful agronomist, marries a veteran officer who, embarking on a new career in agriculture, becomes her deputy. She is clear about the need to support him and lays down the following conditions before their marriage: ' "At work, I am your chief. Mind you don't resent it. But at home, if you want to, I'll submit to you". But when she thought it over, she refined her statement: "But at home, we'll be equals".' At home, she encourages him with his studies, and urges him to catch up and overtake her, and for a particular reason: 'Come along, help me out, catch up. I can't be the boss forever. I'll be having children' (ibid.: 223). This fictional resolution neatly dovetailed with the demographic priorities of the state in the post-war devastation – the problem was that women were not necessarily inclined to follow role models such as the self-sacrificing Shura.

Since urging greater consideration on the part of women did not prove to be a panacea, concern that prescribed Soviet gender roles somehow did not fit together in the desired way was only amplified in the Brezhnev era. Women in the Slavic republics were still not reproducing at the required rate – by the 1970s a 'demographic crisis' was proclaimed[24] – while men were perceived to be becoming damagingly feminised (Lapidus, 1978: 326). In the 1970s and 1980s the press took up a cause which had been current in academic circles in the 1960s about the need to return to 'traditional' sex roles. Journalists were particularly eloquent on the masculinisation of the female personality and the feminisation of the male, and there was a vogue for publishing letters from regretful 'masculinised' women and downtrodden men (Attwood, 1990: 166–9). The Soviet woman, it was claimed, was resentful of weak husbands since she 'finds her own supremacy an unnatural deviation from the rule. She wants to be weak' (*Literaturnaya gazeta*, 10 October 1984, quoted in Attwood, 1990: 168). At the same time as lamenting the erosion of private male authority, however, the same organs continued to emphasise the importance of women's work and to glorify motherhood, as opposed to parenthood, thus legitimising the sources of women's private power and their independence from men. Indeed, this was pointed out by G. Bragrazyan, who charged journalists with 'praising women to the hilt, almost singing hymns to their honour, and letting fathers slip to the periphery of our consciousness' (*Pravda*, 2 September 1984, quoted in Attwood, 1990: 168). This tension between 'communist' and traditional ethics is neatly captured by Irina Tartakovskaya's analysis of the press in 1984 in Chapter 6. While articles in the youth newspaper *Komsomol'skaya Pravda* tended to situate worker-mothers in a world devoid of men where they could give unconditional devotion to the state, its more conservative counterpart, *Sovetskaya Rossiya*, endorsed a more traditional model of the family with the worthy male worker at its head. This difference in emphasis reflected an unresolved problem in official policy. On the one hand, women were implicitly encouraged to give priority to work and motherhood – their twin duties to the state – but on the other, the authorities became increasingly aware that men were not flourishing in a world of 'masculinised' women.

Soviet and traditional values: the tensions in the lives of Soviet men and women

The contradictions in official thinking were not merely of theoretical significance, for what the interview-based studies in this collection reveal is the way in which they found their expression in the perceptions, behaviour, conflicts and frustrations of individual men and women formed within the Soviet system. The evidence presented in several chapters in this volume shows that the gender relations and identities of the Soviet era tended to reflect the combination of traditionalism and radicalism in Bolshevik ideology, and that this was often a cause of tension.

For example, the idea that the gender identities fostered within the Soviet system were somehow 'unnatural' was not simply something dreamt up by the authorities. As Marina Kiblitskaya shows in Chapter 2, this was a feeling shared by many Soviet women. Her female 'breadwinners by default' of the post-Second World War era, for instance, were furious about having to take over the role of main provider in their families. Kiblitskaya's account highlights two important components of Soviet gender relations: first, the frequent disengagement of Soviet men from domestic life, and, second, the traditionalism of women's expectations. Despite the fact that women worked, they wanted men to take on the role of *kormilets* (breadwinner). This, Kiblitskaya argues, resulted from the fact that men were always paid more than women in the Soviet Union, and thus the idea that it was 'natural' for men to be the main providers was never challenged. (Soviet wage scales and pensions, however, were not designed to support a family of dependants on a single income (Lapidus, 1988: 92–3).) Given that their expectations of men were based on ideals from an earlier era, it is not surprising that women were often disappointed by men socialised in Soviet society.

Meanwhile, as far as men were concerned, a key problem was the relationship between their private and public roles. The public sphere was a site in which male domination was legitimised by the regime, but a man's dominance at home was dependent on his position at work rather than simply his sex. As Sergei Kukhterin shows in Chapter 3, this created problems for men who were in humiliating positions at work. In terms of masculine self-definition virtually all that was left open to them was the camaraderie of all-male company, usually involving drink, and the direct domination of women. Moreover, as Elena Meshcherkina shows (see Chapter 5), humiliation and subordination at work were not confined to the lower levels of the occupational ladder: they were products of the hierarchical rigidity of the Soviet system and were experienced at all levels. In this sense, it is no wonder that far from being regarded as wielders of unlimited patriarchal power, Soviet men were often perceived and portrayed as *weak*: inappropriately feminine, drunk, irresponsible, shiftless.

What above all comes through in the interview material presented in this collection is the way in which the gender identities formed in the Soviet era were in conflict with each other. For example, to return to the concept of the male *kormilets*, a continual source of conflict was the fact that men and women perceived the role in a different light. As far as men were concerned, being the main breadwinner was what defined their autonomy: keeping back a section of their earnings (the '*zanachka*' or '*karmannye den'gi*') was important to their masculine identity. (It allowed a man to socialise with his co-workers and demonstrated that he was not under his wife's thumb.) Meanwhile, however, the ideal *kormilets* in the minds of women was a man who pooled his income and eschewed drinking with his workmates: he was a model of sobriety and responsibility. As Kiblitskaya shows, this conflict over different conceptions of the traditional male role caused enormous tension – in particular since it occurred in the Soviet context in which a man's word was no longer law and women had greater potential to protest against their partners' shortcomings.

What resulted from such conflict was prolonged trench warfare and uncomfortable stand-offs: there were no winners.[25] Perceived from the perspective of the state or their wives, men may well have looked 'weak', but this did not mean they could be bullied into changing their behaviour. Part of the reason for this, Kiblitskaya suggests in Chapter 2, is that women's traditional assumptions regarding the role of men acted as a form of self-limitation. For example, since women accepted that it was their duty to run the household, it was difficult even for female breadwinners to attain the kind of engagement in the domestic sphere which they desired from their spouses.[26] Thus, the paradoxical legacy of the Soviet era can be seen as strong, independent women who nevertheless ended up doing all the housework, and weak, 'feminine' men who none the less had the autonomy to relax, drink and escape the domestic arena.

Gender after Soviet rule

The collapse of the Soviet state has enormous implications for gender relations in Russia. The institutional and ideological underpinnings of Soviet-approved gender relations and identities have been removed: work and motherhood are no longer defined as duties to the state; the traditional family has been rehabilitated, and the state no longer monopolises the patriarchal role. Meanwhile, no clear alternative model is being imposed from above: as Irina Tartakovskaya shows in Chapter 6, there is widespread confusion and anxiety regarding the evolution of gender relations in post-Soviet Russia. This has introduced a new ingredient to the already explosive mixture of tradition and radicalism which characterised Soviet gender culture: Western norms and values, with their own set of ambiguities and inconsistencies regarding the proper role of men and women. The new plurality has only intensified the sense of normative uncertainty which characterises the post-communist era.

There has been a tendency to consider the collapse of communism in terms of a balance sheet of losses and gains for women, in a way which recalls the approach of the commentators who sought to determine whether or not the revolution liberated women.[27] This approach is unable to capture the uncertainty and conflicts over gender roles that the demise of the Soviet state has set in train, and it also ignores the fact that men as well as women are challenged by the end of the Soviet era. The contributions to this book aim to identify the main lines of conflict and sources of uncertainty, although it is too early precisely to predict the outcomes of contemporary struggles over the form of gender relations and identities in the new Russia. What is beyond question is that the Soviet model of gender relations is now deeply contested and its inconsistencies ever more visible. This section begins by looking at the implications for women, followed by the implications for men and young people.

What are the implications of the collapse of communism for women? First, in terms of work, the fact that the state is no longer committed to maintaining women's employment raises a number of questions. Soviet women clearly bore a very heavy burden and often worked in appalling conditions. But this does not necessarily imply that they want to be liberated from what was once a state-imposed obligation. As Kiblitskaya shows in Chapter 2, women are playing a key role in keeping many households afloat in the transition era, and are committed to their work and public role. Unless they are forced to do so, women are not simply going to leave the jobs for the boys as unemployment mounts, in the way that some contemporary politicians hope.[28] Indeed, women are showing a remarkable determination to hold on to their jobs. Despite widespread discrimination in the labour market, according to the most recent labour force survey there are still roughly equal proportions of men and women unemployed: in October 1998 the count was 13.7 per cent of men, and 13.3 per cent of women (Goskomstat, 1999: 28). Meanwhile, women's employment (labour participation rate) has fallen by almost exactly the same amount as men's: 8.3 per cent, as against 8.1 per cent for men (ibid.: 8). Since women are not going to leave the labour force voluntarily, it is possible that the labour market will increasingly become the site of competition between the sexes.

Meanwhile, the other element of women's duty to the Soviet state – motherhood – is being redefined as a private institution and responsibility. While during the Soviet era women tended to see having children as a useful and valued service to society[29] now, as Issoupova points out in Chapter 1, they are being taught that 'only you need your child'. The corollary of this is that the state will no longer assume responsibility for the welfare and care of the child. This, combined with the comprehensive destruction of the financial security of the past in the reform era, has undermined the independence of women within the reproductive sphere. Meanwhile, as Issoupova's review of the contemporary press reveals, on a discursive level the role of the father has been completely rehabilitated. The key question, however, is whether men are ready to return to the family to resume their paternal responsibilities. As can be seen from Issoupova's discussion of her interviews, women's views on this issue are sharply divided.

Women are thus responding to the pressures of transition within parameters defined by the Soviet inheritance, but this does not have clear-cut implications. On the one hand, the ideal of the Soviet superwoman who works, runs a household and takes pride in her ability to do so, is still enormously influential: it shines through in the self-presentation of Kiblitskaya's respondents. But on the other hand, the same women frequently harbour a persistent longing for 'strong shoulders' on which to lean. Whether women would appreciate this in practice is one of the big unanswered questions of the transition era,[30] and an issue which runs through the contributions of Kiblitskaya and Kukhterin. Kukhterin's analysis of an attempt to restore patriarchal norms during the transition era suggests that when women say they want 'strong shoulders' behind them, what they mean is that they want some support and male participation in domestic decision-making. They do not want to be forced to obey a traditional patriarch – although it seems that such obedience is what some young men are craving. This is one of the areas where the contradictory imperatives of traditional Russian and Soviet culture are most visible and problematic.

Post-Soviet men might be expected to welcome the new opportunities offered by the collapse of communism: the state is no longer monopolising the patriarchal role, theoretically leaving men free to resume their 'natural' position within the private sphere. But the other side of this is the expectation that men will reassume the traditional 'male' responsibilities which have been abandoned by the state. This implies increased pressure and responsibility in an increasingly competitive economic environment. That is, men are now called on to perform a patriarchal role in a society in which daily survival is difficult.

There is therefore a huge question mark over the ability of Russian men to fill the void left by the retreat of the state. As discussed above, women seem to be looking for two things from men: financial security, and emotional and practical support within the family. In terms of the former, as Kiblitskaya shows in Chapter 4, many men are having great difficulties in providing for their families in the transition era (although what is equally important to such men is the way in which their personal autonomy has been curtailed by their falling living standards). Even when this is not the case, Kukhterin argues that successful young men often have to work much longer hours to secure a level of comfort comparable to that enjoyed by their fathers. Finally, Meshcherkina shows that even 'New

Russian' men have often only attained the status of main breadwinner with the support and collusion of their wives. Her chapter highlights the fact that both men and women are contributing to current vogue for what could be termed 'new traditionalism'. It is women's longing for men to fulfil the role of traditional breadwinner, as much as men's desire to resume their place as head of the family, which is defining the mores of the new elite.

But, as already mentioned, men and women have different visions of what the role of the head of the family entails. While many men hanker after a full return to the past, women usually want only a modified version of tradition. As Meshcherkina illustrates in Chapter 5, women tend to be wary of the idea of a full return to the home even when their husbands want this and can afford to have a non-working wife.[31] What women want, Kukhterin and Issoupova argue, is more involvement from men, both as partners and fathers. This, however, presents even more problems than women's financial expectations. Judging from the evidence presented in this collection, it seems that a substantial proportion of Russian men are not yet psychologically prepared to involve themselves in the despised 'femininity' of the domestic sphere. Meanwhile, though some women may go some way to indulge men's dreams of patriarchal supremacy, there are usually limits to this collusion. As one of the entrepreneurs quoted in Meshcherkina's chapter says, 'I wouldn't be against my wife staying at home. But the time has already passed, and it's too late': women imbued with the Soviet work ethic are going to be hard to chain to the kitchen sink. It therefore seems likely that the redefinition of men's domestic role in the post-communist era is going to be a painful, conflict-ridden process.

The next question is, what of young people? Young Russians are growing up in a new cultural climate. Previously the public sphere was heavily ideologised and organised: socialisation was not left to chance. Now the space in which young people operate is heavily commercialised; they are exposed to a whole range of perspectives within the media and advertising. Much of the material in publications aimed at young people is Western-influenced, although with idiosyncratic Russian twists. In spite of the new plurality in the youth media, however, Elena Omel'chenko's study of youth sexuality in Ul'yanovsk (see Chapter 7) reveals that the young subscribe to fairly traditional ideas regarding gender differences, although it is notable that the ideas of young men are more conservative than those of young women. For example, while women perceive female power as attractive, men still prefer their women to be defenceless. Meanwhile, young men are also far more conservative with regard to homosexuality, reacting to it with 'an almost animal fear'. They cling insistently to the sexual dichotomy, and find ambiguity in issues relating to sexuality disturbing. Whether the intimate relationships of the young will be less fraught than those of their parents is at present difficult to assess, although most are pessimistic about the fate of relationships after marriage.

Are the younger generations who missed out on Soviet socialisation going to consolidate on the traditionalist currents discussed above? For example, are younger Soviet women going to be more receptive to the call of the home than their mothers? At the moment, it does not appear so. The labour force participation of younger women has fallen dramatically since 1992, but there is no evidence that this is connected with a desire to leave work for a life of domestic confinement. First, the most dramatic fall has been in the 16–19 age group, and has affected men equally. Second, although the participation of women in their twenties has fallen by substantially more than that of men, overall this amounts to only 2 per cent of all women in the age group, while the rate of marriage and the birth rate have continued to fall (Clarke, 1998: 85). The decline in young women's labour force participation, therefore, seems overwhelmingly to be explained by the general alienation of young people from participation in formal work, with low and unpaid wages, unhealthy and humiliating working conditions. Indeed, one of the most dramatic changes in values ushered in by the collapse of the Soviet state affects both young men and young women: they appear to be rejecting the self-sacrificing stance of their parents in favour of the pursuit of private comfort. The most extreme expression of this in contemporary post-Soviet culture is the cynical search of a visible minority of young women for a 'sponsor' (rich older man) to cushion them from the travails of transition.[32]

The structure of the book

This book begins with an analysis of the Soviet institution of the worker-mother and her fate in the post-communist era. In Chapter 1, Olga Issoupova deals with the question of motherhood, while in the following chapter Marina Kiblitskaya looks at the issue of women and work, through her examination of the role of female breadwinners in different eras. Sergei Kukhterin, Elena Meshcherkina, and Marina Kiblitskaya consider the response of men to the collapse of the Soviet state. Kukhterin considers the fate of fathers and patriarchs in the Soviet and post-Soviet era in Chapter 3, while Meshcherkina focuses on 'New Russian' men in Chapter 5, and Kiblitskaya on the experience of men whose status is challenged by the loss of employment or a dramatic fall in earnings (see Chapter 4). In Chapter 6, Irina Tartakovskaya contrasts the media representation of gender in the Soviet and post-Soviet eras, through her comparison of the press in 1984 and 1997. Finally, in Chapter 7, Elena Omel'chenko analyses the views of provincial young men and women regarding sex and sexuality.

Notes

1 The 'gender order' refers to the historically constructed pattern of power relations between men and women and definitions of masculinity and feminin-

ity in a given society (Connell, 1987: 98–9), a definition which Connell developed on the basis of the insights of Matthews (1984). For the sake of variety, I use the terms 'gender order' and 'gender system' interchangeably.

2 The state was 'patriarchal' in terms of the social role it performed. Patriarchal is employed here as an adjective and its use does not imply acceptance of the idea that 'patriarchy' is a distinct form of self-reproducing social system comparable to capitalism. As Anna Pollert has convincingly argued in her critique of dual systems theory, 'there is no *intrinsic* motor or dynamic within "patriarchy" which can explain its self-perpetuation' (Pollert, 1996: 643). 'Gender is a mutable dimension of experience and social relationships' (ibid.: 655) and, as such, the specific ways in which gender is articulated in different situations must be analysed empirically rather than explained theoretically through the ahistorical concept of patriarchy. Thus, for example, the idea that 'patriarchy' was a constant systemic feature of Tsarist and Soviet society is empty and meaningless, for though men may have been dominant in both societies, the content of the gender relations was significantly different.

3 There is a variety of feminist approaches to the state, from those who regard it as a tool of patriarchal oppression, to those who perceive it as an instrument of potential benefit to the feminist cause and arena for bargaining among interests, to those, influenced by post-structuralism, who reject the whole notion of a unified state (Rai, 1996: 6–7). Here, the Soviet state is assumed to have been 'patriarchal' in terms of the social role it performed – that is, it arrogated to itself many traditional masculine roles. But the dominance of men within the state machine is *not* perceived to be the basis of this 'patriarchal' character: as will be seen, the state was by no means an unqualified ally of men. The contributors do tend to present the communist state as a coherent whole. While the perception of the state as an 'actor' is not without its problems – there are always factions and fractures within any state – this has proved fruitful as an initial assumption. The post-structuralist approach has been most effective when applied to states in the developing world, which are often distinctly fragmented: by comparison, the Soviet state was notable for its unity. There is, however, clearly room for greater exploration of the conflicts and fissures within the Soviet state with regard to gender politics. One interesting attempt to do this is Deborah Field's (1998) analysis of the different approaches of Soviet moralists and judges with regard to divorce in the Khrushchev era.

4 Wood sees Richard Stites (1978) as an advocate of the emancipatory position, and Gail Lapidus (1978) as tending towards an instrumental view within the paradigm of modernisation. While Wood does not say so, in my view Wendy Goldman (1993) can be placed alongside Stites as an advocate of the proposition that the Bolsheviks were genuinely interested in women's liberation. In Goldman's view, they were prevented from securing this goal by 'a crushing material poverty' (Goldman, 1989: 61). Mary Buckley took a more measured position, while at the same time stressing the Bolsheviks' theoretical commitment to women's liberation and the 'truly revolutionary' nature of their legislation (1985: 34).

5 Official hostility to the family reached its pinnacle during the first five-year plan, when slogans such as 'Down with the kitchen!' and 'The saucepan is the enemy of the Party cell' became watchwords of economic and political transformation (Stites, 1978: 409). It was in 1932 that Pavlik Morozov, a young boy who denounced his father to the authorities for concealing grain and was killed by his family for his pains, was made a hero. Stalin supported Morozov's cult in every possible way, and he remained an idol of the Komsomol throughout the 1930s and 1940s (Laqueur, 1990: 197).

6 One particularly extreme moment in this fervent deliberation was the presentation of castration 'as a symbolic and even logical event' in N. P.

Brukhansky's book *Materials on Sexual Psychopathology*, published in 1927 (Naiman, 1997: 126). Brukhansky presented the case of Anastasia E., whose 'rational faculties' were imperiled by her sexual desire for her husband. She contracted venereal disease from her unfaithful spouse several times, and on one such occasion, in late 1923, he forced her to have intercourse twice in the same evening, which proved very painful because of her infection. The next morning, upon awakening, she cut off his penis. Brukhansky saw this action as the result of Anastasia E.'s desire to 'emancipate herself' (Naiman: 124–6). Such an interpretation was completely in line with the official view expounded by Health commissar Nikolai Semashko, and supported by 'a parade of professors and doctors' that the energy 'wasted' in sex should be used more productively elsewhere (ibid.: 142).

7 The most notable provision of this law was the abolition of the distinction between *de jure* and *de facto* marriages. Although this has been hailed as promoting 'free union' (Goldman, 1989: 75) it actually, rather than attacking the institution of marriage, formalised the *de facto* relationship (Farnsworth, 1978: 162), and thereby provided another means through which the authorities could regulate private life. Again the law was strongly opposed by peasants since it represented a challenge to the integrity of the *dvor* (household). For more details on this conflict of interest see Farnsworth (1978).

8 Lapidus perceives the wider implications of the measures providing the juridical foundations for the independence of women, noting that 'they had as their larger goal the destruction of the network of economic, religious and familial ties that bound women to traditional social solidarities and inhibited their direct and unmediated participation in the larger political and economic arena' (Lapidus, 1978: 62).

9 Despite the Zhenotdel's emphasis on the need to transform the domestic sphere, amid the social chaos of the mid-1920s it effectively accepted the continued existence of the individual household. But while the household was accepted as a functional entity, its privacy was by no means to be respected: women were to be instructed how to perform their domestic tasks, in particular motherhood, through official publications such as *Rabotnitsa* ('Woman Worker') and other Party organs (Fuqua, 1996: 35–9).

10 Although Stites argues that the Zhenotdel represented 'the working out ... in some ways ... of the ... feminist belief, given expression by Lenin in 1919, that "the emancipation of working women is a matter for working women themselves" ' (1978: 345), he also notes the Party's fear that women might begin to define their own agenda. This concern was strikingly demonstrated in the resolution of the Twelfth Party Congress in 1923 which lamented the growth of 'feminist tendencies' that 'could lead to the female contingent of labour breaking away from the common class struggle' (ibid.: 342).

11 One of the important roles of the Zhenotdel was to run literacy classes, for as Lenin observed, 'a person who can neither read nor write is outside politics' (quoted in Lapidus, 1978: 64).

12 Like Aristarkhova and Wood, Fuqua argues that to focus on how far the Bolsheviks succeeded in 'liberating' women is to misunderstand Bolshevik politics. 'The real historical significance of the *zhenotdely* is not whether they eliminated discrimination or transformed women's social position, but how the *zhenotdely* attempted to redefine and reconstitute the domestic sphere, placing women's traditional family roles under state control' (1996: 10).

13 Goldman argues that the progressive potential of the 1920s 'was cut short in the 1930s by the decision ... to end open discussions of women's liberation, and to resurrect the family' (1989: 61). This is a common line of argument. See, for example, Buckley (1985: 38); Einhorn (1993: 31); and Voronina (1994: 46).

14 As Thurston notes, the regime had problems balancing its family policy. Once the cultural *khudzhum* of the 1920s was over, stability was at a premium, especially in the light of the social strains caused by industrialisation. But, at the same time, the authorities needed to feel sure that families were under their control. It is this tension which underlay the swings between endorsing happy families and celebrating those who denounced family members to the state which characterised the 1930s.

15 The labour collective is the Soviet term used to refer to all members of an enterprise, from the director to the cleaner.

16 Between 1928 and 1940 the absolute number of women among workers and employees grew almost fivefold and their proportion of the total rose from 24 to 39 per cent as a result of Stalin's crash industrialisation programme. The Second World War promoted a second mass influx of women into the labour force and by 1945 56 per cent of the workforce was female. Then between 1960 and 1971 labour shortages prompted another massive recruitment drive among the major untapped source of labour power – women remaining in households – and a further 18 million women were drawn into the labour force (all figures from Lapidus, 1978: 164–7). Since 1970 the proportion of working-age women within the labour force has been close to the biological maximum (Shapiro, 1992: 15).

17 For a full account of the terms of women's integration into the labour force see Filtzer (1992: 177–203).

18 The alliance forged between women and the state against drunken men endured for the whole of the Soviet era. My research in a Kuzbass mining community between 1994 and 1998 revealed that, while male workers bitterly resented the Party's encroachment on what they perceived as their right to drink, women workers often cited this as a positive feature of communist rule. As one female worker recounted with approval, 'in 1985 there was a "war against alcohol". It was very strict. We in the Party sent a lot of people for treatment. Wives of men with drinking problems would come to the Party and ask for their husbands to receive treatment. ... The Party disciplined people' (Ashwin, 1999a: 123).

19 Defining the wives of engineers and other prominent men such as managers and shock workers as *obshchestvennitsy* was a way of bringing them within the Party's ambit. It was an ingenious means of simultaneously rendering family life a public concern, and of drawing housewives into work: as well as being charged with looking after and disciplining their husbands, the *obshchestvennitsy* also effectively performed unpaid inspection work in the factories. For more details see Buckley (1996).

20 Given the centrality of production to the Bolshevik project, it is not surprising that one of the abuses which was highlighted was that of men who refused to allow their wives to work (Kotkin, 1995: 189).

21 Post-revolutionary Iran or contemporary Afganistan provide extreme examples of such politics, although more subtle forms of the same approach are widespread. The experience of Iran provides an interesting contrast to Soviet practice, since the politicisation and transformation of private gender relations was likewise central to the self-definition and control strategies of the new revolutionary regime. The difference lay in the content rather than the form of the politics. Like its Soviet counterpart, the Islamic regime was pro-natalist and defined motherhood as duty, but it also strongly supported the confinement of women within the private sphere under the control of men: nurseries, which were denounced as 'dens of subversion', were closed down; mothers of young children were not officially permitted to work, while temporary marriages, polygamy, and the retention of an unlimited number of concubines by men were all permitted (Afshar, 1989).

22 A new scale of decorations for motherhood was introduced in 1944: five children earned a mother a second-class motherhood medal, while at the top of the scale, after three classes of 'Motherhood Glory', a mother of ten was designated a heroine mother (Buckley, 1989: 134).

23 It is ironic to note that, while the 1920s have generally been hailed as the era of women's liberation, the 1940s could arguably be seen as the decade in which women achieved most in terms of advancement within the public sphere. As in the West, this did not prove a permanent settlement – indeed, the pressure on women to create homely comfort, which Dunham (1990) argues is endlessly expressed in post-war Soviet novels, parallels the expectations of feminine domesticity fostered in the cultural climate of the United States in the 1950s.

24 The perceived demographic crisis of the 1970s had a notable impact on official thinking. Not only were measures taken to encourage women to have more children, such as the extension of maternity leave and benefits in the early 1980s, but serious attention was also given to the male role within the family. For example, discussions of child custody in cases of divorce began in the 1980s to question the principle of automatic custody for the mother, something which represented a significant departure from the earlier denigration of the private paternal role (Attwood, 1990: 201).

25 For a description of the 'trench warfare' between men and women over vodka consumption in a Kuzbass mining settlement see Ashwin (1999a: 46–8).

26 The implication of this is that the 'double burden' cannot simply be seen as something which was imposed on women from the outside by the authorities. It was also something which accorded with the gender identity of the average Soviet woman who internalised state ideas regarding the importance of paid work, but also accepted that the domestic sphere was her domain. In this sense, the ideal of the Soviet superwoman was not merely a hollow invention of the state, it was something to which women aspired and helped make sense of their lives. For more on the ideal of the superwoman, see Ashwin (1999b).

27 See, for example, Voronina (1994); and Konstantinova (1994).

28 One of the most notorious expressions of this was the comment of the (then) Russian Labour Minister, Gennadi Melikyan, when asked in 1993 about measures to combat female unemployment: 'Why should we employ women when men are out of work? It's better that men work and women take care of the children and do housework. I don't think women should work when men are doing nothing' (quoted in Morvant, 1995: 5).

29 Elena Zdravomyslova has observed that mothers socialised in the Soviet era tend to claim that their children were something they 'gave the state' (*rodila gosudarstvu*) in return for which they expected certain benefits (Zdravomyslova, 1996b).

30 Similarly, although Russian workers often say that what they want is a 'firm but fair' boss, they often do not appreciate this firmness when they experience it (Ashwin, 1999a: 178–9). It also very likely that, while many Russians say they would like a 'strong' president to replace Boris Yeltsin, such enthusiasm would dissipate when confronted with the realities of political 'strength'.

31 On the difficulties faced by Russian women in adjusting to the role of housewife see Zdravomyslova (1996a).

32 The nature and implications of the sexualised survival strategies pursued by post-Soviet women during the transition are analysed by Jakob Rigi (1999) in his fascinating anthropological account of responses to the transition in Almaty, Kazakhstan.

References

Afshar, H. (1989) 'Women and reproduction in Iran', in N. Yuval-Davis and F. Anthias (eds), *Woman-Nation-State*, Basingstoke: Macmillan: 110–25.

Akiner, S. (1997) 'Between tradition and modernity: The dilemma facing contemporary Central Asian women', in M. Buckley (ed.), *Post-Soviet Women: From the Baltic to Central Asia*, Cambridge: Cambridge University Press: 261–304.

Anthias, F. and Yuval-Davis, N. (1989) 'Introduction', in N. Yuval-Davis and F. Anthias (eds), *Woman-Nation-State*, Basingstoke: Macmillan: 1–15.

Aristarkhova, I. (1995) *Women and Government in Bolshevik Russia*, University of Warwick: Labour Studies Working Papers, 4.

Ashwin, S. (1999a) *Russian Workers: The Anatomy of Patience*, Manchester: Manchester University Press.

—— (1999b) 'Russia's saviours? Women workers in transition from Communism', in M. Neary (ed.), *Global Humanisation: Studies in the Manufacture of Labour*, London: Mansell: 97–126.

Attwood, L. (1990) *The New Soviet Man and Woman: Sex Role Socialisation in the USSR*, Basingstoke: Macmillan.

Buckley, M. (1985) 'Soviet interpretations of the woman question', in B. Holland (ed.), *Soviet Sisterhood: British Feminists on Women in the USSR*, London: Fourth Estate: 24–53.

—— (1989) *Women and Ideology in the Soviet Union*, Hemel Hempstead: Harvester Wheatsheaf.

—— (1996) 'The untold story of obshchestvennitsa in the 1930s', *Europe-Asia Studies* 48 (4): 569–86.

Clark, K. (1977) 'Utopian anthropology as a context for Stalinist literature', in R. Tucker (ed.), *Stalinism: Essays in Historical Interpretation*, New York: W.W. Norton and Company: 180–98.

Clarke, S. (1998) 'Structural adjustment without mass unemployment? Lessons from Russia', in S. Clarke (ed.), *Structural Adjustment without Mass Unemployment? Lessons from Russia*, Aldershot: Edward Elgar: 9–86.

Connell, R. (1987) *Gender and Power: Society, the Person and Sexual Politics*, Cambridge: Polity Press.

Dunham, V. S. (1990) *In Stalin's Time: Middleclass Values in Soviet Fiction* (updated edition), Durham, NC and London: Duke University Press.

Einhorn, B. (1993) *Cinderella Goes to Market: Citizenship, Gender and Women's Movements in East Central Europe*, London and New York: Verso.

Farnsworth, B. B. (1978) 'Bolshevik alternatives and the Soviet family: The 1926 marriage law debate', in D. Atkinson, A. Dallin and G. Lapidus (eds), *Women in Russia*, Brighton: Harvester: 139–67.

Field, D. (1998) 'Irreconcilable differences: Divorce and conceptions of private life in the Khrushchev era', *Russian Review* 57(4): 599–613.

Filtzer, D. (1992) *Soviet Workers and De-Stalinization: The Formation of the Modern System of Soviet Production Relations, 1953–1964*, Cambridge: Cambridge University Press.

Fuqua, M. (1996) *The Politics of the Domestic Sphere: The Zhenotdely, Women's Liberation and the Search for a Novyi Byt in Early Soviet Russia*, paper no. 10, Seattle, WA: The Henry M. Jackson School of International Studies, University of Washington.

Goldman, W. (1989) 'Women, the family and the new revolutionary order in the Soviet Union', in S. Kurks, R. Rapp and M. B. Young (eds), *Promissory Notes: Women in the Transition to Socialism*, New York: Monthly Review Press: 59–81.

—— (1993) *Women, the State and Revolution: Soviet Family Policy and Social Life, 1917–1936*, Cambridge: Cambridge University Press.

—— (1996) 'Industrial politics, peasant rebellion and the death of the proletarian women's movement in the USSR', *Slavic Review* 55(1): 46–77.

Goskomstat (1999) *Statisticheskii byulleten'*, 3(53), Moscow: Goskomstat Rossii.

Haynes, J. (1996) 'When men *were* men: An analysis of gender relations in Stalinist cinema', *Postgraduate Working Papers in Modern Languages at the University of Manchester*, 1, April 1996: 35–45.

Kollontai, A. [1914] (1977) 'Working woman and mother', in A. Holt (ed.), *Selected Writings of Alexandra Kollontai*, London: Allison and Busby: 127–39.

—— [1919] (1977) 'Communism and the family', in A. Holt (ed.), *Selected Writings of Alexandra Kollontai*, London: Allison and Busby: 250–60.

—— [1921a] (1977) 'Thesis on Communist morality in the sphere of marital relations', in A. Holt (ed.), *Selected Writings of Alexandra Kollontai*, London: Allison and Busby: 225–31.

—— [1921b] (1977) 'Prostitution and ways of fighting it', in A. Holt (ed.), *Selected Writings of Alexandra Kollontai*, London: Allison and Busby: 261–75.

—— [1923] (1977) 'Make way for the winged Eros: A letter to working youth', in A. Holt (ed.), *Selected Writings of Alexandra Kollontai*, London: Allison and Busby: 276–92.

Konstantinova, V. (1994) 'No longer totalitarianism, but not yet democracy: The emergence of an independent women's movement in Russia', in A. Podsadskaya, *Women in Russia: A New Era in Russian Feminism*, London and New York: Verso: 57–73.

Kotkin, S. (1995) *Magnetic Mountain: Stalinism as a Civilisation*, Berkeley, Los Angeles and London: University of California Press.

Lapidus, G. (1978) *Women in Soviet Society: Equality, Development and Social Change*, Berkeley, Los Angeles and London: Berkeley University Press

—— (1988) 'The interaction of women's work and family roles in the USSR', *Women and Work: An Annual Review* 3: 87–121.

Laqueur, W. (1990) *Stalin: The Glasnost Revelations*, London: Unwin Hyman.

Lenin, V. I. (n. d.) *On the Emancipation of Women*, Moscow.

—— [1919] (1937) 'The tasks of the working women's movement in the Soviet Republic. Speech delivered at the Fourth Moscow City Non-Party Conference of Women Workers, September 23, 1919', in V. I. Lenin, *Selected Works*, vol. IX, London: Lawrence and Wishart.

—— [1921] (1937) 'International working women's day', in V. I. Lenin, *Selected Works*, vol. IX, London: Lawrence and Wishart.

Massell, G. (1974) *The Surrogate Proletariat: Moslem Women and Revolutionary Strategies in Soviet Central Asia 1919–1929*, Princeton, NJ: Princeton University Press.

Matthews, J. (1984) *Good and Mad Women: The Historical Construction of Femininity in Twentieth Century Australia*, Sydney: George Allen and Unwin.

Morvant, P. (1995) 'Bearing the double burden in Russia', *Transition* 1(16), 8 September 1995: 4–9.

Naiman, E. (1997) *Sex in Public: The Incarnation of Early Soviet Ideology*, Princeton, NJ: Princeton University Press.

Pollert, A. (1996) 'Gender and class revisited: Or, the poverty of "patriarchy" ', *Sociology* 30(4): 639–59.

Rai, S. M. (1996) 'Women and the state in the Third World: Some issues for debate', in S. M. Rai and G. Lievesley (eds), *Women and the State: International Perspectives*, London and Bristol, PA: Taylor and Francis: 5–22.

Reid, S. (1998) 'All Stalin's women: Gender and power in Soviet art of the 1930s', *Slavic Review* 57(1): 133–73.

Rigi, J. (1999) 'Coping with chaos (*bardak*): Networking, sexualised strategies and ethnic tensions in Almaty, Kazakhstan', unpublished Ph.D. thesis, SOAS, University of London.

Shapiro, J. (1992) 'The industrial labour force', in M. Buckley (ed.), *Perestroika and Soviet Women*, Cambridge: Cambridge University Press: 14–38.

Stites, R. (1978) *The Women's Liberation Movement in Russia: Feminism, Nihilism and Bolshevism, 1860–1930*, Princeton, NJ: Princeton University Press.

Thurston, R. (1991) 'The Soviet family during the great terror, 1935–1941', *Soviet Studies* 43(3): 553–74.

Trotsky, L. [1926] (1973) 'Next tasks for worker correspondents', in L. Trotsky, *Problems of Everyday Life: Creating the Foundations for a New Society in Revolutionary Russia*, New York: Pathfinder: 186–94.

Voronina, O. (1994) 'The mythology of women's emancipation in the USSR as the foundation for a policy of discrimination', in A. Podsadskaya (ed.), *Women in Russia: A New Era in Russian Feminism*, London and New York: Verso: 34–56.

Wood, E. (1997) *The Baba and the Comrade: Gender and Politics in Revolutionary Russia*, Bloomington, IN and Indianapolis: Indiana University Press.

Zdravomyslova, E. (1996a) 'Problems of becoming a housewife', in E. Haavio-Mannila and A. Rotkirch, *Women's Voices in Russia Today*, Aldershot: Dartmouth Publishing Company.

—— (1996b) 'Women's unemployment', paper presented to a conference on 'Gender Relations in Transition', Soros Foundation East-East Programme, Samara, Russia, 24–27 May 1996.

Zetkin, C. (1934) *Reminiscences of Lenin*, International Publishers: New York.

1   From duty to pleasure?

Motherhood in Soviet and post-Soviet Russia

Olga Issoupova

This chapter considers the changing construction of motherhood in Soviet and post-Soviet Russia. It is divided into two sections: the first section considers the Soviet approach to motherhood through an analysis of the official state journal *Voprosy materinstva i mladenchestva* ('Questions of Motherhood and Infancy'), between 1926 and 1937, during which time the main elements of the Soviet attitude to motherhood were established.[1] The second half considers the transformation in attitudes towards motherhood set in train by the collapse of the Soviet state. My research is based on two sources: a review of the contemporary Russian press, and interviews with women of child-bearing age, which were designed to gauge how far the change in the ideological climate has been reflected in the subjective perceptions of ordinary women.

Methodology

In terms of the review of the press, the form of analysis which was used to study the two eras – Soviet and post-Soviet Russia – was somewhat different in each case. *Voprosy materinstva i mladenchestva* was a mouthpiece for state policy with regard to motherhood and infancy, and I treat it as such in this chapter. The discussion of this journal is thus a study of state policy and its official representation. By contrast, in the post-Soviet era, there is no 'official' state position on motherhood. I have therefore attempted to capture the main strands of contemporary opinion as presented in the press through studying a representative cross-section of the print media between the period 20 July 1996 to 10 August 1996. In total, I monitored over twenty papers, including the main national newspapers and the Moscow local papers, and analysed all articles which in one way or another related to the subject of motherhood.[2] In 1995–6 three new women's magazines were launched: the Russian editions of *Cosmopolitan*, *Good Housekeeping* (*Domashnii ochag*), and *Motherhood* (*Materinstvo*), and I included the September issues of these magazines in my analysis. I also included issues of the monthly magazines *Rabotnitsa* and *Krest'yanka* ('Woman Worker' and 'Peasant Woman', respectively, the two most popular women's magazines of the Soviet era), published between January and September 1996. Issues of *Sostial'naya zashchita* ('Social Protection') for this period were also included since this publication considers questions relating to social protection of motherhood.

Between 1996 and 1998 I conducted detailed interviews with thirty-three women of child-bearing age, the youngest of whom was 19 and the oldest 40. Whether or not these women had children, I worked from the assumption that all of them would have given some thought to the 'maternal question'. Eleven of the women I interviewed were relinquishing mothers (women who had given up their children for adoption), as I was particularly interested in the motivation of such women during the transition era. As a whole, the women interviewed were in a variety of different situations – childless, married, single, cohabiting, and so forth. My questions focused on the women's motivations regarding motherhood, and their perceptions of the 'prerequisites' of this in the transition era.

The construction of motherhood in early Soviet Russia

The specialist journal *Voprosy materinstva i mladenchestva* ('Questions of Motherhood and Infancy') is an excellent source through which to examine the development of the Soviet conception of motherhood and childcare. The journal was established in 1926 with the goal of medical enlightenment of the population in questions of reproduction, through the transmission of the latest scientific information about pregnancy, birth and child-rearing. At the same time, however, it served as a means through which the state transmitted its policies; indeed, this function gradually began to dominate during the Stalin era. What were the main priorities of the nascent Soviet state? The emerging politics of motherhood and infancy can be examined under three headings. First, reproduction was seen as a *state function*, for which women should be rewarded. Second, in line with this, the state was concerned with the quality of future generations. This implied that women's bodies were valuable vessels in which the state had a legitimate interest. Third, children, once produced, should be brought up as communists. Early plans to socialise childcare completely were abandoned for practical reasons, but the quest to ensure control of child-rearing continued. In place of the development of 'child colonies', the state sought to develop a special alliance with mothers, whose care was to be supplemented by nursery provision. This, however, was at the expense of fathers who were symbolically excluded from the state-mother-child triad.

Motherhood: 'the highest form of service'

In the first issue of *Voprosy materinstva i mladenchestva*, V. Lebedeva (1926) wrote that 'motherhood is the social function of women – this is our watchword'. The aim of the Bolshevik government, in Lebedeva's opinion, was to 'grant women equal conditions at work, take from them the burden of housekeeping and child care' so that they would no longer be 'tired and downtrodden'. In the absence of such reforms society hindered 'a woman's very nature, her maternity'. This article highlights three key Bolshevik positions with regard to maternity: first, that motherhood was not a private matter, but a social one; second, that motherhood was the 'natural' destiny of women; and third, that it was a function which was to be facilitated and rewarded by the state.

If motherhood was a social function, it followed that it should be exercised in accordance with the needs of society (and, as is well known, according to Leninist doctrine, it was only the Communist Party which was capable of discerning where the interests of society lay). In the mid-1920s, however, there was still some room for debate within the Party over what sort of motherhood would best serve Soviet society: 'conscious' or compulsory. In the first year of the journal an article by Rachmanov (1926), entitled 'On the road to conscious motherhood', advocated the use of birth control: pregnancy should be a deliberate choice. He claimed that across the world 'a shift' was occurring: 'men don't want families and women don't want to give birth'. This was also characteristic of many builders of communism in the USSR, for 'it's better to climb mountains unburdened'. In such conditions, the author concluded, children would fare best when they were wanted. Rachmanov was thus appealing to the idea that builders of communism understandably had other priorities. Others, however, did not take such a lenient view of the difficulties of Soviet mountaineers. Levi (1927), for example, focused on the medical profession, warning that 'medical workers are falling behind' in their 'execution of the maternal function'. He produced figures to show what he saw as the lamentably low birth rate among female doctors and nurses, and their over-use of abortion. His stern warning about the backwardness of medical workers was clearly grounded on the assumption that it was a woman's duty to give birth as often as possible.

Paradoxically, once industrialisation began in earnest and many women were taken up with other tasks, the authorities gradually attempted to close off the option of any kind of individual choice with regard to motherhood. This manifested itself most clearly in the area of abortion. Given the unreliability of other forms of contraception available to Soviet women at the time, this was often used as a form of birth control. In 1930, however, the journal reported that women would only be able to have abortions after obtaining permission from a specially created commission.[3] In 1935 it was announced that abortions would henceforth have to be paid for, and the following year they were banned.

The journal treated the 1936 ban on abortion as an issue related to women's health. Nogina (1936) noted that the number of abortions had begun to decrease, and the birth rate increase, before the adoption of the law: that is, the journal attempted to argue that the law had simply confirmed an existing tendency. Failed underground abortions became more common, however; Nogina (1936; 1937) reported that women were turning up in hospital with life-threatening complications. Meanwhile, she noted that in the first month after the ban on abortion many doctors still 'found all sorts of unimportant reasons through which they obtained permission for an abortion' (Nogina, 1937). Another article, entitled 'We will precisely and unerringly implement the government decree on the banning of abortion' (Levi, 1937), dealt in detail with the experience of one Moscow clinic and argued that it was necessary to reduce further the number of abortions carried out on medical grounds. Schizophrenia, tuberculosis and heart defects were only to be considered grounds for abortion in the most extreme cases, while syphilis was completely ruled out as grounds for an abortion. Nogina, meanwhile, wrote with pride about how the birth rate had doubled in comparison with the year before, not because of the ban on abortions, but because 'our women are not afraid to give birth because the Soviet state assists them at all stages of motherhood' (Nogina, 1937). At the same time, however, reporting of the rapid building of new maternity units made it clear that this decree put pressure on the maternity hospitals which were not ready for this upsurge in births (Nogina, 1936; 1937). This pressure was also felt in industry, as can be seen from the publication of articles with such titles as, 'The experience of organisation of breast feeding rooms and breast milk collecting points in factory workshops' (Tsykhanskii, 1937).

Since motherhood was a duty to the state, it was logical that it should be rewarded. At the same time as the ban on abortion, therefore, a number of rewards for motherhood were introduced, including, in principle, the liberation of pregnant women from the prison camps (in practice, however, far from all of them were released). These rewards above all concerned mothers of several children. A woman was entitled to become a heroine mother only when she was the biological mother of ten or more children – step-children, adopted children and children who died were not taken into account. The title 'hero father' was not introduced. The state gave the title and the money to the mother, and thus developed a direct relationship with her as the producer of the children, and the man was excluded from this relationship as an insignificant figure (if not as a competitor for the woman's loyalty). Meanwhile, the status of the mother was increased in relation to that of the woman worker: as Kaminskii proclaimed 'the word "mother" is the most respected, motherhood is the highest form of service to one's people and state' (Kaminskii, 1936).

Kaminskii's words echoed those of Lebedeva (1926), writing in the first issue of *Voprosy materinstva i mladenchestva*. This serves to underline the *continuity* of policy with regard to motherhood during the NEP (New Economic Policy) and Stalin eras. Beginning with Trotsky ([1937] 1972), commentators have tended to treat the ban on abortion as part of the 'Thermidor in the family', a symptom of the reactionary subversion of the revolution by the Stalinist bureaucracy. They have therefore seen the policy of the 1930s as qualitatively different from that of the earlier period. But it is important to stress that since the revolution access to abortion had *always* been regulated; it was never treated as a woman's 'right'.[4] This is not surprising given that, as should be clear from the above account, the Bolsheviks never saw motherhood as a private matter. It was a social function, and, as such, the state had the right to regulate it. The ban on abortion was in this sense a continuation of past policy – it was only the severity of the regulation which distinguished it from the earlier approach.

Protecting the genetic inheritance; controlling the 'living machine'

As well as being concerned with the number of children women produced, the state was also interested in the quality of future generations. This implied that the state had an interest in the 'protection' of women's bodies. A significant proportion of articles in the journal were therefore concerned with promoting what was perceived to be healthy living. This continued a long tradition: the Bolsheviks added only an ideological twist to the pre-revolutionary practice of the Russian intelligentsia for whom medical enlightenment of the (mainly peasant) population had always been a key concern. The main difference between the approach of the Bolsheviks and that of their philanthropic predecessors, however, was that the former extended beyond the propagation of best practice into active control of women's behaviour. Such control was justified on the grounds that women's bodies were the incubators of the new generation of communists.

A typical example of interest taken in the conduct of 'future mothers' was an article by Professor Durnovo, entitled 'Heredity and the new generation', which examined the negative consequences of the destruction of the Civil War on the offspring of the current generation (Durnovo, 1926). This did not fail to mention other negative influences on future generations such as abortion and sexual disease. Having an abortion before the first child was claimed to be a potential cause of sterility. Meanwhile, in other articles written during the same period shocking evidence of the prevalence of syphilis in rural Russia was presented. Although such discussions were obviously in part motivated by genuine medical concern, they also legitimised the proscription of certain types of behaviour deemed to be undesirable by the state. This can be seen, for example, in an article by Grigo entitled 'The work of Soviet power in the area of sexual enlightenment of the female population'. Grigo emphasised the need to protect young women from depravity entailing disease and early abortions 'in order not to upset the living machine: the human being' (Grigo, 1930: 18). The wording here made it clear that the female 'human being' was perceived as just another asset of the Soviet state.

A series of other issues were also considered in terms of their implications for the genetic inheritance of the country. For example, a number of articles looked at the harmful influence of women returning to work too early after childbirth.[5] This was said to be bad for the woman's health and hence for her capacity to work and give birth to healthy children in the future – an idea which was soon to be brushed away amid the fervour of Stalinist industrialisation. Similarly, a scheme to provide medical support and occupational training to homeless women who were pregnant was justified on the grounds that this would improve the quality of their offspring. In fact, however, the author notes that in general the only women who found work as a result of this training were trade union members (Davydov, 1927).

The interest of the state did not stop at 'protecting' future mothers. There was a 'correct' way to do most things, and this included giving birth. For example, a number of articles were published regarding the practice of midwifery by the different peoples of the USSR. The aim of these articles, however, was to harmonise the practice of midwifery through the introduction of one, correct system. This did lead to the abolition of some peculiar practices such as that, for example, existing among certain Caucasian people in which the concern of women to 'preserve their dignity' meant that they removed as few clothes as possible during childbirth, and that the older women who were present gave them virtually no help and, indeed, hardly came near them (Raukhvager, 1926; Yushkevich, 1930). But at the same time, other practices, some of which look progressive from a contemporary point of view, were also condemned. This applied, for example, to the Crimean Tartar practice of giving birth in a squatting position, even though the authors who wrote about it noted how easily these births usually proceeded, with the mother drinking coffee and chatting with the other women present almost immediately afterwards (Bukh, 1927).

While in the 1920s the state concentrated on obstetric enlightenment,[6] in the 1930s it increasingly used coercive force to achieve its ends. By 1935 the possibility of giving birth outside state institutions was completely closed down. Young midwives were charged with finding underground *povitukhi* (folk midwives) and, in the spirit of the time, denouncing them to the authorities (Nogina, 1935; Bryukhanov, 1935). This regulation of midwifery, though it no doubt partly stemmed from concern for the health of the mother and child, also served firmly to quash the idea of childbirth as a private, individual experience. It would henceforth only be conducted under the watchful eyes of the state.

The formation of the communist citizen

Not only was motherhood designated as a state function, child-rearing was also deemed to be a public rather than a private matter. Such was the

Bolshevik hostility to the private family that initially the full socialisation of childcare was advocated by many prominent Party members. Aleksandra Kollontai in particular promoted such ideas, arguing that:

> The old family, narrow and petty, where the parents quarrel and are only interested in their own offspring, is not capable of educating the 'new person'. The playgrounds, gardens, homes and other amenities where the child will spend the greater part of the day under the supervision of qualified educators will, on the other hand, offer an environment in which the child can grow up a conscious communist.
>
> (Kollontai, [1919] 1977: 257)

By the time *Voprosy materinstva i mladenchestva* was established, however, it was recognised that the infant mortality rate in state institutions was too high, rising to 90 per cent in some cases (Lunts, 1926). This, it was believed, was partly due to the deficiency of breastfeeding in these establishments. Wet nurses were recruited among homeless mothers, but there were never enough of them, and hence alongside breast milk children were fed a variety of inadequate (and often noxious) supplements (Al'tgauzen, 1926).[7] Meanwhile, Lunts and other writers also recognised the problem of what they called 'hospitalism', by which they meant that children raised in institutions were deprived of emotional interaction. In addition to these deficiencies, state childcare was also more expensive than that within the family. Given all these problems, the rhetorical question 'nursery or child-colony?' was eventually resolved in favour of a combination of maternal and nursery care.[8] It should be stressed, however, that this acceptance of the role of private care represented a compromise with reality rather than an ideological change of heart.

Thus, for pragmatic reasons, from its inception the journal promoted the 'natural' role of mothers in the upbringing of children. The emphasis on motherhood, however, left the question of the formation of future citizens in private hands. The compromise with mothers was always a slightly uneasy one, and this tension was dealt with in two ways. First, mothers were to be brought under the improving influence of the state, and, second, children were to receive supplementary (and possibly corrective) socialisation at nurseries. The former was precisely the goal the journal was created to serve and its contributors dutifully stressed the idea of the state as the benign protector and champion of mothers. As Shustova enthusiastically proclaimed, 'The Soviet state having announced that the protection of motherhood and infancy is a state task ... has broken the bonds of oppressed motherhood, joyless and lifeless infancy; with its last strength the exhausted proletariat has achieved state protection of motherhood and infancy, which preserves the mother for the child and the child for the mother' (Shustova, 1927). 'State protection of motherhood and infancy' (*okhmatmlad* in the characteristic Soviet abbreviation of the time) was the perfect vehicle for securing greater influence over mothers and their children. This can be seen, for example, in articles that dealt with the further development of state policy with regard to motherhood and infancy, many of which explicitly linked this to social and political control. An article by Krist (1930), for instance, dealt with the creation of local mutual aid funds for mothers. This, it was argued, would help to strengthen ties to the local area, thus helping to develop state control over the movement of citizens. Meanwhile, an article by Grossman (1930) argued for the elimination of differences in the social protection of mothers and infants in different regions, which the author claimed was essential for the implementation of Party policy. Uniformity was a necessary precondition of effective control.

But in spite of the efforts of the authorities to foster a close relationship with mothers, they remained wary of parental discretion: the journal published a number of articles which highlighted the negative influence of parents, not only on the health of their children, but also on their psychological development.[9] In line with this continued suspicion of the private sphere, the idea that parental care should be combined with the public nurseries was a constant theme of the journal. 'The struggle for nurseries' was partly based on the idea that the staff would inculcate communist as opposed to religious values, though after the beginning of the industrialisation programme the 'liberation' of women workers from their children became an increasingly important justification. A typical example of the arguments advanced in favour of nurseries is provided by an approving article detailing the practice of *kolkhoznitsy* (female collective farm workers) at one collective farm during the harvest. After the establishment of the nursery, the women began to leave their children (including those still being breastfed) at the nursery at five o'clock in the morning, and to pick them up at around ten in the evening (Zal'kindson, 1927).[10] This was perceived as a positive means of ensuring the female workforce was used rationally and fully: instead of using one woman to care for one child, forty could be cared for in the nursery. During industrialisation twenty-four-hour factory nurseries were established for the same purpose.[11]

During crash industrialisation the campaign for nurseries became so important that between 1933–4 the journal changed its name to 'Nursery'. By this stage, the journal was giving increasingly open expression to the subordination of the individual to the state. Children were to be brought up not for the parents' benefit, nor for their own benefit, but for the sake of the country. And they should love not their parents, but their country. Therefore, as the President of the Soviet of People's Commissars of the Russian Federation, D.E. Sulimov, put it in a speech to a meeting of nursery employees, 'It is necessary to create an environment in which the child feels from an early age the care the socialist state has given him'

(Sulimov, 1934). At this time the magazine also began to assert that nurseries offered a qualitatively better form of care than children could have at home. It is clear, however, from the mass of material in the journal relating to the 'future improvement' of the nurseries, that infant mortality within these establishments continued to be high (Shaburova, 1934). Moreover, thieving flourished: Shaburova related how children's food, clothes and the material intended for their nappies was stolen by nursery employees. In the discourse of the time this was no longer simply stealing but the 'machinations of the class enemy'.[12]

It should be noted that the history of the 'struggle for nurseries' again casts doubt on the idea of a conservative reaction in family policy during the Stalin era. Although plans for full socialisation of childcare were abandoned for practical reasons, the Stalinist authorities became determined to take as many children as possible from the care of their parents for as long as possible, even when this meant the children attending substandard institutions swarming with thieves. This can hardly be seen as part of a resurrection of the family.

The marginalisation of the father

One very important consequence of the state alliance with the mother, and the attempt to wrest as much control as possible from the parents via nursery provision, was the virtual exclusion of fathers from childcare. The role of fathers in raising children was mentioned very rarely. When fathers featured in the journal it was usually in a negative capacity, in connection with abandonment of children or alimony. A prominent theme of the journal in the late 1920s and early 1930s, for example, was the abandonment of children and the social reasons for this. Klimovskaya (1930), in an article entitled 'Everyday features of the abandonment of children, based on material from Perm children's home', cited cases in which women chose their husbands over their children, or where they left the child with its father, who then took it to the police and declared it abandoned. All this was clearly directed against men. At this stage the women themselves were not blamed; they were seen to have the right to relinquish a child. Indeed, another line of propaganda was the idea that mothers had to be freed from the burden of their children, something which, it seems, a number of women achieved through abandonment.

In 1934, however, the official attitude to relinquishing mothers changed and women became criminally responsible in cases of abandonment, which was considered to be a crime comparable with murder. The legal responsibility of fathers remained akin to that of responsibility for property; in this way, the father–child bond was symbolically relegated to the level of a financial obligation. Meanwhile, the redundancy of fathers was continually underlined by the emphasis placed on the links between mother, state and child.

The rise and fall of *okhmatmlad*

After the end of the Stalin era, some of the more coercive aspects of the practice of *okhmatmlad* were abandoned. The ban on abortion, for example, was lifted in 1955. Nevertheless, the broad outline of policy remained the same until the end of the Soviet era. Motherhood continued to be glorified as the highest duty to the state, while the state monopoly on obstetric services was strengthened. The continual exhortation of the Stalin era was softened, however, and was replaced by less conspicuous normative pressure to conform to certain standards, which included having a family of at least one, or preferably two, children. The continued emphasis on collective duty rather than choice was reflected in the failure of the Soviet state to supply adequate contraception to its people: the 'second contraceptive revolution' of the 1960s passed the Soviet Union by, for the simple reason that it was never treated as a priority (Vishnevskii, 1998: 128). Children were considered to be important, however: an institutional infrastructure of infant and childcare was gradually developed, and a state network of nurseries and kindergartens set in place. Indeed, it was in the 1980s, amid concerns regarding the birth rate, that the policy of maternal protection reached its fullest development. Maternity leave and child benefit was increased to levels which made reliance on the state rather than the individual man quite feasible (although single mothers could not survive on state benefits; they had to work to secure their independence). In this period, the number of children born outside marriage began to increase significantly.

The collapse of the Soviet state changed all this. Motherhood is no longer viewed as a state function, and correspondingly state support for mothers has been reduced. Meanwhile, in the light of the shifting political priorities, nurseries and kindergartens are no longer regarded as an important state service. The post-Soviet state is no longer concerned to ensure it has a role in the socialisation of young children, whom it is happy to consign to the private sphere. The authorities are also not so worried about ensuring full female labour participation – indeed, a fall in this is seen by some policymakers as the best solution to unemployment. What does this shift in attitude imply for the institution of motherhood in the post-Soviet era? The following sections examine this question through an analysis of the popular press in 1996, and interviews with women of childbearing age.

'Only you need your child': an analysis of the contemporary press[13]

The following analysis of the treatment of motherhood in the contemporary Russian press is based on my monitoring of newspapers and magazines in 1996. I did not select the themes that are discussed in advance – the areas of interest that I identify below emerged from my analysis of the data. Clearly, there was a subjective element to this, and the themes that are identified can be seen as the product of the interaction between a 'living author' and a 'living text' (Stanley, 1985). But, overall, the treatment of motherhood in the publications that were studied tended to follow similar lines – the standpoint of 'international' magazines such as *Cosmopolitan*, for example, did not differ significantly from that of Russian magazines, perhaps because of the effort the managers of such publications expend in studying the nature of local markets.

The first point to note regarding the treatment of motherhood in the press is that it clearly reflects the fact that maternity is no longer a state function. In place of a concept of duty, there is a new emphasis on individual choice, responsibility and even pleasure. This can be seen, for example, in the treatment of large families. In the past, having a large number of children was viewed as unquestionably positive; it was a heroic service to the motherland. Now, given that responsibility for reproduction has been transferred to the private sphere, it is viewed in a very different light. A number of authors treat it as ill thought out and self-indulgent behaviour – as a route to poverty which places an unnecessary burden on the social services.[14] Others stress that it is only possible in present conditions if the husband is capable of earning enough money to support the family and the wife is able to economise.[15] Given the new pluralism in the press, however, this is not a unanimous opinion, even though it is a dominant one. There are those who are more optimistic and stress the potential pleasure to be gained from motherhood whatever the financial situation. This, for example, is the attitude of the author of 'You don't have to be Venus to give birth in the sea surf', who claims that 'women in our group are not afraid to give birth. Three children is the norm' (*Komsomol'skaya pravda*, 7 August 1996: 1). The increasing emphasis on pleasure can also be seen in articles relating to the upbringing of children – although the work involved in motherhood is not denied, greater emphasis is placed on its enjoyable aspects. The break with the past implied by this is highlighted by the title of an article by Anna Leont'eva: 'Less heroic exploit, more maternity' (*Krest'yanka*, no. 3, 1996: 36). Such articles clearly highlight the reconceptualisation of motherhood as a private experience – the pleasure is private, as is the financial responsibility.[16]

The gradual privatisation of the maternal experience has opened up a discussion over women's control over their bodies: if they are no longer seen as incubators retained and rewarded by the state, then they clearly have greater rights. Thus, for example, while in the Soviet era strong pressure was put on women to get married and have children when young, now the more liberal press treats the decision to defer having children with greater sympathy. As the author of an article called 'When the mother is over 40' comments:

Many people think that only at this age is it possible to feel the full joy of motherhood, because it is at this age that a person becomes fully mature, when the value of all other pleasures – parties, cinema, sex, professional achievements and so on – is already known to be small in comparison to the possibility of communication with a little one, with your own child.

(*Materinstvo*, no. 1, September 1996: 108)

Unsurprisingly, however, the pro-Communist press is critical of the fact that women have begun to defer motherhood until 'abnormally' late, leading them to have fewer children or to forgo the experience altogether. Meanwhile, the rest of the press continues to see early motherhood as the best option – unless, of course, it is too early, in which case it is deemed to be a problem.[17] Certainly, the tone of much of this shows that the prescriptive proclivity of the Russian press has not been eroded overnight, but at the same time some sections of the press are beginning to accept the validity of individual preference in relation to parenthood.

The greater emphasis on individual choice can also be seen in relation to the discussion of childbirth itself. The state monopoly and rigid control of the obstetric sphere is no longer in operation, and it is therefore possible to discuss alternatives. For example, in some sections of the press, options for improving the experience of childbirth – such as giving birth in water, at home, or with the participation of the father – are discussed.[18] The coverage is less coy and more informative than in the past, and is often accompanied by colour photographs. There are, however, some exceptions – one article, for example, referred to menstruation as 'the womb's tears for the child that wasn't conceived'! (*Rabotnitsa*, 4, 1996: 34). Other articles engage with childbirth in typical old-Soviet style – as an unavoidable form of suffering which confers on every woman who goes through it the status of a heroine:

The men get all the joy of the event and women get all the rest. ... Eternal fear, blood, sweat, tears, the difficulty of producing the first milk, the night cries of babies with dirty nappies, weakness – you can't even lift a kettle, let alone a baby ... in the words of one doctor 'Well, love, birth, it is always a tragedy. We'll manage it.'

(*Sobesednik*, no. 28, July 1996: 8–9)

None the less, although some of the attitudes of the past persist, the idea that women have the right to make decisions over how to give birth has begun to take root.

In some other post-communist countries women have been liberated from the demographic demands of the state only to be subjected to the moral strictures of the church – most notably in Poland where abortion has been banned since the collapse of communism. This has so far not occurred in Russia. Nor, it seems, is abortion a particularly contentious issue. None of the papers in the period of my review contain anti-abortion articles. The attention paid to contraception also suggests that the idea that sex and reproduction can be separate issues is beginning to gain ground.[19]

While the retreat of the state has begun to hand women potential control of their bodies, it has also cleared the way for the reclamation of the institution of fatherhood. The general sentiment of the press in this connection can be summed up thus: 'Fathers, return to the family!' The space created for the individual father by the retreat of the state is explicitly recognised in an article entitled 'A secondary role':

> Today our Russian post-Soviet fathers have gained the chance to oc-cupy an appropriate place in the family. As soon as the economy be-came market-oriented, it required the development of traditional male qualities, and a man obtained the possibility of returning to his normal and natural role. His destiny is now in his own hands. ... He can (if he wants, if he gets up from the sofa and makes an effort) provide for his family. Now he himself must take responsibility for the children, and not delegate it to Big Daddy: the state.
>
> (*Materinstvo*, no. 1, September 1996: 91)

The author of this article, Lina Tarkhova, stresses that, 'the role of the father is designed for an active and responsible man'. She is optimistic, claiming that the Russian family is becoming more similar to that of the Protestant tradition 'where the role of the husband and father is especially important' and much larger in comparison to the Orthodox tradition (ibid.: 91). What is interesting about this article is Tarkhova's emphasis on the *potential* of men to play a greater role: whether they will actually stir themselves to substitute for Big Daddy is an open question. This highlights one of the key areas of tension in Russia's new pattern of gender relations.

Tarkhova seems mainly concerned with the question of financial provi-sion, but other commentators have a wider concept of paternal participa-tion. The other strand to such discussion is the idea that men should play a greater role in the upbringing of children, feeding, washing and caring for them in the same way that women do. Even more striking is the attention given to the idea that fathers should be present at the birth of their children, which, it is argued, strengthens the biological link between father and child. This represents a complete break with Soviet obstetric practice, which ensured that men were not allowed to see their wives or their children until five days after the birth, as well as with Soviet discourse which placed very little emphasis on the father–child link. For example, an article entitled 'I was the first person you saw', argues that, 'when the fathers are allowed to play an active role in childcare they become equally good baby-sitters as the mothers'. The article provides a mother's moving description of the formation of this bond: 'it was simply born and it said, "hi Daddy" (coming from my ... belly into daddy's trembling hands)' (*Krest'yanka*, no. 8, 1996: 32). Another indication of the new importance placed on fatherhood is the attention given to new reproductive technologies designed to help men who are suffering from infertility. The scars of the past are still visible, however, and many articles are devoted to tales of egotistical, cold and absent fathers. But single mothers no longer stand alone as the victims of indifferent partners – the phenomenon of the single father, left by his uncaring wife to care for their children, has also entered the popular consciousness. In a complete reversal of usual gender stereotypes one article, entitled 'How the Pope of Rome became a single father', examines the experience of an abandoned man. The mother of the children fits the usual press profile of the irresponsible father: '[His] six children do not object to his new marriage. The main thing as far as they are concerned is that their future mother shouldn't be a heavy-drinking brawler' (*Komsomol'skaya pravda*, 7 August 1996: 6).

Although the possibility of fathers returning to the family is welcomed, there is some ambivalence about the desertion of the former 'father' of all Soviet children – the state. Many articles imply that the post-communist state has reneged on what still tend to be perceived as its parental responsibilities. This is underlined, for example, in an article entitled 'A good deed lasts for two centuries', about a priest and his wife who organised a shelter for abandoned children and the elderly. The author asks the rhetorical question, 'How can such a large family be provided for? The state gave no help. Private individuals and enterprises helped' (*Moskovskii novosti*, 28 July–4 August 1996: 23). What is usually noted in such articles is the insufficiency of state support, and the consequent fall in the birth rate and increased incidence of child poverty. For example, Eduard Grafov relates a sad tale of a girl called Arina who died of hunger because her father had not been paid for several months: '80 per cent of parents give their children all they can. But how much have they got to give?' He then proceeds to examine the gloomy statistics regarding the incidence of child poverty (*Vechernyaya Moskva*, 7 August 1996: 1). The subject which above all induces a craving for state action, however, is the perception that Russia is facing a demographic crisis. The fact that women are refraining from having children is often noted. One article, for example, claimed those women who wanted children were being forced to flee Russia: 'Future and potential mothers all try to marry abroad, to emigrate, to run away and who can blame them? People don't want to starve and don't want their children to starve. Everyone saves themselves as best they can' (*Sotsial'naya zashchita*, no. 3, 1996: 135). Another article painted a grim picture of depopulation, which in the author's view resulted from the state failing to provide work for women: 'In these conditions [the mass unemployment of women] it is difficult to decide to have a child. According to surveys only 24 per cent of women plan to have children and of these 41 per cent want to have only one' (*Pravda-5*, 3 August 1996: 3).

Most authors at least imply that such problems are created by the state which is seen to have deserted parents: 'Society must finally recognise its responsibility for the creation of the best conditions for increasing the population. It must share responsibility with parents' (*Sotsial'naya zashita*, no. 2, 1996: 99). Such calls to action are often couched in national terms, with the Russian nation replacing communism as the altar of maternal sacrifice. A typical example is an article entitled 'How many Russians are left in the world?', which lamented that, 'Russia has entered a period of demographic collapse: mortality is higher than fertility ... Russians have become a divided and dying people. It's a pity that it's like that' (*Sobesednik*, 28 July 1996: 4). This highlights the fact that the changing politics of motherhood is closely tied up with wider political struggles in Russia: were either nationalists or communists to triumph, the control of the bodies of 'future mothers' could once again be seen by those in power as a legitimate concern of the state.

Fears regarding the future of Russia are also reflected in the treatment of the symbol of the nation, Mother Russia. In the Soviet era, Mother Russia was portrayed as a monumental and heroic figure, an exacting standard against which the citizen-children were measured (and inevitably found wanting). In contemporary Russia, by contrast, she is portrayed as suffering, weak and unattractive, while her child (the future of Russia) is hunted by evil forces. This hunt is graphically described by Aleksandr Prokhanov in an article entitled 'We are from Russian civilisation':

> Our country – like a future mother, who as a result of feeling the first movement of her child, calms down, loses her beauty, avoids any superficial fuss, concentrates on her internal life, on the mysterious growth [inside her] – not feeling ashamed that it was called 'stagnant', gathered its resources to pour into its future extraordinary child, and prepared itself for the birth. ... As in the story of King Herod (for Orthodox Christians, Yel'tsin is equivalent to King Herod), murderers searched for this future hero and saviour and mercilessly crushed the screaming mother.
>
> (*Zavtra*, no. 31, August 1996)

The main exception to such tragic musings on Mother Russia is the treatment of the soldiers' mothers, which recalls earlier Soviet maternal imagery. These mothers, it is argued, 'must' stop the war in Chechnya. A whole issue of *Moskvichka* (no. 17, 1996) was devoted to this theme, and was rich in 'heroic' maternal imagery. Nearly all those who contributed thought that mothers had a special role to play, summed up especially well by a deputy of the Ingush state Duma, who argued that politics must be performed with clean hands, 'what can be cleaner than women's hands, mothers' hands?' Meanwhile, Eset Gorchkanova, the leader of the women's movement in Urus-Martan in Chechnya, appealed to Russian mothers: 'Dear Russian women, take your sons from Chechnya and we will take our sons' – a plea which implies a boundless maternal authority.

Soviet propaganda and iconography was built upon pre-existing ideas regarding the significance of motherhood, and its centrality to the life of every woman. Such ideas continue to be expressed, as does the notion of the mother as the guarantor of world order. A good example of both these preoccupations is provided by Ekaterina Kozhukhova, writing in *Rabotnitsa* (no. 2, 1996): 'A Russian mother knew that the hour would come when God would ask her not what kind of boss she was at work, not how well dressed she was, nor what were her life achievements, but what kind of mother she was.' She also pointed out that the main beam supporting the traditional Russian house was known as the *matitsa*, a word derived from the Russian word for mother: 'the Russian woman spiritually preserved the [integrity of] the family and the fatherland'.[20] In this sense, motherhood is still perceived as the natural and special mission of women. In contrast to this, one article (*Materinstvo*, no. 1, September 1996: 25) links the symbolic status of the mother in Russia with the popularity of *mat*, the Russian sub-language of curses, implying that the mother is both revered and hated. Igor Martynov argues that the increased use of *mat* is related to greater freedom and the sexualisation of society (*Komsomol'skaya pravda*, 27 July 1996: 4). This suggests that with the increasing emphasis on women as sexual beings, the emphasis on their maternal potential is weakening.

A common perception in the press is that hand in hand with the increasing sexualisation of Russian society has come a rise in violence: both tend to be viewed as unwelcome products of liberalisation. It is therefore not surprising that a major preoccupation of the press is the cruel and unjust treatment of children found in articles concerning abandonment; child murder, including that carried out by mothers; child prostitution; the sale of children; and other forms of criminal use of children by parents or guardians. For example, a typical article discussed illegal adoption, arguing, 'This is one business which the crisis won't ruin. In Russia there is a trade in children and there will continue to be a trade in children. As the criminal argues, "It is better to be sold to kind people than to be killed by your own mother" ' (*Moskovskii komsomolets*, 7 August 1996: 2).[21] It is notable that the theme of adoption occurs more often in relation to discussions of the trade in children than it does in relation to infertility. Such issues were not discussed in the Soviet era, and in the rare cases when they were mentioned it was as cruel and bizarre exceptions.

Meanwhile, a relatively familiar subject from the early Soviet period – the means of dealing with orphans and abandoned children – also features in these discussions. Particular prominence is given to children's 'family' homes of the type in which abandoned children are given a 'mother' – in the best case a spinster with no children of her own – and a place in a house where she acts as their guardian. These articles reveal the extent to which the private family has been rehabilitated: institutional care-givers are now praised for mimicking the family. 'Fathers' for these homes are not envisaged, however. It seems that fathers, in comparison to mothers, are still seen as something of a luxury.[22] Having said this, however, one of the articles in *Krest'yanka*, a magazine which is notable for the amount of attention it gives to fatherhood, does publicise the existence of a children's home headed by a man, a veteran of the war in Afghanistan who is quoted as saying, 'All 56 battles [in Afghanistan] are mine. And 57 children are also mine.' He can 'talk to each child as if he were his only [child], and he was his natural and only father'. The veteran claimed to find it 'incredibly interesting' (*Krest'yanka*, no. 8, 1996: 12).

Infertility is another new topic for the press. Although, as mentioned above, there is still a tendency to view motherhood as a universal and central part of any woman's life, those suffering from infertility are often advised to concentrate on other interests in life. Other suggestions are to adopt children, or, for example, to marry a single father.[23] At the same time, however, there is still a tendency to privilege biological motherhood over social motherhood. For example, an article entitled 'new maids' – about women who have chosen to become 'old maids' – is very negative about the behaviour of such women, some of whom adopt only daughters. The author of the article writes about this scathingly, arguing that this is not true motherhood because it doesn't involve bringing a new child into the world (*Rabotnitsa*, no. 9, 1996: 34). In cases where disputes arise between a surrogate mother and the biological mother, the journalist's sympathy usually lies with the latter. This attitude is clearly visible in an article by Tat'yana Gur'yanova and Tat'yana Ressina on this topic. They begin by asserting, 'Isn't it a joy for the mother to know that the child, even if it was carried by another woman, sometimes a complete stranger, is genetically a continuation of her line?' They then note that the views of the husband of the surrogate mother are not considered when the baby is handed over 'and thank God! ... the infertile couple ... at any moment risk losing the child with their own blood, which it has been so hard for them to obtain' (*Moskovskii komsomolets*, 18 June 1996: 7).

This review of the contemporary press makes it clear that a transformation in the approach to motherhood has occurred within Russian society. In particular, it is increasingly seen as an individual choice, responsibility and pleasure. The extent to which the state should support parents is a matter for debate, but the father is no longer viewed as a competitor with the state. He is perceived to have a legitimate place in the family, which has likewise been fully rehabilitated as an institution. None the less, motherhood is still privileged over the notion of parenthood, and a tendency to view motherhood as the destiny of women persists. The pro-natalist bias of the press is also still very much in place, as can be seen in the continuation of the Soviet tradition of seeing biological parenthood as superior to social parenting, and the regularity with which despairing articles about the birth rate are published.

Motherhood, fatherhood, parenthood: the views of contemporary Russian women

The previous section leads us to ask the following: 'Are these changes in the public portrayal of motherhood, and the shift in state policy, reflected in the subjective perceptions of women?'[24] Assessing this question presents some methodological problems; for although it is possible to chart changes in state policy and public discourse regarding motherhood, it is difficult to assess what impact these had on women in the past, and therefore to discuss the nature of any shifts which have occurred in the post-communist era. For example, it is clear that there has been a shift from the idea of motherhood as a duty to the state, towards the idea that it is an individual's choice and responsibility. What is harder to assess, however, is whether women themselves perceived having children as a civic duty in the Soviet era. Regardless of the propaganda directed at them, the idea that women did not see having children as an individual choice seems hard to sustain. Why, if this was the case, was the abortion rate so high? And if women meekly accepted their duty to be mothers, why was all the propaganda necessary?

Given such difficulties, it is not very easy to compare past and present attitudes of women. What I propose to do here, therefore, is take one 'hot topic' of the post-Soviet era – the role of the father – and examine how women are dealing with this. As mentioned above, by the end of the Soviet era, state support for mothers was reasonably well developed. In addition to this, Soviet society was becoming less traditional and more tolerant. It was thus becoming progressively easier for women to 'go it alone', and in the 1980s the number of children born outside marriage rose sharply. Indeed, within this environment single motherhood became quite socially acceptable.

After the collapse of the Soviet Union, however, the two-parent family has become the new ideal, and fathers have been expected to fill the void left by the state. Moreover, in line with the opinions expressed in the press, there is a widespread perception that it is now financially impossible to have children without male support, especially given the erosion of state benefits. This, for example, was a typical comment of one of my respondents, Raya, who was born in 1962. She has one daughter, but relinquished her son after his father left her in the fourth month of her pregnancy. She claimed, 'in an economic sense, it [motherhood] was easier [before]. ... Now a child means that the wife won't work, that the husband alone will work: that is, that there will be some deprivation in many areas. To divide one pay packet in two will be pretty difficult.' This comment also highlights the beginnings of another potential cultural shift: the idea that it is impossible to be a working mother. This possibly reflects the decline in pre-school provision, and also the fact that a whole section of the economy – the new private sector, where the highest wages are often to be found – does not honour the maternity leave provisions, which guarantee that a woman can return to her job within three years of having a child. In the light of such problems, having a man may seem to some women to be a prerequisite of having children.

Meanwhile, at an ideological level, the idea that two-parent families are a 'good thing' is in the ascendant.[25] This had certainly had an impact on some of my respondents. They had for the most part grown up during the 1970s and many of them recall that to become a single mother at that time was acceptable. Indeed, some of them had even planned on it, as the following quotations reveal:

> As a child it definitely seemed to me that if the role of the man was … simply to create the child biologically, then it's really strange, why do you have to live with him afterwards? You've also got to get on with him, wash his socks, and it's not even clear what you get out of it. Not everyone wants that.
>
> (Irina)

> Yes, I always thought that I didn't need a man, a husband, no way, I just needed a child.
>
> (Marina)

Both these women had, however, markedly altered their views with time. Irina is now married with one child which she had with the help of fertility treatment, while Marina is also married with a child which she had within wedlock. They commented:

> Then I began to want to involve a man in this thing, and it suddenly seemed to me that it is unfair and it is not in everyone's interest [that men are not included], for a man, because nobody needs him, for a woman, because she is overworked, and for the child, because it would be better for the child to be able to communicate with a father. In addition, the economic situation has changed. And, also, I began to meet these sorts of men in real life, the good men, who, as I found out, want this themselves.
>
> (Irina)

> And then I thought – well, OK, I do not want a husband, but did I ask the child about that? Did I ask him whether he needs a father or not? If, for example, I asked him and he said that there was no need [for a father] then that is another thing. And, also, if something were to happen to me, my mother is not very healthy, so, then, would a child

have no close relatives in this situation? While ... [with a father] he will have a father and this father's parents.

(Marina)

Obviously, the role of personal factors in these changes in perception cannot be ruled out, but they have none the less taken place within a conducive environment: these women have moved with the times.

There is a big problem with the putative return of the father, however. Are men ready for the new role which they are expected to play? Many women would answer a categorical 'no' to this question, believing that single motherhood is still preferable to involvement with a man. Vera, a single mother and founder of a self-help organisation called 'Only Mummy' comprised of fifty single mothers, was unequivocal in her response when asked whether she thought it was important to have a man around as a father for the child:

> Trousers? You don't need trousers. That is, the sort of man who's simply in the house, but he doesn't give anything to the children, not money, not joy, nor a feeling of protection, you don't need that sort – you're better off without.

Lyudmila, a woman who loved her job, was opposed to marriage and as yet had no children, had a similar opinion:

> What do you need that sort of husband for if he can't even stand beside you? One of my friends got married, and he [her husband] couldn't even stand up in the registry office; he was so drunk that he fell down.

Similarly, Nina, who was married with eight children, when asked why her mother had not married for a second time, replied: 'What's the point of getting married – to be beaten? Once is enough.' Galya, meanwhile, who had adopted a daughter because of infertility, spoke approvingly of the conscious decision of one of her friends to go it alone:

> She had already lost hope of getting married, and decided to have a child. [Her] mother was in shock at first [but] now she's resigned to it. N. was coming to this [idea] for two years and now it's matured. She's already 29.

These sceptical views of the benefits of having a man around provide some explanation of why, despite the prevalence of the idea that it is impossible for women to survive alone, the proportion of children being born outside marriage has not declined since the 1980s.

This does not mean, however, that some women do not suffer for the lack of a man. With only one exception, all the mothers I interviewed who had given up their children at birth had done so either for economic reasons or because of a lack of support (whether from the father or a wider social network). Many relinquishing mothers and those who planned to relinquish but then re-thought had ended up having an unwanted child as a result of a 'struggle for a man'. One woman, Nastya, had given birth to not one but three children in the (fruitless) struggle to catch the same man. She ended up relinquishing her third child after the father cut off contact with her. As Raya, the relinquishing mother quoted above (p. 47), recognised: 'The idea came into my head that perhaps it happened so that he wouldn't leave … that if I have a child he'd stay with me, and all that.' In other cases where either the child is important in its own right, or the mother has the resources to support herself and her child, the 'struggle for a man' will result in single motherhood, as it did in the case of Vera, the organiser of 'Only Mummy'. This, however, can be difficult. The state no longer has a policy of trying to keep mother and child together as an 'indivisible whole'. The implications of this are illustrated by the story of Tamara who was planning to relinquish her daughter at birth. On seeing the child, however, she felt a 'maternal instinct' and changed her mind. All the same, she was obliged to put the child into state care with the option of taking her back within a year since she was a student with no money and nowhere to live and keep the child.

The above discussion implies that the new family ideal in which the man plays a key role does not as yet match reality. Women are continually disappointed by men, something which can result in a mother relinquishing her child if she does not have sufficient support, or can lead to single motherhood. This is not surprising, given that the Soviet state had usurped the role of men in the private sphere to such an extent that it had all but ceased to exist. The retreat of the state, meanwhile, though it may have contributed to raising women's expectations, has not had an immediate impact on male behaviour. As Tarkhova implies in her interesting reflections on fatherhood, it is getting men 'off the sofa' and inducing them to 'make an effort' which is the problem for would-be female partners (*Materinstvo*, no. 1, September 1996: 91). In this sense, the future of motherhood, fatherhood and parenthood is still in the balance, with the gulf between the new ideals and the existing reality likely to do little to resolve the gender tensions bequeathed by the Soviet state.

Notes

1 The journal changed its name several times during the pre-war period. Between 1926–32 it was published under the title *Okhrana materinstva i mladenchestva* ('The Protection of Motherhood and Infancy'); the 1933 issues and the first three issues of 1934 were entitled *Yasli* ('Nursery'), while for the remainder of 1934 it was known as *Materinstvo i mladenchestvo* ('Motherhood and Infancy'). Between 1935–41 it was published under the title, *Voprosy*

materinstva i mladenchestva ('Questions of Motherhood and Infancy'). I use
the latter title here because it is the library catalogue listing.

2 The following publications were monitored: *Argumenty i fakty, Dochki-
materi, Izvestia, Komsomol'skaya pravda, Kul'tura, Kuranty, Megapolis-
ekspress, Moskvichka, Moskovskaya pravda, Moskovskii komsomolets,
Moskovskie novosti, Pravda, Pravda-5, Nezavisimaya gazeta, Rabochaya
tribuna, Semeinyi sovet, Semya, Segodnya, Sobesednik, Sudarushka, Trud,
Vechernii klub, Vechernyaya Moskva, Vek,* and *Zavtra.*

3 These commissions already existed, although in the 1920s their function had
been to decide who would receive *free* abortions.

4 This point has also been recently made by Fuqua (1996: 19), Vishnevskii
(1998: 127), and Wood (1997: 106–7). Wood notes that Lenin castigated 'neo-
Malthusianism' as 'a tendency of the egotistical and unfeeling bourgeois
couple' and rejected all teachings of family limitation (Wood, 1997: 107),
while Fuqua and Vishnevskii note that the 1920 decree legalising abortion was
explicitly written with the aim of protecting the interests of *the collective* rather
than the individual woman. Abortion was still noted in the decree to be 'an evil
for the collective' (Vishnevskii, 1998: 127). [SA]

5 See, for example, Seletskii (1927).

6 In the 1920s the folk-healers were the subject of hostile propaganda
campaigns, with posters boasting such slogans as 'the folk-healer will cripple
your health'. In the posters peasant women, symbolised by headscarves tied
under their chins, were typically shown risking their health with the *babka*,
while conscious workers, their scarves tied behind their heads, were shown
visiting the clean, Bolshevik clinic (Bernstein, 1998). [SA]

7 In fact, however, though inadequate feeding may have been part of the
problem, infant mortality among foundlings consigned to the (not so tender)
care of peasant wet nurses was lower than in state institutions.

8 A 1930 article with this question as its title came down firmly in favour of the
former option (Erman, 1930).

9 See, for example, Mitina (1926) and Klimanova (1926).

10 The long hours themselves were nothing new. As Barbara Engel notes, in the
pre-revolutionary period peasant children born during the busy summer
months – known as 'the time of suffering' (*stradnaya pora*) – were far less
likely to survive, since their mothers took them into the fields with them while
they worked, leaving them unsupervised in the shade and returning to them
rarely for brief feeds (Engel, 1994: 49).

11 With the launch of the first five-year plan childcare itself was to be put on an
'industrial' footing: for example, one article of this era argued that it was
necessary to transform factory nurseries into 'another form of workshop, a
nursery workshop for the factory' (Feder, 1931).

12 The importance attached to the provision of uniform socialisation can be
adduced from the recognition that even class enemies required nurseries:
Kopelyanskaya (1934), for example, in an article typical of the purge era,
earnestly stressed the need for nurseries to be established in prisons.

13 'Only you need your child' was a comment that I heard, made by a doctor in a
Moscow clinic. To my mind, it sums up the official attitude to motherhood in
post-communist Russia.

14 See, for example, 'Put my mother in prison' (*Vechernyaya Moskva*, 7 August
1996: 1).

15 This is an attitude which is often manifested in relation to the decision to have
any children at all. As one article put it, 'in order to decide to have a child it is
necessary not only to be brave, but also not to be poor' (*Komsomol'skaya
pravda*, 1 June 1996: 1).

16 The retreat of the state is also highlighted by the discussion of new private means of protecting the rights of children – such as the conclusion of agreements regarding alimony, prenuptial agreements and the like. See, for example, Elena Mushkina in *Vek*, no. 31, 9–15 August 1996: 12.
17 See, for example, *Sem'ya*, no. 31: 6.
18 Examples of this are the article by Anastasia Pleshakova, 'A person is born' (*Komsomol'skaya pravda*, 1 June 1996: 1), and Marina Kupratsevich's, 'You don't have to be Venus to give birth in the sea surf', an article about giving birth in the Black Sea (*Komsomol'skaya pravda*, 7 August 1996: 1).
19 See, for example, Marina Korchagina in *Nezavisimaya gazeta*, 23 July 1996: 8.
20 It should be noted, however, that some authors have begun to rebel against the idea that the mission of Mother Russia is to save the world. As one author ironically notes: 'Enough of [this idea that] we carry the world on our shoulders! If we move away it won't fall down!' (*Komsomol'skaya pravda*, 27 July 1996: 4).
21 Other examples of the preoccupation with cruelty are the articles, 'Put my mother in prison' (*Vechernyaya Moskva*, 7 August 1996: 1); 'Hunting butterflies with a knife', an article about a schizophrenic mother who killed her sons with a knife (*Sobesednik*, 30 August 1996: 7); and 'Concentration camp in Pervomaika', a story of serious parental neglect (*Trud*, 3 August 1996: 2).
22 An example of this is an article entitled 'Mamka, mama, mamochka' (*Moskovskii komsomolets*, 26 July 1996: 4).
23 For example, an article entitled 'A twist of fate' relates how an infertile young woman began living with a single father whose wife had been killed in a car accident (*Domashnii ochag*, September 1996).
24 For a more detailed examination of the women's motivation for decisions regarding motherhood, see Issoupova (forthcoming).
25 It should be noted that Irina Tartakovskaya's review of the press in 1984 (this volume) revealed a diversity of views regarding single motherhood. *Izvestia* and *Sovetskaya Rossiya* may have favoured the two-parent family, but the youth paper *Komsomol'skaya pravda* glorified the single worker-mother.

References

Al'tgauzen, N. F. (1926) 'Ocherki po grudnomu vskarmlivaniyu', *Voprosy materinstva i mladenchestva*, 1: 21–9.
Bernstein, F. (1998) 'Envisioning health in revolutionary Russia: The politics of gender in sexual-enlightenment posters of the 1920s', *Russian Review*, 57: 191–217.
Bryukhanov, N. D. (1935) 'Rabota akusherskogo punkta v kolkhozakh Moskovskoi oblasti', *Voprosy materinstva i mladenchestva*, 1: 34– 5.
Bukh (1927) 'Rabota akusherskogo punkta v tatarskom poselke', *Voprosy materinstva i mladenchestva*, 3: 39–44.
Davydov, I. (1927) 'Trudovoe obshchezhitie dlya besprizornykh materei v g. Taganroge', *Voprosy materinstva i mladenchestva*, 12: 30– 3.
Durnovo, A. S. (1926) 'Nasledstvennost' i novoe pokolenie', *Voprosy materinstva i mladenchestva*, 1: 10–16.
Engel, B. (1994) *Between the Fields and the City: Women, Work and the Family in Russia, 1861–1914*, Cambridge: Cambridge University Press.
Erman, S. (1930) 'Yasli ili detkolonii?', *Voprosy materinstva i mladenchestva*, 6: 27–8.

Feder, E. A. (1931) 'Litsom k proizvodstvu', *Voprosy materinstva i mladenchestva*, 1: 10–13.

Fuqua, M. (1996) *The Politics of the Domestic Sphere: The Zhenotdely, Women's Liberation and the Search for a Novyi Byt in Early Soviet Russia*, paper no. 10, Seattle, WA: The Henry M. Jackson School of International Studies, University of Washington.

Grigo, Yu. (1930) 'Rabota Sovetskoi vlasti v oblasti polovogo prosveshcheniya zhenskogo naseleniya', *Voprosy materinstva i mladenchestva*, 5: 17–19.

Grossman, Ya. (1930) 'Rabota po standartizatsii v oblasti okhrany materinstva i mladenchestva sotsial'nogo sektora', *Voprosy materinstva i mladenchestva*, 3: 22–3.

Issoupova, I. (forthcoming) 'Problematic motherhood: child abandonment, abortion, adoption and single motherhood in Russia in the 1990s', *Slavonica*.

Kaminskii, G. N. (1936) 'Rech' narkoma zdravookhraneniya na vtoroi sessii Vserossiiskogo TsIK XVI sozyva', *Voprosy materinstva i mladenchestva*, 3: 1–4.

Klimanova, A. B. (1926) 'O detskom lyubopytstve', *Voprosy materinstva i mladenchestva*, 8: 12–16.

Klimovskaya, M. A. (1930) 'Bytovye shtrikhi o podkidyvanii detei po materialam Permskogo doma mladentsa', *Voprosy materinstva i mladenchestva*, 8–9: 19–21.

Kollontai, A. [1919] (1977) 'Communism and the Family' in A. Holt (ed.), *Selected Writings of Alexandra Kollontai*, London: Allison and Busby.

Kopelyanskaya, O. E. (1934) 'Sotsial'no-pravovaya pomoshch' materi i rebenku', *Voprosy materinstva i mladenchestva*, 3: 30–5.

Krist, E. (1930) 'Kassy vsaimopomoshchi materei', *Voprosy materinstva i mladenchestva*, 2: 22–6.

Lebedeva, V. (1926) 'Zadachi i puti okhrany materinstva i mladenchestva', *Voprosy materinstva i mladenchestva*, 1: 6–9.

Levi, M. F. (1927) 'Nekotorye osobennosti otpravleniya funktsii materinstva u meditsinskikh rabotnits', *Voprosy materinstva i mladenchestva*, 3: 3–9.

—— (1937) 'Budem tochno i neuklonno vypolnyat' postanovlenie pravitel'stva o zapreshchenii abortov', *Voprosy materinstva i mladenchestva*, 1: 30–5.

Lunts, R. O. (1926) 'Glavneishie defekty ukhoda i ikh vliyanie na razvitie grudnykh detei', *Voprosy materinstva i mladenchestva*, 2: 13–17.

Mitina, A. D. (1926) 'O znachenii podrazhaniya v zhizni' rebenka', *Voprosy materinstva i mladenchestva*, 5: 16–20.

Nogina, O. P. (1935) 'Zadachi okhrany materinstva i mladenchestva v 1935 godu', *Voprosy materinstva i mladenchestva*, 1: 1–12.

—— (1936) 'Puti razvertyvaniya meropriyatii po okhrane materinstva i mladenchestva v svyazi s zakonoproektom ot 25.05.36', *Voprosy materinstva i mladenchestva*, 7: 12–22.

—— (1937) 'Konstitutsiya narodov SSSR i gosudarstvennaya okhrana materinstva i mladenchestva', *Voprosy materinstva i mladenchestva*, 1: 19–25.

Rachmanov, A. N. (1926) 'Na puti k soznatel'nomu materinstvu', *Voprosy materinstva i mladenchestva*, 3: 3–8.

Raukhvager, R.V. (1926) 'Bytovoe polozhenie chechenskoi zhenshchiny', *Voprosy materinstva i mladenchestva*, 8: 32–6.

Seletskii, S. A. (1927) 'O rannem vstavanii posle rodov', *Voprosy materinstva i mladenchestva*, 6: 3–8.

Shaburova, M. A. (1934) 'Rech' na soveshchanii yasel'nykh rabotnikov', *Voprosy materinstva i mladenchestva*, 1: 15–22.

Shustova, M. (1927) 'Okhrana materinstva i mladenchestva k 10-i godovshchine Oktyabrya v Ivanovo-Voznesenskoi Gubernii', *Voprosy materinstva i mladenchestva*, 11: 55–9.

Stanley, L. (1985) 'Accounting for the fall of Peter Sutcliffe and the rise of the so-called "Yorkshire Ripper" ', *Occasional Paper no. 15*, Manchester: Department of Sociology, University of Manchester.

Sulimov, D. E. (1934) 'Rech' na soveshchanii yasel'nykh rabotnikov', *Voprosy materinstva i mladenchestva*, 1: 5–9.

Trotsky, L. [1937] (1972) *The Revolution Betrayed: What is the Soviet Union and Where is it Going?*, New York: Pathfinder.

Tsykhanskii, L. S. (1937) 'Opyt organizatsii v tsekhakh fabrik komnat dlya kormleniya detei i punktov po sboru zhenskogo moloka', *Voprosy materinstva i mladenchestva*, 3: 15–18.

Vishnevskii, A. (1998) *Serp i rubl': Konservativnaya modernizatsiya v SSSR*, Moscow: OGI.

Yushkevich, S, (1930) 'Byt gorskikh zhenshchin', *Voprosy materinstva i mladenchestva*, 7: 22–6.

Wood, E. (1997) *The Baba and the Comrade: Gender and Politics in Revolutionary Russia*, Bloomington and Indianapolis: Indiana University Press.

Zal'kindson, S. (1927) 'Istoriya Zaozerskikh letnikh yaslei', *Voprosy materinstva i mladenchestva*, 2: 35–7.

2 Russia's female breadwinners

The changing subjective experience

Marina Kiblitskaya

This chapter looks at the changing experience of female breadwinners in three distinct eras – the Stalin era, the post-war era, and the post-Soviet era. In each case, I highlight particular subjective features of the women's experience, especially their relationship to the state, work, men and the family. The first group comprises women born in the 1920s and 1930s who grew up and worked during the Stalin era; this group I characterise as being 'married to the state'. I argue that during this period a particular female work ethic was inculcated: women were taught that the meaning of life was to be found in work and that personal life was to come second. Although this ethic has been modified over time, its legacy can be seen today in women's response to the challenges of transition. The women breadwinners born in the post-Second World War era I see as 'breadwinners by default'. These women also saw work as important, but their motivation was somewhat different. Ideology was less a part of their lives: they did see work as a duty, but not necessarily one which they conceptualised in relation to the state. They were also driven by their sense of responsibility for the comfort of the family. When married women ended up as 'breadwinners by default' it was usually because their husbands did not share this feeling of responsibility and did not live up to what women saw as their duty to provide.[1] Meanwhile, post-Soviet female breadwinners can be described as 'divorced from the state', in that they have discarded the ideological baggage surrounding their work, and their main aim is to protect their families. In the transition era, women's primary role within the family is something which pushes them to be active and adaptable in the labour market – and in a few cases leads them into successful new careers.

The following account is based on the analysis of fifteen life history interviews with Muscovite women from different generations. I also had access to thirty work history interviews with female breadwinners conducted by my colleagues in the Syktyvkar branch of the Institute for Comparative Labour Relations Research (ISITO), which I used to check my findings. Life history is an appropriate means to examine the subjective experience of respondents. The main idea of this approach is to follow the life path of the respondent in such a way that she herself places emphasis on what she perceives to be the most important aspects of her life. While it is difficult to assess the extent to which my findings can be generalised, the differences between the attitudes of the generations were sufficiently marked for me to be confident that I have identified distinct types of subjective experience of the female breadwinner role.

Married to the state

This section analyses the relationship of women to work, family and personal life during the Stalin era. What is remarkable about this generation of female breadwinners is the extent to which they internalised the state's prescriptions regarding the centrality of work. I describe them as 'married to the state' because, notwithstanding the personal tragedies they experienced under Stalin, they sacrificed their private lives for the sake of work, which crowded out personal concerns. Certainly, 'circumstances' – crash industrialisation, collectivisation, the purges and the Second World War – played an important role in the formation of this generation. It was difficult to form a personal life in such an environment, while losing a husband was an everyday phenomenon. But it would be wrong to downplay the role of ideology and belief in shaping the lives of these women: their commitment to work was by no means instrumental.

The following section highlights the process through which this generation's sense of duty was formed, using the life histories of two Muscovites, Maria and Aleksandra. Both these 'brides of the state' came with their families from provincial Russia to Moscow in the Stalin era. Both began their working lives as teenagers after their mothers became widows – Maria's father died in the gulag after being arrested in 1935, and Aleksandra's father was killed at the front during the Second World War. As such, they came from families on the verge of destitution. This section looks at their description of their childhood years. As will be seen, both women were forced to learn the importance of work and responsibility at an early age.

Maria was born in 1924. Her story reveals not only the necessity which initially drove her out to work, but also the contradictory character of many women's relationship with the state in the Stalin era. The state impinged forcefully and brutally on her childhood – as it did on that of countless others. But, as will be seen, Maria was none the less induced to devote her life to work in its service:

> My childhood was very hard. I can't talk about it [begins crying]. The whole family came to Moscow; my father was called here to work. He was a mechanic in a textile institute. All the heating, all the stokers were under his command. In 1935 he was sentenced. (Now I've gathered all the documents posthumously to rehabilitate him). And it was

then that our hard times began. Tattered, ragged, hungry. My mother was immediately sacked from the institute. They wouldn't take her back for a very long time. Then they took her back at the textile institute. She worked on a machine – combing sheet wadding. Somehow her right arm got caught in the machine, and she lost it, and was left an invalid. She and I went round doing washing [weeps]. We'd ask 'Have you got anything that needs washing, some towel or other?' Some people would give something. And some would say, 'get out of here you beggars'. And we lived like that until 1938. I used to get kerosene for everyone. Then there were rich people, but we were the poorest. 'Masha, go and get the kerosene', they'd give 20 kopeks and I'd go and buy something for 20 kopeks. ... 'Masha, go and wash the floor', 'Masha go and feed the cock' ...

And I didn't have anything to walk in. My mother gave me her size thirty-nine shoes. And I was size thirty-four. And you drag along. You get to school and they don't let you in. 'Take them off. Dirty shoes will make the school dirty.' There was one boy who studied with me at school. Vanya Romanov. I often think about him. I often looked at him and he at me. But we understood that we were from families where someone was in prison [*tyuremshchiki*]. We understood that he had nothing to wear. At break he used to stand in his socks and warm himself on the radiator. And I did the same. ... I wanted to ask 'Who in your family?' (That is, I wanted to know who in his family had been repressed, but in the end I decided not to ask.) So the two of us we went around in rags ...

In 1939 my mother got married for a second time. I don't know who the man she married was. It seemed to me that he was a military man. He did time in prison, but I don't think it was that much. Perhaps they let him go, decided that he was in prison by mistake. They let him out. He helped us, he was good at sewing, and we began to get back on our feet. And then my younger brother was born. On 14 June 1941 I finished school ... and on 21 June the war began. My stepfather was immediately sent to the front. And my mother was left with a young child.

As soon as the war began I went to work at Likhachev factory, or as it was then called, Stalina. They took me on as a radial drill operator. I worked there until the 16 October 1941. And then, because the Germans were advancing on Moscow, they evacuated the factory. I stayed here in Moscow, because I didn't have anything to feed the children. My mother was an invalid and I had to stay behind in order to feed the children. I couldn't be evacuated. I couldn't even think about evacuation.

Aleksandra, by contrast, was not so much a victim of the state as of the Nazis. Nevertheless, the effect was similar – she was forced to become tough and responsible from a young age. She was born in 1928 in a village in Orlovskaya *oblast'*. Her parents were agricultural workers; her brother was killed during the war. In the following extract, she describes her childhood:

> [It was] very hard. When I was 4 years old my parents had to move to Voronezh. My mother worked at an arms factory and my father worked in a public canteen. Until the war we lived in Voronezh, and then we were evacuated to Uzbekistan. It was a very hard time, especially during the period of evacuation. I was evacuated with strangers. And my mother during the time of the attack returned to my father to be with him. Since the town withstood [the attack] we returned to Voronezh, lived there for a little while, and then we had to evacuate to Tambov and then Moscow. In 1942 we turned up in Moscow. Our aunt took us in and we lived with her. My father was killed in Vitebsk. I was 14 years old, and because of the evacuation I had missed two years [at school]. Then I went to school no. 279 on Prospekt Mira. I finished seventh grade and then went to study at the instrument technical college of Kalibr factory. I got a place in a day-time section, but as things were very tough at home (my mother had to work as a caretaker because of the apartment), I moved from [studying] in a day section to [studying] at night. [During the day] I went to work at the Kalibr factory.

Thus, like Maria, Aleksandra not only began her working life when she was young, but also, on beginning work, immediately became the main breadwinner in her family. But as will be seen in the following section these women were not only motivated by their need to provide for their families: the authorities' continual emphasis on the intrinsic value of work played an important role in shaping their attitudes.

'All our generation was in love with work'

All through childhood women such as Maria and Aleksandra heard one message from the state: work, work, work. To work in the Soviet Union was to work for the state – and to work for the state was seen to be the highest purpose in life. For such women, the slogan, 'social interests take precedence over personal ones' (*obshchestvennye interesy vyshe lichnykh*) was not simply empty propaganda, but an idea that helped make sense of their lives.

After the outbreak of war, Maria was sent (through the Komsomol) to work felling trees to build anti-tank defences. Then, in 1942, she began 'top secret' work, building a bomb shelter for the government. This was even more arduous than her previous job – because of the confidential nature of the work, the workers were shut underground for fourteen hours a day. Maria describes her life:

> Working underground, building a metro is very hard work. ... It's a mine, it's rock, clay, water. ... There were shifts; we began at five in the morning. They shut us in at six o'clock in the morning, because we walked [to work] through the metro tunnels, and we had to get through before the trains began working. So we began at five in the morning and finished at eight in the evening. There was an hour for lunch. But Stalin gave us a ration. A little roll and 100–150 grams of sausage. And money, of course. ... We finished the bomb shelter, though Stalin didn't come. ... They also proposed building him one in Kuibyshev, and they built one, but he liked Mayakovskaya Metro station, and until the end of the war he spent nearly all his time at Mayakovskaya.

Maria's attitude to her work in this period of her life is complex. On the one hand, she was no friend of the regime that killed her father, but on the other hand, she felt some pride at having attained secret work in the service of the same regime. Meanwhile, although the work was very arduous, Maria was grateful for it because it was well paid and allowed her to support her mother (who was not working) and younger brother. Most interestingly of all, while she vividly recalls the privations she endured, Maria also sees this as one of the happiest and most interesting periods of her life.

She does not, however, see herself as any kind of heroine. Maria's attitude to her experience is well captured by her response whenever I conveyed sympathy or admiration: 'Oh, who am I? There were millions like me.'[2] Maria explained her acceptance of her lot in terms of the ideological environment of the time: she argued that a whole generation was induced to see work as the most important thing in life. The pressure to work was all-pervasive; it was experienced 'everywhere, in small doses' (*vezde ponemnogu*). Maria felt it most strongly at the enterprise:

> There were a lot of good things in the past at the factory ... But there they always exhorted us to work. Come on work, things will get better. Work! ... They were always saying 'Work! The most important thing in life is your profession. It's for the future. It's for your old age.' [Ironically] And now look at us in our old age. ...
>
> They always said we had to work and we worked. We were afraid of being sacked. Now – you can just shrug your shoulders and leave. But then we valued our jobs. And so we got used to work. Now you can ask any old worker [and they will tell you] – then work was the most important thing for us, and family life came second. And after that leisure. ... All our generation was in love with work. Every day

they went on at us, 'You, watch out, be on time.' To the workers [they'd say]: 'You, watch out, don't get drunk.' When we were paid the foreman would say, 'Watch out, you, I won't cover for you any-more.' From my early childhood [they'd say] 'Masha, why do you walk to school so slowly?' And so you end up going faster ...

Above all, what I want to tell you is that our generation didn't put their personal lives first. Above all they exhorted us to work. Nothing else. And personal life – take it as it comes [*u kogo kak*]. And that's it.

The mixture of coercion and belief in such women's attitude to work is well captured in this quotation. On the one hand, workers were under constant pressure from the authorities to work, but on the other they were 'in love with work'. They were afraid of being sacked, but not just for economic reasons: 'work was the most important thing for us'. In this hot-house environment of ideological exhortation and fear, devotion to work became second nature: 'you end up going faster'. The process through which Aleksandra's work ethic was formed was similar, although in this case she felt the pressure to work most strongly in her family:

In my family they always paid a lot of attention to what I did, and always asked, 'Have you fulfilled [what you were supposed to]? Have you done it?' And so, gradually, I developed a responsible attitude in everything. I did all the errands I was given. I considered that I was obliged to do it. And [now] if I don't get things done at work, I take work home. I won't sleep all night, but I'll get it done.

Again, from this quotation it is clear that, although work and responsibility were initially thrust upon the young Aleksandra, she ended up embracing work as her *raison d'être*, her Stakhanovism long outlasting the circum-stances in which it was formed.

This love affair with work had severe consequences in other areas. Both Maria and Aleksandra neglected their private lives, and seem to have no fond memories of them. In response to questions regarding their personal histories, Maria replied with a decisive, 'it's not interesting', while Aleksandra confined herself to the terse response, 'My personal life worked out in such a way that my husband died.' Asked where she met him, she was unable to recall, and simply restated that he had died, when her son was 6 years old. In response to a question about her son, she replied with pride – her enthusiasm for the interview returning – that he worked alongside her at the Moscow metro. The metro was her reason for living: 'I gave my whole life to the *Metropoliten* and I can't live without the *Metro-politen*. Well, I can't live without it.' Aleksandra claimed to have no regrets about this, arguing that she had 'lived well' and had liked the way she had worked. At this point in the interview she began reading out her *adresa* (personalised records of achievement). She had several of these, in gold hand-written calligraphy, signed by all the prominent figures at her enterprise, as well as by her own collective. Although no material rewards are attached to these records of achievement, Aleksandra, who at 72 years of age is still working for the metro because she cannot live on her pension, values them very highly. According to those who work with her at the enterprise, Aleksandra's enthusiasm for work has in no way slackened with age.

In contrast, Maria was more circumspect about how she had lived her life. She said that if she had her time over again she would live 'differently. For the state, and for myself.' She would have skated more, skied more. She also told a wistful story about the day a man had turned up at her enterprise with a huge bunch of roses. He had given it to one of her friends and said, 'Tell Masha that I have loved her all my life.' She didn't even know who he was. She now sees her solitude as regrettable, and thinks that her generation were 'fools'. None the less, from her own account it is easy to see how work assumed such importance.

Both of these women lived alone for most of their lives and their status as workers came to form the core of their identity. They were 'married to the state' in the sense that their duty to the state – in the form of work – was their main priority. The role of fear and necessity cannot be ignored in their histories, but these factors cannot fully account for the overwhelming sense of duty felt by such women. Obviously, some of this generation of women regret their past more than others, but at the time such sacrifice was considered to be normal: social interests took priority over personal lives.

Breadwinners by default

Although the power of ideology waned after the end of the 'heroic' Stalin era, the normative pressure on women to work remained strong and labour participation continued to be regarded as a 'duty'. None the less, workers were not expected to devote their whole lives to work: they were allowed the space to develop their private lives. Women of this era still did not have much time for skating and skiing, however, because the domestic sphere was seen as their responsibility (and they generally accepted this role). Meanwhile, men usually took on the role of main breadwinner: it is estimated that women received 65–70 per cent of men's wages in the Soviet era (Lapidus 1988: 95). But in a sizeable minority of families the male wage was either low or unreliable, and in these cases women became 'breadwinners by default'.[3] Since they perceived the domestic sphere as their responsibility, women would take it upon themselves to provide for the family when their spouse failed to provide what they perceived as the requisite level of comfort. In this way, the 'breadwinners by default' would come to occupy all the central roles in the family. This section begins by exploring the life histories of three such breadwinners – under communism and during the transition – before moving on to analyse what it was about the Soviet gender order which promoted the types of marital relations in which such women were immersed.

The motivation of the 'breadwinners by default' can be illustrated by the story of Olga, whose working career began in the 1950s. After an unhappy first marriage to a man who beat her, she married for a second time, although this marriage also eventually ended in divorce after twenty-eight years. The main problem in this case was money: Olga felt that the family did not have enough to live on. Her husband was a skilled joiner, a profession which, she emphasised, would have allowed him to find additional employment had he wished to look for it. But when Olga encouraged him to do so he answered, 'If my pay isn't big enough for you, economise. I'm not going to go out stealing.' Although she didn't know exactly how much her husband earned, Olga claimed that it was very little; she had always earned more:

> In general, of course, I fed him [her husband] ... I had two jobs [at the same time], I had three jobs ... And when I worked in the hotel 'Rossiya' I went there at seven and stayed until midnight and some-times until one in the morning and came home after one. And at the same time I had a second job. When I had a break from my main job I ran to do cleaning. ...
>
> On his pay we'd have ended up as beggars. ... Why couldn't he [earn more money]? He didn't want to, I reckon. He didn't feel he needed it. When it was necessary to buy something or other, he'd say 'it's dead capital'. When my son went to work, I began to buy every-thing. I bought everything with my money, did some extra work and bought [things]. It was all bought with my money. My own money. ... Everything that we had in the home was bought by me. ... And he began to drink from the very beginning. He drank even in the very beginning when he worked for the police. But he didn't drink in the way that he did in the end. He loved to drink, but not like that.

The key features of this story are the perceived indifference of the husband to family financial needs (as defined by the wife),[4] and the wife's heroic rectification of his failings. Her husband failed to provide what Olga deemed was necessary for the household, and she was, in her view, forced to do several jobs at once to bridge the gap. The other feature of this story, which crops up frequently in the accounts of other women, is the husband's drink problem, which is often considered by women to be the root of their financial difficulties. In this case, Olga was fairly certain that she earned more than her husband, although often the status of 'breadwinner by default' would be attained because the husband's drinking meant his contribution to the family finances was perceived as unreliable.

Such problems have only intensified during the transition era, as can be seen in the following two histories. The first concerns a typical female provider, Alla, an economist, who married in 1984. She eventually left a job at a military enterprise which she 'really loved', because wages began to be paid late. Meanwhile her husband, in her opinion, had done nothing to keep the family afloat:

> Gradually our relationship came to nothing. Now we live on the verge of divorce. He's constantly moaning, 'Oh, life is so hard.' Well I think that it's shameful for a 40-year-old man to go on about how expensive everything is and how he's not paid. And he says, 'they don't pay me, but [at least] they don't pester me'. I left a job I loved in order to earn money. And he says, 'if you haven't got enough money you think how to get some'. Later he didn't even raise the issue of money. He says, 'You're the rich one here.' But he isn't an invalid is he? At the end of the day you find money, go and unload wagons.
>
> He goes into the faculty, works for two hours and then he's free. He's not used to working from seven until five in the evening. He needs to come home and lie down. I graduated with the recommendation that I should do post-graduate work, but I went to work in a factory. For him it's a problem to get up early in the morning. He's the only son of a mother who never worked. The father did everything. He [her husband] wasn't in the army. He was in a military faculty...[5]
>
> We've got separate budgets. Financially now everything is on my shoulders. I consider myself to be financially independent. I send the child to a holiday home, and I haven't got any money. I said to him, 'The child's going to the holiday home, we've got to pay for the voucher.' He says, 'I haven't got any money.' What does that mean, no money? Borrow it, take it, steal it.

Alla's anger about her husband's inability to earn money is palpable. She feels that she has to take responsibility for everything, that she is the one who has made all the sacrifices to keep the family afloat. In her opinion, her husband's indolence and indifference has forced her to forgo post-graduate study, and to leave her favourite job. Her husband, meanwhile, has sacrificed nothing. Given that he is a healthy man who could easily 'unload wagons', Alla feels that her husband's position is 'shameful'.

Strikingly similar sentiments were expressed by Irina. She married for the second time when she was 29 years old, and at the time of the interview had been with her husband for eighteen years. Initially, she worked in the planning department of an enterprise and her husband was a section chief at an institute, earning more than twice her wage. At this stage 'everything was OK'. During the *perestroika* period, however, her husband's institute began to experience financial difficulties and gradually his pay was reduced to 'peanuts'. At this stage, Irina claimed, 'if it hadn't been for my pay we wouldn't have survived'. Her husband stayed at the institute until 1995, until they ceased paying him altogether. Finally, his friend found him a job at a waterworks as a fitter and caretaker, a job which he took, even though he found it psychologically difficult to adjust to such work. 'But now he has gradually come to the opinion that it's not necessary to have work simply for your soul, but simply, quite simply, to feed your family.' Even though her husband, a man with higher education, has taken extremely low status work simply in order to earn money, Irina is unhappy. She would have preferred a man who took responsibility; who would take charge:

> Now I have a completely different outlook on life. I'd have done better to stay on my own. ... You know, in essence I'm a family woman. For me, the family comes first. I'm simply tired of being a nanny. I want a man who will look after me, who will support me. And all the rest. I've brought up my children, and now I have to bring up my husband. I'm already sick of it.

When asked what she meant by having 'to bring him up', Irina replied:

> Well, he's a little bit – you know – he drinks. In order to feel self-assured. Of course, when he worked at the institute, he tried to earn money and kind of support the family. But all that didn't work out. ... My husband has one big failing. He can come home drunk. If he didn't have that failing then everything in life would have suited me. ... He loves the strong stuff. I've struggled with it the whole seventeen years ... perhaps we should have split up immediately. But that, of course, is his only failing. Now, of course, another one has arisen, the fact that he doesn't earn very much. ... In general, they say that a woman gets the man she deserves. That's what they say on the television. But I none the less say to myself that I deserve better.

As in the case of Olga, drink has played a role in Irina's husband's failure to provide. Meanwhile, like Alla, Irina laments her husband's weakness, and the fact that she is forced to be in control.

The similarity of these women's descriptions of their relationships is notable, but what explains this phenomenon? I would argue that the family dynamics described here are products of the Soviet gender order. The first thing to note about the comments of the breadwinners by default is the way in which they endorse both Soviet and traditional values. It is this combination which causes much of the conflict. Women such as Olga and Alla have, like Aleksandra and Maria, internalised the Soviet work ethic: running away from work is clearly a cardinal sin in their moral universe. Women and men alike are seen as having a duty to work. But, while they see their involvement in work as 'natural',[6] such women also hanker after the pre-revolutionary figure of the male breadwinner (*kormilets*). Their critique of their husbands is based on the idea that a real man provides for his family. This was an idea which the Bolsheviks sought to combat: women were supposed to look to the state and their work for support, not to individual men.[7] But even though, as a result of deliberate state policy, Soviet men rarely earned enough to support non-working wives, the ideal of the *kormilets* lived on in popular consciousness.

Not only did state policy prevent men from being the sole breadwinner, it also served to loosen the ties between men and the family.[8] Meanwhile, in the case of women, the effect of the state was precisely the opposite. Soviet policy was based on the assumption of women's 'natural' responsibility towards the family, while the encouragement of female labour participation strengthened the ability of women to provide for family members. It is within this framework that the biographies of the breadwinners by default should be understood. The dynamics of the relationships analysed all highlight women's acute sense of *responsibility* for the family, and men's sense of disconnection from it.[9] Thus, given that women's expectations of men continued to be fairly traditional, Soviet state policy made a significant contribution to the production of men and women who were in many cases ill-matched.

Once established, the dynamic between 'breadwinners by default' and their husbands tended to intensify over time: the more the wife did, the less the husband did (and the more he drank). On the evidence cited above, it seems that, having failed to live up to his wife's expectations, the husband of a female breadwinner would turn to alcohol increasingly frequently in order to bolster his flagging self-assurance. It matters little who was to blame or 'who started it': 'nagging' wives and 'deadbeat' husbands were predictable products of the Soviet gender order. Irina's commentary on her situation, quoted above, supports this assertion. She argued that, 'in our family I took on the role of the man ... in him [her husband] there's a lot that's feminine. And because of the lack of male qualities I began to fulfil a male role.' She felt that had she been with a more masculine man, 'more feminine qualities might have developed in me'. But instead she had been forced to grit her teeth and fulfil a role she saw as unnatural. There are several points to be made here. First, by a more masculine man, Irina undoubtedly means a sober, high-earning, responsible man. But, as I show in Chapter 4 of this volume, drinking and spending time with other men was a crucial component of masculinity for many Soviet men. Second, it is notable that within the Soviet institutional framework it was possible for women to take on what they perceived to be a male role. In doing so, they often ended up fulfilling all the main roles in the family, while their husbands were increasingly marginalised. Third, despite the fact that women performed such roles, they always resented it and believed that they were forced into such a position by their husband's failure.

How do the breadwinners by default compare with the breadwinners of the Stalin era? What they had in common was a well-developed work ethic, but their motivations differed. Women such as Maria and Aleksandra had a commitment to work which was partly fostered by a sense of duty inculcated by the state. Although this may not have been entirely absent in the later generations, their sense of responsibility for the household was the prime reason for their activism: they keenly felt the need for a comfortable home, for their children to have holidays, and so on. If their husbands failed to provide what they thought was reasonable, then they saw it as their duty to step into the breach. It was this which determined their position as breadwinners by default.

Female breadwinners in transition

As can be seen, Irina's and Alla's experience was very similar to that of Olga's, the main difference being that their husbands' problems were not simply the result of alcohol-induced lethargy, but stemmed mainly from the changes set in train by economic reform. Is there anything new about women's experience in the transition era? This section examines two distinctive features of the present period in post-Soviet Russia. First, any residue of duty to the state which may have prevailed in the late Soviet era has been eroded. In today's Russia, responsibility to the family is the female breadwinner's prime motivation. Second, in a minority of cases, the privations of transition have pushed women into developing lucrative or interesting new careers. While this is clearly not a representative experience, it does show that women's sense of responsibility for ensuring household survival can have positive as well as negative connotations: their past experience of labour market activism can sometimes stand 'breadwinners by default' in good stead.

Female breadwinners of the transition era can be characterised as 'divorced from the state'. Their attitudes are graphically voiced by Elena, a 39-year-old planner at an industrial enterprise:

> Our state spat on me, it doesn't care how I live, how I manage to survive. It doesn't care about me at all. It's only concern is to rob me, to take my last penny. And in return I have nothing to do with this state. I spit on this state as well. I am not interested in its business, its problems, and so on. I don't pay attention to its internal or foreign policy. I think only about my family. This is the most important thing in my life. I know that I should feed my family, support my family and I am doing my best to minimise the impact of this damn state on me and my family.

Thus, women feel deserted by the state, which no longer guarantees them employment, no longer glorifies and supports their role as mothers, and no longer provides them with a safety net. As a result, they have begun turned inwards, to concentrate on their families.

Meanwhile, as shown above, many women whose husbands were previously successful, high-earners by Soviet standards have been knocked back by the transition, and have found it hard to regain their footing. Women's sense of responsibility, meanwhile, has in some cases pushed them to be extremely resourceful. This can be illustrated using the example of Tanya, an accountant in her early forties. Tanya has a strong work ethic: 'I always worked alongside my main job … I never walked away from work. If there's work – it's necessary to work.' Tanya's husband worked as a manager in television but his wages, though substantial, were unreliable: 'I could never be sure how much he'd give me, and how much he'd keep for his own expenses.' And so Tanya, in a characteristic gesture, took the responsibility for provision on herself.

In the transition era, both Tanya and her husband experienced difficulties, but because of her past labour market activism, she was better prepared to deal with them. When it seemed that the institute where she had worked for seventeen years was collapsing, she left and re-trained. She experienced many problems in the organisations she worked for subsequently. Indeed, after leaving the institute she was obliged at different times to attend five separate courses in order to keep or find work: first she trained to work in the patents office, then she did accounting and auditing courses; in her present job she is obliged to keep up-to-date with the frequent legal changes that take place. When asked about her motivation, she replied that it was to provide for her two children:

> What is there to do? The children are growing, they've got to be clothed, fed and have shoes on their feet. There's loads of things we need and while the possibility of finding work that pays exists you've got to use that chance. … I've never run away from work, I've never been scared of work.

In 1996 Tanya set up her own small firm and she also earns an additional income at another firm. Again this activism was prompted by her perception of her responsibilities to her family. As she put it, she 'had to do something':

> My mum was very ill … If I didn't [take responsibility] who was going to? And where was the money going to come from? Nowhere. The doctor cost such a lot. And my brother died four years ago, leaving two children. The girl's still young. I had to help. So I had to go [to work] somewhere or other.

Meanwhile, during this period her husband lost his managerial position in television. He, however, was not mentally prepared for this event – 'he thought that the television [job] would always be there' – and did not look for another job:

> It's more like he's waiting. And if he's looking then it's in a shy way, not insistently. A friend offered him a job, but there you've got to do everything. ... My husband said, 'I can't do manual work.' He was a manager for so many years, with 2,000 people subordinate to him. He's used to managing. ... He values himself, and I can't influence him or push him. ... He does nothing. He mainly sits on the sofa and watches the television. We're constantly fighting at home. Because I took on the role, the function of earning money, and I go out early in the morning and come in about nine or ten at night.

This story clearly illustrates the way in which women's sense of responsibility pushes them to act, while also highlighting difficulties of adaptation experienced by men in the transition era. Does this mean that the transition holds out the prospect of greater equality, as active women, driven by their urge to provide, overtake men? If Tanya's case were representative, the answer might be yes. She has re-trained and increased her earning power. It is more usual, however, for women's activism to push them to take any job, however unpleasant, in their drive to feed the family. Thus, while there are proportionally no more unemployed women than men, there is no sign of the wage gap being closed. None the less, Tanya's case does show that women's sense of responsibility can be the basis for creativity and success.[10]

It is important to make one qualification to this optimistic picture, however. When women take on responsibility for providing for the family, and even when they are highly successful, this does not necessarily result in a transformation of domestic power relations. This can be explained by the fact that, while women may appear to be in control, they generally still accept the idea that the man *should* be in control. This traditional conception of gender roles tends to undermine any power that a woman might gain through her role as breadwinner. Thus, for example, Olga, the disgruntled divorcee quoted above (p. 66), revealed that when she finally divorced her husband he ended up with all the consumer durables she had paid for. This was 'painful' for her, but she was unable to provide a satisfactory account of how it happened. It seems that in the last resort her husband prevailed. Meanwhile, even spectacularly energetic Tanya had not been able to use her position as breadwinner to induce her husband to help her at home. Asked who did the housework now her husband was out of work she replied, 'Who? Me, of course.' In this sense, women's longing for a traditional man can be seen as a form of self-limitation which prevents them from achieving a more equal distribution of burdens in their existing relationships.

Conclusion

The terror and propaganda of the Stalin era inculcated a strong work ethic and sense of duty upon women: work was perceived as the most important thing in life. This, combined with the pressure of economic circumstances, often meant that women of this generation were effectively 'married to the state', the space in which they could have conducted a personal life having been taken up by work. The breadwinners of later generations, meanwhile, were mainly motivated by their sense of responsibility to their family, and their vision of what family life should be like. If a husband did not, or could not, provide what his wife saw as the appropriate standard of living, then she, as a worker, was in a position to take on the role of breadwinner. This, however, was a situation many women resented: the role of men as defined by state policy did not match the women's aspirations. This problem has been exacerbated in the transition era. In many instances, the survival of the family in post-Soviet Russia depends on the woman's ability to find work. Although women have become 'divorced from the state', many of them are still waiting for the *kormilets* of their dreams to walk through the door. This would not induce them to stop work altogether, but, they claim, would simply rid them of the sensation that *all* the cares of the world rest upon their shoulders.

Notes

1 In this chapter I am mainly concerned with *married* female breadwinners. I have conducted separate research on single mothers, funded by the MacArther Fund (Grant no. 98–52242). For a preliminary discussion of the results of this research see Kiblitskaya (1999).

2 Her status as a dispensable resource was made abundantly clear to Maria at the end of the war, at which point the female tunnel builders were told that they could no longer work underground: 'They said "get a job wherever you want", and I went to work at a factory.'

3 Since it was not income level as such which determined whether or not women became the *de facto* main breadwinners in their families it is difficult to quantify this phenomenon. On the basis of my qualitative research, and that of my colleagues within ISITO, however, I would estimate that the characterisation developed below applies, at the very least, to a sizeable minority of women who were raised during the Khrushchev and Brezhnev eras.

4 Women's definitions of household needs usually include things which make life more comfortable such as furniture and televisions, and sometimes personal items like fur coats.

5 Studying in a military faculty is a way of being exempted from military service.

6 Note Alla's disdainful comments about her mother-in-law, who she perceives to be partly responsible for her husband's frailty: the fact that she didn't work means that he has been set a bad example and over-indulged.

7 Kollontai was disgusted by the idea of a woman 'finding herself a breadwinner' (Kollontai [1921] 1977: 269), claiming it was unnecessary under communism. Kept women were playing a 'sad and intolerable part' in the workers' state (ibid.: 272). [SA]

8 See Kukhterin, Chapter 3, this volume.

9 Variants of this dynamic do exist in other countries, especially in parts of Latin

America and the Caribbean. Martha Roldan's (1988) analysis of household relations in Mexico, for example, stresses that women tend to devote their earnings to meeting collective rather than individual needs. Meanwhile, in households where incomes are pooled, conflict between men and women tends to focus on the level of the man's personal expenditure. The main distinguishing feature of Soviet gender relations in this regard was the attachment of women to the labour market, and the fact that their labour participation was considered to be 'normal'. (In Roldan's study women's work was a potential source of controversy, which was the reason why the subjects of her study had chosen to do low-paid domestic outwork.) This means that in the Russian context, rather than simply taking responsibility for the domestic sphere, women take over all the key roles in the family. [SA]

10 I have recently assisted Annette Robertson with a research project for TACIS (no. 98–2338) entitled, 'Women's responses to economic and social change in coal mining areas'. We found that women were the most active in taking up opportunities to train as entrepreneurs: they vastly outnumbered the male trainees in the courses we visited in the Kuzbass and in Rostov. We saw a number of examples of successful small businesses run by women. We also found that women made up the majority of the *chelnoki* (shuttle traders), something which supports the findings of Marina Ilyina's research in Syktyvkar (1996), where she found that women made up the majority of the Russian (as opposed to Caucasian) *chelnoki*.

References

Ilyina, M. (1996) 'Sthrikhi k portretu "chelnoka": Keis-stadi veshchevogo rynka Syktyvkara', paper presented to ISITO seminar, Syktyvkar, September 1996.

Kiblitskaya, M. (1999) 'Dnevniki kak metod gendernoi sostiologii: strategii vyzhivanniya odinokikh materei', in I. Aristarkhova (ed.), *Zhenshchina ne sushchestvuet: Sovremennye issledovaniya polovogo razlichiya*, Syktyvkar: Syktyvkar University Press: 143–58.

Kollontai, A. ([1921] 1977) 'Prostitution and ways of fighting it', in A. Holt (ed.), *Selected Writings of Alexandra Kollontai*, London: Allison and Busby: 261–75.

Lapidus, G. (1988) 'The interaction of women's work and family roles in the USSR', *Women and Work: An Annual Review*, 3: 87–121.

Roldan, M. (1988) 'Renegotiating the marital contract: intrahousehold patterns of money allocation and women's subordination among domestic outworkers in Mexico', in D. Dwyer and J. Bruce (eds), *A Home Divided: Women and Income in the Third World*, Stanford: Stanford University Press.

3   Fathers and patriarchs in communist and post-communist Russia

Sergei Kukhterin

Masculinity and fatherhood are neglected themes in the study of gender in Soviet and post-Soviet Russia. A major reason for this is that the research agenda has been shaped by the Bolsheviks' claim that communism would liberate women from patriarchal oppression, and researchers, therefore, have tended to concentrate on looking at how far the Bolsheviks lived up to their promises. This chapter focuses on the other side of the issue – on the fathers and patriarchs whose power the regime sought to limit. In contrast to the traditional approach which sees this as a laudable, if unrealised, aim, I argue that the destruction of patriarchal institutions such as the church and the traditional family unit did not have as its primary aim the liberation of women. Rather, the aim was to enlarge the public sphere at the expense of the private, in an attempt to render individuals more amenable to state control. As Kollontai put it: 'Bourgeois morality demanded all for the loved one. The morality of the proletariat demands all for the collective' (Kollontai, [1923] 1977: 291). The individual men who stood at the head of the family acted as a barrier, limiting the influence of the state on other family members. In order to achieve control of society, therefore, the state had to challenge the power of the patriarchs. It did this through legislation, state violence and direct repression of individual men, aimed at transforming the state into a universal and exclusive 'father'. I begin by examining this process and then, on the basis of individual life histories, go on to examine how far these totalitarian aspirations were realised. Finally, I consider the implications of the collapse of the Soviet state for the institution of fatherhood in the transition era.

The research presented here is in two parts. First, the attitude of the Soviet authorities to masculinity is examined, on the basis of an analysis of documents from the Soviet era, including Soviet legislation to do with marriage and the family. Second, I consider the implications of Soviet policy on individual men – how they perceive their role as workers and family men – through the analysis of thirty-five interviews conducted between 1996 and 1998. My main emphasis was on interviews with men and women from three generations of five Muscovite families. In addition, I conducted fourteen interviews with individual men. Respondents, all of them Muscovites, were chosen to capture the experience of different age groups – their ages ranged from 21 to 90 – and they covered a variety of educational and professional backgrounds. All the men who were interviewed were heterosexual.

Soviet power and the family

The traditional family unit had always been perceived as problematic within Marxist ideology. Its role had been the subject of hostile analysis in influential works in the Marxist canon, in particular Engels' 'The origin of the family, private property and the state', and Bebel's 'Woman and socialism'. The family was seen as the guarantor of the preservation of private property, and its transference through the male line. The Bolsheviks thus inherited an ideological aversion to the family, which was strengthened by the idea that the patriarchal family was the mainstay of Tsarist society. Nevertheless, the family was a fact of life which had to be somehow accommodated. This tension expressed itself in anxious debates about the family of the 1920s, which centred on the question of what sort of accommodation the Party should reach with this institution. Some, such as Aron Sol'ts, advocated the transformation of families into primary cells of Soviet society, and the strict subordination of the family lives of Party members to the discipline of the Party:

> The family question is a question about what sort of life the Party member should have in his family. N.K. Krupskaya expressed this best. I first heard from her the felicitous formulation that the family of a Party member should be ... a supportive cell. It should be the kind of group of comrades in which the individual in the family lives in approximately the same way as he lives outside the family, and all family members should in all their work and life represent something similar to a supportive cell. As a result of the activity of the control commissions, many cases are known when all accomplished crimes were committed under the influence of bourgeois wives, who have sometimes taken on the mask of communists. But there haven't been cases in which the control commission has laid down divorce as a condition of remaining in the Party. In some cases this would be very much in place and would achieve appropriate results.
>
> (Sol'ts, 1925: 15–16)

Others, such as Martyn Lyadov, went further, however, arguing that the new Soviet individual could not be formed within the private family:

> A sharp break in the whole business of the education of our children is needed. If, through its schools and children's homes, bourgeois society was able to achieve the artificial education of the petty bourgeois,

which went against life itself, then we must ... change above all the business of educating our children. Is it possible to raise the collective person in the individual family? To this it is necessary to give the categorical answer – no! The collective-minded child can only be educated in a public environment. In this respect, the best parents spoil their children by bringing them up at home.

(Lyadov, 1925: 24–5)

As Olga Issoupova argues (see Chapter 1, this volume), the debate about child colonies versus family care supplemented by the state was eventually resolved in favour of the latter. This compromise, however, was achieved precisely at the expense of the father. The state forged an alliance with the mother and child unit which it 'protected', leaving the individual man redundant on the edge of the family. The foundations of this alliance are examined in the following section.

Legislation: the state takes on the family and the patriarch

Some of the first Soviet laws to be put in place were directed specifically towards the destruction of the traditional model of the family, and, especially, individual fatherhood. The decrees of 18 December 1917 and 19 December 1917 were significantly different from the family law of Imperial Russia, which enjoined a woman 'to follow her husband as the head of the family to respect and to love him, to submit to him in everything' (Svod zakonov, v. X, part 1, clauses 1–5). The new decrees laid down the following principles of family life: the legalisation of a civil marriage, which was to be registered only through ZAGS (Soviet registry offices); monogamy; that marriages should be entered into freely by mutual consent; equality for men and women in all aspects of family life; free divorce on request of both parties; state protection of motherhood; and equal rights for children, regardless of whether they were born within or outside registered marriages. The legal father of a child born outside marriage was deemed to be any man who had had sexual relations with the mother of the child in the approximate period of conception. At the same time, certain pre-communist laws were retained: husbands were still responsible for their wives, while parents were still expected to bring up their own children. In January 1918, the church was separated from the state and this meant that all marriages proclaimed by the church lost their legal status. Children from such marriages thus became illegitimate, but, as mentioned above, they retained equal rights with children of registered marriages. In October 1918, these decrees were generalised in the first code of the laws to do with civil registration of death, births and marriages (Kodeks zakonov ob aktakh grazhdanskogo sostoyaniya, brachnom, semeynom i opekunskom prave, 1920: 149–71).

It is clear that these laws reflected not so much the desire of the state to destroy the bourgeois family unit, but its desire to replace patriarchal authority with the authority of the state, on whom the family would now principally depend. The state removed the legal duty of wives to their husbands, and allowed them to leave marriages if they wished to do so. Meanwhile, the protection of motherhood was proclaimed to be a state duty. A key implication of this was that individual fatherhood was deprived of its economic and legislative base, and fatherly responsibility was reduced to the payment of alimony. In particular, the final provision regarding the determination of the paternity of children born outside marriage was so vague that more than one man could be recognised as the father of a child: something which clearly undermined the status of individual fatherhood. Moreover, the fact that the right to alimony and the division of property after divorce only applied to marriages registered in the ZAGS also weakened the institution of fatherhood: men had an opportunity to avoid responsibility.

The further development of family law was required to remove some of the contradictions in the first decrees. The 1926 code of laws on marriage, the family and guardianship has usually been seen as a measure which further strengthened the position of women in the family, but in reality it served to strengthen the control which the state had in the private sphere. The most important provisions of this code were:

- The recognition of *de facto* marriages: that is, any sexual relationship could henceforth be viewed as a *de facto* marriage. Evidence of a *de facto* marriage was: cohabitation; the acquisition of joint property during the period of cohabitation; a declaration of marital relations in the form of a letter or other document, witnessed by a third person; and, also, depending on circumstances, mutual financial help, joint child-rearing, and so on.
- The introduction of the concept of 'jointly acquired property' and the equal division of such property between the spouses after divorce.
- The simplification of the process of divorce. If, under the code of 1918, divorce was registered after the presentation of an application certified by both parties, now it was enough to have an application from one party.
- Payment of alimony for one year after a divorce.

(Kodeks zakonov o brake, sem'e i opeke, 1926: 124–48)

This law implied a further infringement of patriarchal authority – not for the benefit of women, but for the benefit of the state, which acquired new opportunities to intervene in private life and the individual property relations of citizens under the guise of protecting their interests. As Irina Aristarkhova has argued, the elimination of the difference between *de jure* and *de facto* marriages 'institutionalized and publicized private and voluntary connections via property relations' since common property of 'marriages' should be divided (Aristarkhova, 1995: 16). Meanwhile, the division of women in the new law into 'registered wives', 'non-registered wives' and 'casual lovers' implied a strengthening of control in the private sphere, since it was the state which assigned such labels. The law caused particular discontent in rural areas, where a divorce implied a division of the *dvor*, the peasant household, which according to the Land Code of 1922 belonged to household members. The law stipulated that the division of the property on divorce should be determined in conformity with the Land Code. But the peasants correctly perceived that the law weakened the rights of all members of peasant families, since the property of the whole household would be divided in the case of divorce. The law was a deliberate strike at traditionalism in the peasant household. By giving itself the right to 'protect' the property rights of wives – whether *de facto* or *de jure* – the state gained access to the peasant household, and acquired new ammunition to use in its struggle against traditional peasant Russia.

Thus, as a result of these legislative initiatives, the legal basis of the patriarchal family was removed, while the status of fatherhood as an institution was radically undermined. Although superficially women appeared to gain from this, they were actually being used as levers through which the state could gain access to the internal affairs of the private household, in particular the peasant household. A key result of this interference was increased gender conflict.

Gender conflict in the 1920s

The Bolsheviks' intervention into the private life of citizens stirred up considerable gender conflict. It could be argued that this was inevitable – the Bolsheviks informed women that they had new rights which the state was prepared to defend, and therefore it was likely that, in their newly enlightened incarnation, women would come into conflict with the source of their oppression – men. However, this is to over-simplify the situation. This section analyses the nature of the emerging pattern of gender relations, using as its source letters written by ordinary Russians to the Communist Party authorities between 1917 and 1927. These letters highlight precisely the way in which the state established itself as the third party in gender relations – the fact that people wrote letters about the details of their everyday life to newspapers and Party leaders is itself illustrative of the way in which private life and gender questions became the business of the state.

First, the letters highlight the impact of the state's attempt at the enlightenment of women. The following extract from a letter regarding a mass meeting conveys the atmosphere of the time. The writer of the letter

was very impressed by a speech by a girl from the sixth grade at a local
school:

> She spoke for fifteen minutes, and she spoke very well. Savel'eva
> described the situation of women workers and peasants in bourgeois
> countries [and] spoke about how our Russian woman was enslaved
> under the rule of the barbarians, [under] Tsarism. But thanks to the
> Great October, the woman has been liberated, given her freedom, been
> made equal, given the same rights used and rightfully enjoyed by men.
> In passing, as part of her greeting, she recited a poem of Obradovin
> 'Working woman', which begins, '[Her] destiny was gloomy, black,
> impersonal' etc. ...
>   She finished her greetings with the slogans, 'Long live the world Oc-
> tober which has liberated the woman', 'Long live the free woman'. In
> the audience there were cries of admiration, and loud applause which
> lasted three minutes. ... From all of the above it is possible to con-
> clude: the mood of the women was good, and now our women will not
> sleep, but will work. They have promised to be active workers.
>   (Letter from the typist P. Besova to *Krest'yanka*, 1925,
>   quoted in Livshin and Orlov, 1998: 409–10)

It is clear that such agitation was not always welcomed so ecstatically.
While women may have been receptive to the idea that they had equal
rights with men, they were far less attracted by ideas connected with the
socialisation of domestic life, and anything which implied the destruction
of the family, as is clear from the following extract:

> About a third of all the women in the whole village gathered, and sat
> there, not uttering a word. When asked why they didn't speak in the
> debate, the women said 'we're shy because of the presence of men
> here'. It was necessary to remove all the men, and then things were
> ironed out. They began to speak ... Above all, they said that it is
> impossible for a woman to give up cooking, that a woman is bound
> hand and foot to the family. But in the end they all agreed that a
> woman is not a slave in Soviet construction and that a woman has the
> same rights as men. At the end of the meeting four girls were elected to
> the raion conference in Kerch'.
>   (Letter from a rural correspondent, P. Mezentseva, published in
>   *Krest'yanka*, 1925, quoted in ibid.: 432)

What this extract also highlights is the way in which the authorities
became a player in gender relations – removing men when they were not
wanted, coaxing women to alter the terms of their private relationships
and involving women in conferences.

Alongside such tales of attempted liberation, the other main theme of the letters with respect to gender relations was male drunkenness and the impact this had on women. These included, for example, stories of the ruin brought to villages by the availability of 40 per cent-proof vodka (ibid.: 451–2), and, equally, the devastation caused by home-brewed spirits (*samogon*).[1] The after-effects of the latter were graphically described: 'when they [the drunken men] return home, some of them drive out the family, the wife gets the worst treatment of all, and if he finds out that his wife was at a woman's conference, it's already time for her to flee before her husband sobers up' (Letter of S. K. Gorbatikova, published in *Batrak*, Belorussia, quoted in ibid.: 367). Given such problems, individuals called on the state to intervene to support women in their struggle against drunkenness. The following, for example, is a classic example of such a plea, in this case addressed to Stalin in his capacity as General Secretary of the Party. The letter begins with praise for the activism of the War Communist era, when 'delegates came from the town to the villages and explained to the peasant woman, that she should not be so subordinate to her husband in the household, but should be equal with him as a house-keeper'. This activity had been curtailed, in the letter-writer's opinion to the detriment of the village, since women held the key to socialist development:

> The development of women would decrease drunkenness, or even almost stop it altogether, because the majority of village women, or nearly all of them, don't like to get drunk, and are even opponents of it. But … they are absolutely not in the condition to struggle with drunkenness. As it is, the husband drinks, he comes home drunk, his wife says: 'What are you doing, you daft idiot [*golovushka sadovaya*]? The children are naked and barefoot, and you get drunk.' The husband says: 'Your job is to keep quiet.' … And in her mind the wife begins to swear at the moonshine producers or wine dealers, whom she is prepared to put away anywhere she can, but her husband will give her a dressing down for that – she's afraid. But, look, if she knew that he doesn't have the right to hit and curse [her], when he's the one who's guilty, then, of course, there wouldn't be any moonshine producers and wine dealers. …
>
> So, Comrade Stalin, it is necessary, in my opinion, in the first place to awaken the woman-peasant … Socialism will not happen without women. And so, … through the education of women in the Soviet spirit, the remaining road to socialism is short. … Therefore women need to have their own revolution. It's true that women certainly couldn't make a revolution with weapons in their hands, as we had to do at the very beginning. … But they, women, could carry out a huge revolution on the domestic front. … And when they pass into a world where the husbands are not drunk and don't have hangovers, and their

[women's] hands are untied, then it won't be necessary to drag people to meetings, but [people] living at home will have several meetings a day, discussing every question in life, and whom to elect to the soviet and co-operative.

(Letter from a peasant, I. D. Denisov, to Stalin, 25 December 1925, quoted in ibid.: 460–3)

The concept of an alliance between women and the state is clearly expressed here. Liberated, Soviet-spirited women would act as a disciplining agent, helping to cajole the men of rural Russia out of their backwardness. Women would denounce the alcohol-vending wreckers to the state, and their newly dutiful husbands would return to the family. The problem with this was that – for reasons that are too complex to explore here – Soviet women never did pass into a world without drunkenness and hangovers. The important point, however, is that what was achieved was a halfway house. Women gained just enough autonomy to denounce and divorce their husbands, but domestic power dynamics were not transformed;[2] indeed, women themselves were ambivalent about effecting such a transformation.[3] What emerged was a situation in which women relied increasingly on the state as the omnipresent, reliable father and husband, while men were effectively marginalised, their domestic power curtailed, along with their ultimate responsibility to and for their families. While this may have served to moderate the worst of male excesses, its main effect was to fix and institutionalise female responsibility for the household.

Fatherhood in Soviet and post-Soviet Russia: the subjective dimension

How did individual men respond to the transformation of their lot? What were the implications for the development of masculine identity, and for Soviet fathers? How did the triangular relations between men, women and the state influence the position of men within the family? The following sections examine these questions through the perspective of different generations of respondents. The first section examines the clash between the Bolsheviks and individual patriarchs. This is followed by a section looking at Soviet fatherhood and its contradictions. The final section discusses fatherhood in the transition era.

The patriarch meets Soviet power

In the pre-revolutionary period, the role of the patriarchal head of the family was fully legitimised by the Russian Orthodox Church and the state. The Tsar was the Holy Father and ruler of the nation, and the individual father likewise had absolute authority within the family. He was thus a bulwark of the Tsarist regime, the Holy Father in microcosm. This was particularly the case in the peasant family. The typical peasant father was an aloof, powerful figure. The following reminiscences by man about his own father (who grew up in a peasant milieu, and managed to escape repression) capture the role of this type of father:

> [My] father's authority was absolute in the family. When he came home after work, first of all mother served him supper, then he had a rest and mother didn't permit us to disturb him. We played separately and looked over at him when he went to the chair, and sometimes when he was not so tired he asked us about something or just put his hand on my head or my brother's head, and then it was the feeling, I remember it now, it was like total happiness for me, I don't know with what I can compare it, it was like the touch of a God. He touched us very rarely and I remember his hand. Mother was jealous about his relationships with us and kept us away from him. But really we didn't have a special relationship, he never spoke to us much when we were young, he never beat us, I think because it might have destroyed his dignity. To this day I admire how clever and wise he was, without having an education and having only a peasant background.
>
> (Aleksandr 1, 56 years old, two daughters and one son,
> three marriages)

It was this absolute, quasi-divine paternal authority which the Bolsheviks sought to undermine with the measures outlined above.

The legislative incursions of the new communist authorities into the private sphere did not go unnoticed – men keenly sensed the threat to their power which such measures implied. They knew that the basis of patriarchal power was at stake in the new provisions. This is starkly illustrated by the following family history, told by Grigorii, now over 80, who grew up in the early Soviet era. Grigorii's father was a small-scale private producer. He first had to endure strangers being billeted in his house during the Civil War, strangers who, he claimed, ruined his house. Then at the end of 1920, his economic status obliged him to flee with his family from Moscow to the Black Sea town of Adler to avoid persecution. But his greatest complaint about the new authorities concerned Bolshevik family policy:

> My father had a great dislike for Soviet power. His worst insult was the word 'Bolshevik'. ... He very much disliked the fact that they abolished church weddings, and he scorned civil marriages. 'They've already confiscated property, and now they want to appropriate wives and children.' When he got drunk he always went on about Soviet power, it always upset him and he would say things like, 'how it is that I got married to my wife in church and it turns out [because of] that she doesn't belong to me and doesn't answer for anything and the

child is, it's not clear what, illegal it turns out'. He would then explain everything to me, that a man is not a master [*khozyain*] without his own home, without a wife and his own children.

(Grigorii, 80 years old, one daughter, two marriages)

Grigorii's father was so enraged by Soviet power that he was unable to keep his complaints to himself, even during the increasingly repressive Stalin era. Despite his wife's pleas, he would loudly condemn Stalin, something which eventually led to his being denounced and arrested in 1941, never to be heard of by his family again. Such traditionalists rightly perceived in the Soviet authorities a competitor for their control over women and children – and in this case the patriarch eventually paid for his insubordination with his life. This story underlines the fact that the struggle with the traditional patriarch was by no means confined to the legislative and ideological levels. Men who stood up for what they perceived as their God-given rights could be repressed, which in many cases meant their death.

The story of Grigorii's father is in many senses symbolic of the fate of the traditional patriarch who was master in his own home, had the right to treat his wife however he saw fit, and could hand on his property to his children. He was defeated and banished by the Bolsheviks. This was done in the name of female emancipation, but served to strengthen state control – neither women nor feminists were authors of the agenda which landed Grigorii's father in the camps.

Soviet fatherhood: the ideal and the reality

Deprived of his patriarchal authority and his property, what role could the new Soviet man play? The authorities had a clear answer: work was the centre of the Soviet man's life. This was to be his means of self-realisation – a form of realisation which, rather than being strictly individual, was linked with the development of the state. Correspondingly, fatherhood for the Soviet man was to be a formal affair. Looking after children was a distraction from his *real work*. From an early age, his children would spend much of their lives outside the family – in nurseries, kindergartens, in school, at pioneer camp, and so on. Supposedly, the state would provide superior care. Meanwhile, the woman was accorded a far more significant role in child-rearing. In return for the physical feat of motherhood, her links with her children were legitimised by the Party. In effect, she was designated as the moral keeper of the private sphere. This, at least, was the implicit model laid down by the state. But how far did this model correspond with reality?

Without a doubt, the destruction of male legal privileges had a big impact. But while the legal basis of male power and privilege may have been eroded, patriarchal ideology proved far more resistant. Paradoxically, one reason for this was the Soviet definition of work in the public sphere as a duty of men and women alike. This meant that both mothers and fathers were often absent, and while state care was in principle available, in practice there were big gaps in provision. These gaps were plugged by grandparents. As one of my respondents explained:

> Yurii Yakovlevich (my father-in-law) plays with Denis, does things with him, and Vera Ivanova (my mother-in-law) says, 'Well, what a turn up for the books, how he plays with Denis – he didn't take any notice at all of his own children for ten years.' Those were her very words.
>
> (Elena, 27 years old, one child, one marriage)

It is a well-known fact that Soviet children were often closer to their grandparents than to their parents, something which mitigated against the regime's control of socialisation: alongside their lessons about Lenin, children were exposed to the views of their grandparents. This was a means through which more traditional values were preserved – in particular ideas regarding the proper role of men and women. Bolshevism itself was an ideology which combined traditionalism with radicalism, and this duality was inadvertently strengthened through the part-public and part-private pattern of socialisation of citizens which emerged as a result of state policy.

It was not only the role of grandparents which was subversive. Whatever its aspirations, the state was not entirely able to colonise private relations. While the policies and discourse of the regime tacitly supported the model of fatherhood outlined above, many men did not conform to this ideal type; although some fathers may have had the requisite distance from their children, many did not. Which type of relations developed probably had as much to do with personality differences as with the impact of the state. Many of my respondents recalled having what they saw as warm and positive relations with their fathers during the Soviet era. The following quotations illustrate that some sons did not perceive their fathers as indifferent strangers – Lenin may have been 'always with us', but he did not replace individual fathers in the eyes of individual sons:

> I would say that in my upbringing my father was more important. Because, I don't know, … it was because my mum was too strict, and my father was too loyal. Of course, I was more drawn to my father. … I liked to do boxing, and to go car racing. My father always said, 'You want to? Please, there's no problem, as long as you like it'. My mother, of course – tried to interfere in everything, to get to the bottom of everything. She had to control [things].
>
> (Aleksandr 2, 28 years old, one son, one marriage)

My father didn't speak with me much. It always seemed to me that we understood each other well without long conversations, well, I didn't need that, I liked my father's silence. When I was around him I felt so manly [*po-muzhki*], well, you see, such strength, superiority, I felt just like a man [*muzhik*]. For example, we're sitting at the table, dad had come home from work, we're eating supper, in silence, and I start to tell him about school, what I did with the lads, and he listens, nods. Well, my mum tells me to shush, 'What are you doing? You're not giving your father time to eat, he's come in from work tired', you know, the same old tune, and my father smiled into his moustache. And, do you know what, in front of my father, my mother never snapped, around him there was this feeling of superiority.

(Victor, 56 years old, one son, three marriages)

These quotations illustrate that sons grew up with a strong sense of gender difference from a young age, and they identified strongly with their fathers. The idea of innate male superiority was preserved. Meanwhile, though the basis of inheritance via the male line may have been abolished, the emotional links between fathers and sons remained intact.

What these extracts also highlight, however, is the dominance of women within the family – they were the ones who laid down and enforced the rules. In this case, the Soviet intervention into gender relations can be said to have contributed to strengthening women's position. My respondents did report that their fathers would usually have a right of veto over their wives' decisions. But this was generally used sparingly – the times when it was were remembered as red letter days in the lives of sons:

I really loved it when he [my father] took me hunting and fishing. I always looked forward to that, and was happy when we left the house together. And my mother didn't want me to go and got angry, but she couldn't say anything, because my father had already decided, and he and I were together. And I was proud of myself and felt myself really grown up.

(Aleksandr 1)

As this quotation illustrates, women still accepted men's right to command. But within the family men's power was largely latent; fathers usually confined themselves to ironic smiles into their moustaches, and left their wives to get on with it. The definition of the home as a female-policed realm was supported by the Party. Notwithstanding the earlier Bolshevik idea that it would be the wives of communists who would woo their men from the Party's path, the Party came to act chiefly as an ally of women in the struggle for a socialist *byt* (everyday life). This can be seen in the reminiscences of the following respondent:

For instance, if a man [*muzhik*] drank, then, if he was a communist, they could call him to the Party cell, to really shake him up. The sort of thing they could do is remove him from his post, deprive him of his salary, and some such things. And because of that, it kept people within bounds. And now ... there's no limits [*bespredel*]. I think that in the Soviet system ... the controlling factors were far greater than now. ... And now there's chaos.

(Sergei, 44 years old, one daughter, two marriages)

In the Soviet environment, it became accepted practice for wives to attempt to control their husbands, an endeavour which was supported by the Party (which was interested in orderly families and sober workers). Men were seen as the weak link in the family – there was always a question mark over their behaviour, particularly in relation to drink. This is highlighted by the comments of an admiring son talking about his father's life. Although it was clear from his earlier comments that his father was a capable and responsible man, the son nevertheless felt the need to point out that his father was not a drinker or a wife-beater:

I never saw my father hit my mother, there was never such a thing in our life! That is, they could swear, they could shout at each other. But, in principle, as I say, we had a successful [*blagopoluchnaya*] family. My father didn't drink, my mother didn't hit him on the head with a frying pan. That is, it was like the model primary cell of society in the socialist, stagnant period. ... Everyone approached their responsibilities as if they were duties.

(Aleksandr 3, 29 years old, one son, one marriage)

These comments highlight typical Soviet stereotypes: women were expected to be intensely reactive (lashing out with the frying pan, for example), but men were assumed to be the real wreckers on the domestic front with their potential for alcoholism and violence. Gradually, therefore, the social definition of a 'good' Soviet family became one in which the husband was sober and agreed with his wife. Where this was not the case, the family descended into an endless round of quarrels and scandals.

The above discussion illustrates that traditional patriarchal conceptions of gender relations were preserved within Soviet society. But the state did not give institutional support to male dominance in the family, rather it supported the cause of women as a force for order on the home front. What the state offered men was the opportunity to realise themselves in the public sphere – it was here that they could be powerful. For men who were able to succeed in this way, this offered a satisfying form of self-realisation, as the following quotation from the son of the 'model' family quoted above illustrates:

[With regard to] the position of my father in society – as I say, our town was small. That is, 25,000 inhabitants. Put it this way, three-quarters of the whole working-age population worked at the power station. And a person who held one of the leading positions at the power station held one of the leading positions in the town, and people related to him accordingly. My father was a boss at work, and, at least in the family, he always had the last word. What he said, went. We didn't discuss paternal decisions, that is, it was possible to discuss them, but my father, of course, had the last word. ... I think he was sure of his role in society! ... Everyone knew him, everyone respected him.

(Aleksandr 3)

Thus, Aleksandr's father felt self-assured, and his success at work was the basis for a strong position at home.[4] (The benevolent dictatorship of successful Soviet managers at home was something the regime did not object to, because such dominance had been 'earned'). This man was, then, a Soviet success: he could respect himself, and command respect from others (including, crucially, his wife).

But many other men found themselves in humiliating positions at work, and the basis of their masculine identity was thus far more shaky. The uncertainty of such men is captured by the comments of the following respondent. When asked about self-realisation, he immediately links this to the idea of work. But work is clearly not the sphere in which he feels himself a man. Finally, he concludes that it is only when he is directly dominating a woman that he feels any sense of masculine self-realisation:

So, you're talking about my self-realisation as a man through children. What questions you ask! What kind of realisation? In general, I can say of myself – I'll say straight away: I'm not a careerist. I perhaps have my parents' genes – I haven't reached certain heights or stars and I haven't tried to. It's not important for me. Probably family is more interesting than a career. I don't know. A man should always remain a man. I am a man who has given life to people, strictly speaking, one little person; I am a man who has built a house; I am a man who has planted I don't know how many trees. That is, after me [there'll be] some kind of memory for my descendants. That's all, enough. ... To me it's all the same whether a child is a boy or a girl. And in general, perhaps I realise myself more through sex. That I fucked a girl and I already feel good afterwards because I fucked her. And, take note, I [fucked] her, not she, me.

(Sergei, 44 years old, one daughter, two marriages)

The desperation to 'remain a man' exhibited in the above extract sharply captures the dilemmas of Soviet men. Work was a legitimate arena for male domination, but an uncertain one. The chief means through which

Sergei perceived he could define his masculinity was the direct domination of women. But as a general strategy this was more difficult to sustain in Soviet, as opposed to Tsarist, Russia: women had no problems in obtaining a divorce and custody of the children; they had a guaranteed right to work, and thus were able to support themselves – the state was prepared to stand in for the husband and father.

In this sense, the position of Soviet men was highly contradictory. On the one hand, Soviet men and women tended to adhere to traditional ideas regarding natural sexual difference. On the other, the state was jealous of patriarchal prerogatives in the private sphere, and wanted men to direct their energy into their work. The Party perceived in women a means through which it could open up the private sphere, and attempt to bring male behaviour under control. It therefore supported the position of women within the family. Meanwhile, men were given preference in the world of work. For men who were unable to realise themselves in this realm, however, there was little on offer. This caused particular problems given most people believed that men *should* show themselves to be superior to women.

Post-Soviet man and the retreat of the state

In the post-communist era the state no longer aspires to be the father to its citizens. The retreat of the state has created a space in which men can define a new role for themselves within the family and as fathers. Men are responding to this opportunity in different ways. Some are carrying on as before, leaving women in control, a small minority are experimenting with a nurturing role, while a significant section of younger men are attempting to secure a more dominant position in the family. It is this group on whom the following discussion focuses, since they have been the subject of a good deal of speculation in the transition era. As is revealed below, regaining control of the private sphere is no easy matter.

The problems are well illustrated by the story of the following young couple. Aleksandr, the son of the power station boss quoted above, wants to be head of the family, like his father. Moreover, he recognises that the collapse of the communist state has created an important new role for fathers:

> Before we all really lived – 'Lenin lived! Lenin's alive! Lenin will live!' Now we already sort of live differently. There are some different ideals in life. Of course, you can't compare what existed ten years ago with what there is now. Everything has changed. Relations between father and son have changed. If, as it were, before relations were like those on the posters, that is, everything as it should be [*vse kak polozheno*], well now, well, they're not over-familiar, but they are too open. That is, a father now has to give more information to his child, and not be

oriented towards various dogmas and postulates that come from above. Because children need fathers. Without a father is just – fatherlessness. [With] only a mother it's not a normal home.

(Aleksandr 3)

Aleksandr sees that a father's role is being redefined in the present period. He feels that fathers are now more important than ever, because the state no longer defines how its citizens should live. At the same time, however, he is uncomfortable with the new openness that he feels is required of him. He wants to be a father, but he is not sure what his precise role should be, as can be seen in his tautological examination of the consequences of fatherlessness.

Asked about the proper role of husbands and wives, Aleksandr expounded a pre-Soviet conception of the family in which the wife stayed at home and performed the domestic duties, while the man earned the money. He is attempting to live in this way, but there are barriers to the realisation of his dreams:

I wish that my wife chattered less and worked more ... on family matters, on her own [things]. Yes! So that ... her husband would get up to go to work at eight o'clock, he'd kick her and she'd go and prepare him something to eat! That'd be OK! And not so that half an hour goes by while I'm kicking her. Well, so that she took her responsibilities seriously. Perhaps that applies to me too, but at the moment I try, I try. ...

I see my role in the family as ... I clothe them, put shoes on their feet, feed them, that is I carry the, let's say, financial [responsibility]. That is, I bring money into the family, and my wife looks after everyday things [*byt*], comfort and so on. ...

I see my child rarely; my father paid me more attention, but that's because things were arranged in a different way then. People worked from bell to bell, and he was home more than I am. ... what the family meant to my father I don't know, but for me: well, what can the family mean for a normal person? It could be said that the family is everything! No more, no less. Well, look, let's say I imagine myself without my family, without my wife, my children. ... I try to dedicate my life to my family. Perhaps it doesn't always work out, but I try. ...

Because of his financial obligations Aleksandr is obliged to spend long hours at work, and evenings drinking with his colleagues – 'it's essential, if you don't drink vodka they get offended'. He sees himself as operating in an altogether more demanding climate than his father:

Having a career isn't a goal for me, the family is more important....
But, on the other hand, I have to work harder than, say, my

father. Naturally, harder, because it's got harder to earn the same money. Naturally, I have to spend more time at work. And that means paying less attention to the family. Moreover, as much as two times less than my father. ... But I wouldn't say that I've ceased to have the kind of authority that my father had in our family. Authority is not defined by the amount of time you spend with the family. Authority and use of time are, it seems to me, different things. Authority is authority and the amount of time you spend with the family is something completely different.

Elena, his wife, does not concur with this reasoning, however. (And, judging by her reaction to her husband's kicks, doesn't respond very well to his 'authority' either!) He himself suggested as much, saying:

I can easily create the position of leader for myself, without being laughed at, in actual fact I have this position. Of course, my wife tries to play a bigger role than, say, my mother. I don't like it, but she tries. Well I think that for another five years we will, of course, suffer, and then we'll sort of come to a final consensus.

Elena resents her husband's absence, and is contemplating looking for work because of her loneliness and boredom:

I would like at least some minimal help with the domestic chores. ... And then, of course, his relations to the child really get to me. He just doesn't see the child, doesn't notice him; doesn't need him. ... Before he said to me, 'Look, he's small. I'm not going to take him for a walk, because he doesn't know how to do anything. Do you think I going to push him round in a pram like an idiot?' But now ... the child is nearly 5 years old. His father hasn't taken him out for a walk once. He hasn't tried. He loves him, of course, in his own way. I don't want to say that he doesn't love him, but he doesn't play any kind of role in his upbringing.

(Elena, 27 years old, one son, one marriage)

It seems unlikely that their 'final consensus' will be to Aleksandr's taste because Elena was categorical in her assertion that, 'I don't want our family to be a copy of his family!' She stated openly that she was not adverse to her husband being head of the family, but her concept of this was different to her husband's thoughts on the matter. She thought that he should be a participative father, and should be present in the home. She did not want, like his mother, to shoulder all the responsibility for the domestic sphere while doing a full-time job.[5] This highlights a major difficulty in the return of men to the family: men and women may have very different ideas of what their new role should be. For women, a head of the family is someone who takes over some of the responsibility for the home, while men seem to perceive the role as that of a breadwinner whose word is treated as law.

This conflict is not an isolated incident, but an example of a wider struggle over the redefinition of family and gender relations in the post-Soviet period. Men recognise that more is demanded of them, but it is hard to live up to their new role: earning money in post-Soviet Russia is a time-consuming business, and, at the same time, many men are not used to participating in family life. Their wives, meanwhile, have been socialised in a society in which women were expected to work, and the 'authority' of husbands did not need to be taken too seriously. In this environment, it will not be easy for young Russian men to be respected as legitimate heads of their families.

Conclusion

The Soviet state fought a battle with family men for control over the private sphere of their lives. The Bolsheviks succeeded in removing the legal basis of male dominance, but the idea of natural male superiority was preserved in Soviet society. Indeed, the regime contributed to its preservation by allowing men to dominant in the public sphere. The domestic power of women was buttressed and extended, however, through the extension of female employment (which gave women independence); the availability of divorce; the institutional support for maternal control over children, and the presence of the Party as a sympathetic ear to which errant husbands could be denounced. What did this imply for Soviet men? If they were able to demonstrate their supposed superiority in the workplace, then their masculine identity was secure. If, however, they did not find the possibility of self-realisation at work, then the alternatives were not promising – drink and violence being the most obvious outcomes. In the post-Soviet era, men have the opportunity to gain some control over the domestic sphere – and some of them are clearly keen to do so. This, however, is not an easy thing to achieve. Women, it seems, would welcome the presence of a father for their children, but a return of the old-style patriarch is altogether a different matter.

Notes

1 In the immediate aftermath of the revolution wine and spirit factories were closed and the illicit manufacture of alcohol was deemed a criminal offence and carried a sentence of not less than ten years' imprisonment. However, in 1925 all restrictions on the strength of alcohol were removed, while in 1926 the production of home brew for personal use was allowed.

2 It is important to stress that the state did not support a transformation of the domestic division of labour. Although the Bolsheviks wanted women to have enough autonomy to attend meetings and go out to work, they did not devote

serious attention to the question of who would wash and cook before the promised public facilities were developed.

3 While women certainly would have preferred their husbands not to drink, they did generally adhere to traditional conceptions of gender roles. This can be seen, for example, in Marina Kiblitskaya's analysis of the preservation of the male breadwinner ideal in the Soviet era in Chapter 4, this volume.

4 None the less, elsewhere in the interview Aleksandr recalled that, 'My father didn't go to the shops. My mum carried all the family [responsibilities] in our home.'

5 This marital conflict also raises important questions about women's views regarding work and motherhood, although there is not space to discuss them here. Two things are worth noting, however. One is that, in contrast to her mother-in-law, Elena expects help with the family chores, but, paradoxically, unlike her mother-in-law she does not have a job. The other is that her experiment with housewifery has not been a particularly happy one: she feels bored, neglected and resentful.

References

Aristarkhova, I. (1995) *Women and Government in Bolshevik Russia*, University of Warwick: Labour Studies Working Papers, no. 4.

Kollontai, A. ([1923] (1977) 'Make way for the winged Eros: A letter to working youth', in A. Holt (ed.), *Selected Writings of Alexandra Kollontai*, London: Allison and Busby: 27–92.

Kodeks zakonov o brake, sem'e i opeke (1926), *III Sessia Vserossiiskogo Tsentral'nogo Ispolnitel'nogo Komiteta XII Sozyva (1926): Postanovlenia*, Moscow: Yuridicheskoe izdatel'stvo.

Kodeks zakonov ob aktakh grazhdanskogo sostoyaniya, brachnom, semeynom i opekunskom prave (1920), *Sobranie uzakonenii i rasporyazhenii Rabochego i krest'yanskogo pravitel'stva RSFSR: Sbornik dekretov 1917–1918*, Moscow: Gosudarstvennoe izdatel'stvo.

Livshin, A. and Orlov, I. (1998) *Pis'ma vo vlast' 1917–1927: Zayavleniya, zhaloby, donosy, pis'ma v gosudarstvennye struktury i bol'shevistskim vozhdyam*, Moscow: Rossiiskaya politicheskaya entsiklopediya.

Lyadov, M. (1925) *Voprosy byta*, Moscow: Kommunisticheskyi Universitet imeni Sverdlova.

Sol'ts, A. (1925) *O partetike*, Moscow: Kommunisticheskyi Universitet imeni Sverdlova.

Svod zakonov (1914), Moscow.

4 'Once we were kings'

Male experiences of loss of status at work in post-communist Russia

Marina Kiblitskaya

One of the results of the enormous economic and poltical upheaval afflicting post-communist Russia has been a loss of status for many male workers who were once seen as the heroes of the Soviet Union. The economic reforms that have taken place since *perestroika* have plunged the country into deep recession, with the result that many people have experienced a dramatic decline in living standards. This has led to a large increase in poverty which would have been unheard of under the old Soviet regime. Whatever its faults, the communist system provided a safety net for its citizens, whereas in post-communist Russia many people have to struggle simply to ensure their survival. My analysis here focuses on the experiences of men because they were in a more privileged position with regard to work during the Soviet era, and, correspondingly, have further to fall under the new system. I consider the impact that the late payment of wages, falling real wages, and the threat of unemployment has had on Russian men's sense of identity. This is done by analysing the male breadwinner norm which, despite the full labour participation of women, was preserved during the Soviet era. I show that the concept of the male *kormilets* (breadwinner) had a number of dimensions, and these provide a basis for understanding the men's subjective experience of the loss of status, in particular with regard to their sense of masculine identity. The implications of the challenge to the *kormilets* are examined under two headings. First, I look at the impact on relations within the family, and, second, I analyse the changing position of men at work, focusing on the experience of those who work in declining industries and professions. Within the family unit, many men have been faced with unwelcome evidence of how far the respect they were accorded in the past was dependent on their social status, rather than their innate superiority. Meanwhile, paradoxically, the higher status that men enjoyed at work has in some cases made it more difficult for them to adapt to the new economic climate of the transition era.

My research is based on fifteen in-depth interviews, supplemented by the transcripts of over 100 work history interviews.[1] The fifteen interviews conducted specifically for this study were all with Muscovite men, ranging in age from 40 to 60 years old. Of these, three were academics, five were workers, three were specialists, and four were unemployed.

The male breadwinner norm in the Soviet era

The idea of the male breadwinner is well established in Russian culture. In pre-revolutionary peasant culture a son was seen as a future provider for the family, while it was expected that a daughter would marry and leave for another family. This was reflected in the upbringing of and parental attitudes to boys and girls: girls were unwelcome, while boys were valued (Pushkareva, 1997); an attitude that can be seen in such pre-revolutionary popular sayings as, 'Feed your son for a while, the time will come when your son will feed you' (the person who would do the feeding was, of course, the mother). Another saying equated the husband with a fifty kopek piece (a substantial sum of money in the nineteenth century) and a woman with a piece of cloth 'they go together, and so live well' (Mikhailov, 1988). This identified women with domesticity and men with money.

The Bolsheviks sought to erase these patriarchal traditions: instead of being dependent on men, women were to be independent workers who could rely on the state to support them as mothers and pensioners. But though full female employment was achieved under the Soviet regime, the idea of the male breadwinner was maintained in Russian culture. Soviet men continued to think of themselves as breadwinners, and were taught from childhood that a 'real man' was one who could earn money.

The preservation of traditional male roles can clearly be seen in the interviews of my respondents. This, for example, was the view on the issue of a 61-year-old scientific employee of an institute:

> My starting point is that a man is the breadwinner [kormilets] – this question was always paramount for us. We grew up with the idea that a man should bring money into the home. The wife is a sort of second-order breadwinner. She says, 'provide for the family'. I can support this with my own family history. My father was killed young – in 1940 when I was 4 years old. My step-father married my mother with three children. He had the main job in terms of earning money and he was paid reasonably well. He used to say, 'I've earned the money, and now you make sure that I'm full.' In this way there's a sort of division [of labour] in family relations: one earns the money and the other uses this rationally for the good of the family.

Traditional views such as the one above are by no means uncommon among male workers, regardless of whether or not their wives work. In one sense, the persistence of such ideas is something of a puzzle given the highly visible presence of women within the Soviet labour force and the fact that many women had to cope without the support of men, in particular in the immediate post-Second World War era. It could be argued that the ideal of the male *kormilets* is a cultural residue of the pre-revolutionary period. But the continued prevalence of this ideal within Russian society cannot simply be put down to some kind of folk memory. The Soviet state itself contributed to the perpetuation of such ideas through the systematic privileging of 'male' industries and professions over female ones (Filtzer, 1992: 179). Obviously, the mechanisms through which this occurred were complex. It was not official policy to pay men more; rather, that deeply ingrained gender prejudices guided the development of the Soviet industrial system at every level. But the result was clear – Soviet women had a secondary position within the Soviet labour force. This contributed to the preservation of the concept of a male breadwinner, in so much as it reinforced the idea that it was 'natural' for men to earn more. This comes out strongly in the following quotation, from a 57-year-old senior scientific employee at a steel and alloy institute, who used the wage gap between the sexes to justify his idea of different male and female destinies:

> The man should be the main breadwinner. ... The whole system of society is laid out in this way. They paid men more. And it was more difficult for women in this regard. In this way according to the structure of society men should be at the head and the breadwinner, and the wife should look after the family hearth. In accordance with her destiny, a wife is better adapted for this. And a man's role is to earn money.

Thus, the impact of high labour participation of Soviet women on popular consciousness was limited by the fact that the traditional gender hierarchy was reproduced in the Soviet workplace, leaving male supremacy more or less intact.

What were the components of the male breadwinner ideal? One notable finding of my research is that it had different meanings for men and women. As has been shown in Chapter 2, Soviet women also believed that men should be the main wage earners. Their interpretation of the breadwinner's duties was that he should bring home a decent wage, not spend too much of it – and not drink too much of it. A high wage earner did not qualify as a *kormilets* if he drank his wages. In contrast, however, though men also talk about their role in bringing money into the family, a key component of their vision of the *kormilets* was the idea that, alongside providing for the family, he should have his own personal pocket money (*zanachka* or *karmannye den'gi*). As an employee of a scientific institute, aged 51, noted, this was 'about 20 per cent of my pay. For beer, for presents, and for other things' (estimates of the *zanachka* vary between 10 and 20 per cent). This pocket money was justified on the grounds that the man was the main breadwinner, a fact which gave him the psychological freedom and right to spend some of the money. As one respondent explained:

> Men are by nature more companionable, more open [*raskovannye*], freer in their spending than women. Moreover, the fact that women themselves were not the main wage earners [*dobytchiki*] left an imprint on their behaviour. They were sort of accountable to men – that is, those who brought the main income into the family. And so women had a stricter approach to the use of resources and couldn't allow themselves anything superfluous. Besides, it was already arranged in our state that it was easier for a man to do work on the side. And so, if he was more wilful in the use of money it was only because he knew that it was his responsibility to earn it.

Having money available for personal expenditure was seen as crucial to a man's dignity. As another former employee of a scientific institute, now a pensioner, explained:

> The *zanachka* was no more than 10–15 per cent. However, this money, as a rule, we kept in our pockets. Well, I can't turn up at the institute without a few kopeks in my pocket can I? You've got to have basic human dignity.

Moreover, being able to spend money independently was an important component of masculine identity, especially that of industrial workers. Being accountable to the wife (*podotcheten svoei babe*) was something which was perceived very negatively in male work collectives. Any man who took too much account of his wife's opinion was always open to the accusation that he was not a real man (*muzhik*). Within this climate it was considered shameful for a man not to have personal spending money: a key sign that he was *podotcheten svoei babe*. This was made clear as soon as a man entered the enterprise – a whole series of traditions served to reinforce this norm. The following, for example, is an account of one such ritual from a respondent who was forced to begin work at a factory at the age of 14 in order to help his mother support a large family:

> I started at the factory on 21 August 1951. I was short. On 15 November I was going to be 15. I wasn't tall enough to reach the machine. They put a special stool there so I could reach. After two weeks the day of my first pay packet arrived. As is well known, in Russia there's a tradition that you drink your first pay packet. With your first pay you drink, and treat the foreman, and the teacher who taught you (in my case an instrument fitter). And so there were three blokes – the foreman, the teacher and me. We went to one of the small

cafés which were near the factory. They said to me: 'Petrovich – today is your celebration. Well, what, shall we order [ourselves] 150 grams [of vodka] and glasses of beer? And for you – 50 grams and that's enough. Take the rest of the money home.' I was small and by the end of it I was completely drunk.

In such ways, men were introduced to an industrial culture in which drinking with their workmates was a key signifier of their manhood. Traditions such as keeping *zanachka* and going for drinks with co-workers were important informal buttresses to masculine identity. Certainly, such practices were not officially condoned by authorities obsessed by increasing production, while many women spent their entire married lives fighting to curb such expressions of male autonomy (see Chapter 2). Under communism, the efforts of both the Party, with its periodic anti-drunkenness drives, and women, with their tenacious rearguard action, were in vain: the cultural norms surrounding masculine behaviour were not challenged. In the transition era, by contrast, men have found their autonomy curbed by economic forces seemingly beyond their control.

Men's loss of status

As noted at the beginning of this chapter, the secure environment in which men were able, if they so wished, to live up to the ideal of the *kormilets* has now been destroyed by major reforms within the Russian economy. Real wages have fallen sharply, first of all under the impact of price liberalisation between 1992–3, and then more slowly in 1994 and 1995. By mid-1998, despite some recovery over the previous two years, statistical real wages were still only a little over half of the 1985 level, and in August 1998 they fell again to less than a third of the December 1991 level. Moreover, some people suffered far greater wage erosion than others, as inequality doubled in Russia under the impact of reform (all figures from Clarke, 1999: 120). Meanwhile, overdue wages reported on 1 July 1998, before the new crisis struck, amounted to 70 billion new roubles, which implies an average of slightly over one month's delay for every employed person in Russia. Again, however, the wage debts are very unevenly distributed, with some regions and industries far worse afflicted than others (ibid.: 114).

At the beginning of the transition period, many commentators predicted that it would be women who would bear the brunt of reform, while men would be relatively protected. This, however, has not proved to be the case (Ashwin and Bowers, 1997). In October 1998, for example, there were still approximately equal numbers of working age men and women unemployed on the labour force survey figures: 51 per cent of the unemployed were men, 49 per cent were women (Goskomstat, 1999: 28). Meanwhile, the withdrawal from labour market activity has been concentrated among the young and those of pension age, and only to a very limited degree by the exit of women from the labour force (Clarke, 1999: 118). The 'losers' of the reform process have therefore not been conveniently confined to one sex. 'Male' industries such as mining and metallurgy have been devastated along with 'female' industries such as textiles and garment manufacturing; men suffer wage delays along with women. Indeed, it may be that men feel the decline of their position more keenly given that they were in a stronger position to start off with.

There is some evidence that men have had more problems adapting to the problems of reform than women. The strongest indirect evidence of this lies in the life expectancy of men, which has declined dramatically during the transition era. The gap in life expectancy between Russian men and women is now one of the highest in the world, with only the Baltic states (which are undergoing a similar transition) in a worse position. As can be seen from the following table (based on the most up-to-date figures available from Goskomstat), the life expectancy of Russian men is one of the lowest in the world (seven years lower than China; one year lower than India).

Table 4.1   Life expectancy at birth for men and women

Country	Year	Men	Women
Russia	1997	60.9	72.8
Armenia	1996	69.3	76.2
UK	1995	74.1	79.3
USA	1995	74	80
Brazil	1996	64.1	70.6
Egypt	1995	64	66
China	1996	68	71
India	1996	62	62
Vietnam	1996	66	69

Source: Goskomstat, 1998: 392–3.

The difference in life expectancy between Russian men and women is mainly accounted for by the deaths of working age men, who are more than four times as likely to die than women of working age, from all causes (Goskomstat, 1998: 270–1). They are more than five times as likely to die of heart disease, 4.7 times as likely to die from alcohol poisoning, and more than seven times as likely to commit suicide (ibid.). Although these differences have remained more or less constant in proportional terms during the transition, it is clear that men's health problems, many of which are related to lifestyle, have only been exacerbated by the reform process.

The subjective dimension: male experiences of loss of status

The above statistics certainly paint a grim picture of the fate of men during the transition era. But how do the men themselves view this situation? Why have the privations of the transition era had such a dramatic impact on them? Why do a substantial number of men appear to be less able to cope than women, particularly when one considers the inherent advantages they possess within the labour market? The following sections attempt to explore the problems faced by men whose position at work – both in terms of pay and status – has been eroded by economic reform.

The home front

Tatiana Klimenkova argues that in order to retain his masculinity, a man must constantly battle with the shame of becoming a woman (1997: 13). This certainly accords with the portrait of Soviet masculinity sketched above: being too 'feminine', too influenced by his wife, meant that a man's status as a real man, a *muzhik*, was called into question. That is, the acceptable boundaries of masculinity were policed in the public sphere by male friends and co-workers, while the individual man was responsible for withstanding 'feminising' influences in the domestic sphere. As has been noted in previous chapters, in the Soviet era the latter element posed some problems given that the traditional role of the patriarch had been de-legitimised by the communist regime. For this reason, male status at work became the key to their position at home: the *kormilets* was the vital link which legitimised the extension of male status at work into the domestic realm. The role of breadwinner was thus central to the Soviet man's concept of self – as well as his wife's set of expectations.

What happens to men when they are deprived of the status of *kormilets*? And what happens to relations within the family when the material basis of established gender identities is undermined? Reproduced below is one man's account of what occurred when he lost his status as main breadwinner. Yura is a 59-year-old worker at an industrial enterprise, who is married with an 18-year-old daughter. Having worked at the enterprise for over twenty years, he has a high-skill grade, and was previously a respected member of the workforce. Now, however, the enterprise is on the verge of bankruptcy, and at the time of the interview Yura was owed seven months' wages. He argued that the younger workers at the factory – up to the age of 40 – had managed to find work elsewhere, but for workers like him it was impossible:

> We're 55, 58, 60 [years old]. There's nothing to discuss here. People around pension age – it's unlikely that they're going to get a job

somewhere. They don't take you. Here there's a pensioner – 72 years old and still working. Can't live on the pension – has to work.

My wife gets a pension. I get an invalidity pension of 220,000 roubles. And pay – you wait for them to give it to you. If only they'd give us that money. But they don't ... And every month inflation goes up. You go to the shop and look at the prices – they're one thing one month and something different the next. And the pay is today one thing and tomorrow another. ... We don't see any kind of way out. I've got four months left until my pension. If they don't drive me out in that time – I'll work up to then. And they drive you out saying, 'live on your own crusts'. And now my wife keeps me.

Having to be financially dependent on a woman raises complex emotions, as can be seen from Yura's description of his plight:

Before, of course, I knew for definite, I would bring home money on the 10th and the 22nd [of the month]. I lived like a king [*Ya khodil korolem*]. And now I don't open my mouth. My wife gets a pension. And she asks me from the doorstep, 'have you brought some money?' I say, 'no'. She says, 'What's the matter with you?' A man counts for nothing these days! [*Muzhika ni za chto ne schitayut!*]. I'm scared. I've got a daughter of 18. I've still got to raise her. To feed her. Put shoes on her feet. She's studying at a medical technical college. If only I had just 2 million [roubles]. As it is – I don't know how we're going to live. Things will be bad for us ...

At home, of course, my wife takes me into account. We've lived together for twenty-five years. But I feel as if I owe her. If I brought her home wages every month then she'd be satisfied. But as it is – you miss out on going visiting. New Year is almost here. And so you should pay people. So that people could celebrate a little bit. If only they paid us for one of the months [they owe]. Say, for September. I can't speak for the others [his colleagues], but if only they gave our workshop something or other.

There are three points that stand out in Yura's comments. First, he notes his loss of *personal* autonomy. Later in the interview, he repeated the evocative phrase, '*Ya khodil korolem*' ('I lived like a king'), continuing, 'and now I can't buy anything. At home I don't even open my mouth.' This highlights two key components of his previous 'kingly' status: he had money to spend and he had authority at home as a result of his status as the main breadwinner. The loss of his spending power and domestic status is clearly hard to bear. Second, his wife uses the idea of the male *kormilets* to call him to account, waiting on the doorstep for him to bring home the bacon, and expressing her frustration when he fails to do so. It seems that, to a certain extent, Yura agrees with his wife's criticism, since he no longer feels able to 'open his mouth' at home: failing to perform his allotted role appears to leave him without the right or the confidence to speak. At the same time, however, he feels that this situation violates the natural order of things: 'A man counts for nothing these days!' His discomfort about his relations with his wife is also visible when he slightly contradicts his earlier description of her, and stresses that, of course, she takes him into account. For her not to do so – as it seems she sometimes does not – is a violation of what he feels *should* be his naturally superior position as a man. Third, it is evident that Yura is worried about providing for his family. He feels he should find the money to educate his daughter and is concerned about her future. He is likewise preoccupied with obtaining at least enough money to be able to celebrate New Year (a traditional family festival in Russia, equal in status to Christmas in the UK.) Yura's reaction thus fully supports the argument that the ideal of the male *kormilets* was dualistic; it entailed responsibility for familial financial provision, but, equally important, it implied masculine independence. The former provided the basis for male power within the family, while the latter was crucial to their status among their peers. The challenge to the position of the male *kormilets* in the transition era has thus exposed the fact that male status was socially defined rather than naturally given.

Yura's sense of disorientation is replicated in the comments of another worker from the same factory, also called Yura. Yura 2 was equally despondent:

> They've completely killed me. This state. I always had money. If I needed a suite [of furniture] – I earned the money. If I needed a car – I did officially registered supplementary work at a school. I was a Party member for twenty-four years. But the Party didn't give me anything. I lived like a king [*Ya khodil korolem*] ...
>
> My wife works in a school. But now I'm going out of my mind [*krysha u menya edet*]. Honestly speaking, I don't know what to do. ... [Before *perestroika*] I lived, I didn't suffer. *Perestroika* got me into trouble. My fridge was always full, and now it's empty.

Significantly, Yura 2 also emphasises that he lived like a king (though no thanks to the Party, who he now feels has betrayed him). He notes that he had money in the past – that everything was attainable. His comments reinforce the point that for men the sense of having money *in their own* pockets was as important as their ability to provide.

The stories of these two men illustrate just how central waged work was to masculine identity. Work was the legitimate sphere of male self-realisation; it gave them a defined status in the family, and it usually entailed entrance to a male culture of comradeship, which played the role of reinforcing informal norms of masculine behaviour. The decline or closure of their workplaces has thus left the men who have not been able to recreate themselves bereft, 'scared' and at a loss as to what to do. Their world has been turned upside down, not least because what they saw as an enduring law of nature – their superior status in relation to women – has been revealed to be conditional.

It is therefore not surprising that the other emotion experienced by these men is anger. In many cases this is directed towards the state or the President, as can be seen in the comments of Yura 2: 'I think that if they don't get rid of Yeltsin I won't find a way out [of my problems]. Gorbachev began [everything], he gave his Party to Yeltsin. They destroyed everything. … They, of course, brought me down, but they didn't completely break me.' Such comments – and many far stronger – are commonplace. The other outlet for anger is, of course, the family. Given that domestic violence is about the exertion and confirmation of power, it seems likely that the disruption in domestic power relations caused by the loss of the status of breadwinner may lead some men to resort to violence. (Given the unreliability of data in this area it is difficult to assess whether domestic violence has increased during the transition era). This was obviously something that was difficult to discuss in interviews with male respondents, although one of my female respondents did shed some light on the way in which male frustration can express itself within the family. Her husband was unemployed for nearly two years, and this had had a dramatic impact on their marriage:

We had a very difficult period. He was depressed for a year and a half. He was like a gloomy black cloud. He didn't do anything at home. I was developing on all fronts. And he basically lay on the sofa and watched television. He couldn't find himself any work after managing for all those years: he couldn't force himself to work in a non-managerial position. What was going on at home – I can't tell you. One time I came home from work, sat in front of the computer, and he was watching the television. My work was urgent, and he sat re-laxing, watching television programmes. I asked him to turn the vol-ume down slightly – and he threw a slipper at me – my printer was bothering him. How much I put up with – only God knows. The only thing that saved me from divorce was the fact that our two children were growing up.

But recently he found a job – and immediately everything changed. With his first pay packet he brought home an enormous bunch of roses. He became a normal human being again.

This story does not reveal startling abuse, and it has a happy ending. But given that many men will not find work, it is likely that the problem is more severe in a substantial minority of families.

Work: kings without their crowns

One of the key arguments put forward in this volume is that in the Soviet era, the key to men's status was their position at work: work was a legitimate sphere of male domination which was tacitly underwritten by the communist authorities. The question is: in post-Soviet Russia, apart from the fact that wages have been drastically eroded, and are often paid late, what constitutes the male identity crisis in relation to work? First, in the context of industrial decline, male autonomy at work – that is, shop-floor power – has been seriously curtailed. Spontaneous, impulsive behaviour of the kind that was previously seen to befit the *muzhik* at work is now rather dangerous. Second, working-class masculine identity was very much tied up with the performance of particular kinds of work – 'real' work with metal, coal, machines, and so on. The decline of heavy industry has undermined this position. Meanwhile, for men outside industry, often what was important was their concept of professionalism, something which in many cases has also been undermined by economic transition. Finally, given that male status at work was the key to their overall identity (at home as well as among their peers), any fall in professional status is a blow to the individual man, rather than a local difficulty. Particularly in the case of older male workers, this may serve to inhibit the kind of flexibility demanded by the new Russian labour market.

Under communism, skilled workers were always in demand. It was often difficult to find and retain certain types of workers, who acquired the status of gold. Managers were scared of losing good workers because it was hard to replace them. These workers, therefore, had a certain amount of autonomy and were secure in their position: this meant they could talk back to their managers, and could occasionally even appear at work drunk without any serious consequences. Meanwhile, if they decided to leave, it was not difficult for them to find another job. The contrast to the workers' situation in post-Soviet Russia could not be more stark. Workers in many branches of heavy industry have found their position transformed: now, in the context of economic collapse, they are constantly at risk of losing their jobs. Behaviour that went with their privileged position in the past – for example, showing disrespect to a manager – is now highly risky. Such men find the decline in their fortunes very difficult to come to terms with, as the reflections of Yura 2 sharply illustrate:

[Before] nobody swore at me. I always knew my work. It suited me. The boss couldn't bellow at me, because there was nothing I couldn't teach him. And now I haven't been paid for seven months. [Before] I always walked along with my nose in the air. ... I always said what I wanted. But now they've crushed me. I shouted that I'll leave. And then I bit my tongue and thought 'why am I shouting? I've only got two months left to work out [until my pension]'. Then an order came to them to make fifty people redundant. And I'd been drunk. They said they'd sack me. And I answered them, 'go on then, sack me'. And then I realised what it meant.

This quotation illustrates just how hard it is for some workers to adjust to the new economic climate. Yura 2 finds himself slipping back into his old ways – drinking, answering back, threatening to leave – but then remembers that he no longer has the power to behave in this way. Threatening to leave no longer has the same impact as before, since there are not the same plan targets to be kept; he will simply be brushed off with the typical managerial retort of the transition era, 'if you don't like it, leave'.

These workers also find it hard to come to terms with the declining status of the old-style male professions. They perceived their work in industry as 'real work', while the more lucrative professions of the transition era – most of them connected with trade – are not seen as work worthy of 'real men'. Yura 2, assessing his limited job prospects, was categorical on this point: 'I am a peasant by nature. I will work with iron and soil. But to buy and sell – it's not my thing.' Such views are commonly encountered among industrial workers, who grew up with the idea that to work in heavy industry was a noble calling. The Soviet value system which despised trade as a capitalistic, parasitic venture is deep-rooted: younger generations may be able to adapt to the new Russia, but older industrial workers are finding it almost impossible. As Yura 1, asked if he could do some additional work to supplement his income, put it: 'Where? In trade? If I was 18 years old I'd do it. But soon I'll be 60. At 60 years old it's completely different.'

Professionals in areas which have not flourished during the transition period, such as scientists and academics, find themselves in a similar position. This is illustrated by the case of Andrei, an academic at a scientific institute. His institute had suffered under *perestroika*, and, while some of his colleagues had managed to reorient themselves, Andrei had been unable to do so. Although his monthly pay amounted to only $15, he felt constrained by his own sense of professionalism from changing direction:

Professionalism – it's what I've striven for all my life. It took me too long to get there. And with the result that I've become highly professional in something that, in essence, nobody needs now. Meanwhile, many of my colleagues very quickly reoriented themselves and re-qualified. They began to sell anything they could: metal, cheese, computers. But my observation is that very often business and commerce are connected with ... 'banditry'. I would like, if it were possible, to develop a lawful operation. Using my knowledge, my experience. But, unfortunately, it is practically impossible. This is probably connected to [my] upbringing – some people became businessmen because they could get round the law, so that they made a profit and they had enough. In my understanding, a man's attributes should be nobility, the ability to respect and understand people, and many other qualities for which there is no room in contemporary business.

Andrei's sense of what a man should be – professional, noble and honest – prevents him doing what he thinks is necessary to succeed in today's Russia. Of course, it is possible that this is just an excuse, a form of sour grapes, but such ideas are sufficiently widely encountered to suggest that in many cases, masculine professional identities developed under communism have become an obstacle to success in the transition period.

It is therefore possible to argue that while women's secondary status in the Soviet labour force allows women to endure the privations of 'flexibility' without too much damage being done to their self-esteem, the opposite is true for men. The fact that their superior status was defined by their position in the labour force means that it is more difficult for men to adapt. Exchanging the status of a skilled worker for that of a trader or security guard is a blow to a man's gender identity. Of course, some men are able to deal with this change in status, while others are not, but it is a difficult issue for any man who has to face it. This, for example, was the comment of one engineer who realised that his determination to hold on to his profession against all the odds had limited his prospects:

> I sat at home for a year and a half. Of course, I didn't just sit there, I worked. I tried to register as unemployed, but at the employment service they humiliated me, by telling me that I was an old man. That's at 40-odd. I began to work for myself. I set myself the goal of not losing my qualifications and to work in my specialism. It cost me a lot that saving of my face.

Saving face, however, is not a superficial matter – in this case a man's whole identity is at stake. Often it requires a major crisis to change the situation, as can be seen in the comments of the following junior academic at a Moscow institute:

> I think that if something particular happens – then I'll go and get a job somewhere. I'll even take a job as a caretaker. However, now I think – well it hasn't reached that critical point where I have to drop everything and find something. Of course, I'm absolutely not paid enough for what I do, and it's difficult to live on my pay. But all the same I think, yes, give me my pay. While they're shooting each other in the government and reforming everything, I'll wait. But if what money I get stops – then I'll go and look.

Although men are generally more mobile in the labour market than women, it is none the less the case that many older men in what are now obsolete or declining professions find it difficult to search for better paid work when this entails a fall in professional status.

Conclusion

This chapter has argued that men as well as women have lost out in the transition era. This has had major implications for the masculine identity of those affected. Men's status as the main breadwinners was a crucial buttress to masculinity in the Soviet era: it was the key to their position at home, while their primary position in the labour force allowed them a degree of autonomy at work. In the transition era, however, many men have lost their *kormilets* status, altering both their work and home life. Male worker identities that were based on the concept of 'real' men's work, and the sense of indispensability and freedom that went with having certain labour skills in the communist era, have been challenged by reform. In addition, many older men who in the past enjoyed a secure professional position, have found it difficult to accept the indignities thrust upon them in the contemporary labour market. It seems likely that the depression and anxiety associated with this situation is a contributory factor to the health crisis among older working age men. Vodka is the easiest way to obtain temporary relief from anxiety, but its use also causes or exacerbates many of the complaints which are responsible for the deaths of middle-aged men.

Meanwhile, the loss of male status at work has also had a profound effect on men's domestic relations. Men who fail to live up to what many regard as their 'masculine duty' to provide are symbolically 'castrated', and their status within the family is undermined. This leaves them with two options: they can either accept subordination, or fight back. Tragically, however, the only target against whom they are likely to score any 'victories' is their wives.[2]

Notes

1 The work history interviews were conducted for a project entitled 'The restructuring of employment and the formation of a labour market in Russia', which was headed by Professor Simon Clarke at the University of Warwick, UK. I was one of the researchers involved in this project.
2 In theory, these men could respond to their situation collectively, attempting to defend their position through trade unions or other workers' organisations. But although there have been sporadic, spontaneous protests during the transition era, there has been little effective co-ordinated activity on the part of workers' organisations. The reasons for this are complex; and for more details see Ashwin (1999).

References

Ashwin, S. (1999) *Russian Workers: The Anatomy of Patience*, Manchester: Manchester University Press.

Ashwin, S. and Bowers, E. (1997) 'Do Russian women want to work?', in M. Buckley (ed.), *Post-Soviet Women*, Cambridge: Cambridge University Press: 21–37.

Clarke, S. (1999) *New Forms of Employment and Household Survival Strategies in Russia*, Coventry, Moscow: ISITO/CCLS.

Filtzer, D. (1992) *Soviet Workers and De-Stalinization: The Formation of the Modern System of Soviet Production Relations, 1953–1964*, Cambridge: Cambridge University Press.

Goskomstat (1998) *The Demographic Yearbook of Russia*, Moscow: Goskomstat Rossii.

—— (1999) *Statisticheskii byulleten'*, 3, 53, Moscow: Goskomstat Rossii.

Klimenkova, T. (1997) *Zhenshchina kak fenomen kul'tury*, Moscow: Preobrazhenie.

Mikhailov, Yu. (1988) *Russkie poslovitsy i pogovorki*, Moscow: Khudozhestvennaya literatura.

Pushkareva, N. (1997) *Chastnaya zhizn' russkoi zhenshchiny: nevesta, zhena, lyubovnitsa*, Moscow: Ladomir.

5   New Russian men

Masculinity regained?

Elena Meshcherkina

'New Russian' is a journalistic term that is used to refer to Russia's new rich, a social group which has emerged during the transition era. In this chapter I look at the redefinition of masculinity among 'new Russian' men, using as my informants successful entrepreneurs in a variety of different fields. As the most wealthy section of Russian society, 'new Russians' are one of the few groups free to live as they choose. Moreover, as the new elite of Russian society, the forms of masculine identity that are forged by men in this group are likely to be influential in wider society. My analysis proceeds from the basis that masculinity is a relational phenomenon – that is, masculinity is formed through interaction both among men, and between men and women.[1] I identify four key fields in which masculinity is defined: in relationships among men in the public sphere; in relationships between the sexes in the public sphere; in private relations between men; and in private relations between men and women (for the purposes of this chapter, I focus on relations between spouses). My main findings concern the redefinition of gendered hierarchies in the public sphere, and the shifting balance of power in the private sphere. In both areas *perestroika* and the reform that followed it led to disruption, but the entrepreneurs who are the focus of my study were able to adapt to their new situation in a way which protected their sense of masculine identity.

My findings are based on fifteen life history interviews conducted specifically for research for this chapter, although I also drew on previous research on life histories which I conducted for a number of other projects.[2] The reason for the use of life history research is that no individual can be seen as atomised – every situation in which s/he finds her/himself has been partially created by wider social factors. This does not mean that it is possible to claim that generalisations based on life histories are universal, but that every life history can highlight features of the environment in which a given individual is inserted.

The public sphere: the recreation of hierarchy

To be a man in Soviet society was to have a place in a rigid hierarchy, and individual men were forced to adapt to this hierarchy. In this sense, the social standing and identity of the individual man was defined by his position in relation to the state. This subordination was keenly experienced at a subjective level. In post-communist Russia, horizontal relations between individual men have assumed a far greater importance, and now men who want to succeed have to define their position in relation to their peers. That is, they are striving for success in a new hierarchy of their own creation.

The nature of the hierarchy in the Soviet era can be illustrated using extracts from the life history of G., a *nomenklaturshik* (state bureaucrat). G. was born in 1938 to a peasant family. His elevation to the ranks of the *nomenklatura* was thus a great one, something which was possible at the time through the Soviet education system. After obtaining a place at the prestigious Moscow Institute for International Relations, he stayed on there to work after completing his studies. He then completed an internship in Canada, before obtaining a position working for the Soviet government at the United Nations (UN) in Geneva, where he was secretary of the Party organisation. As G. himself readily acknowledged, he formed part of the Soviet elite.

His comments on the nature of the environment in which he used to work reveal the workings of the state hierarchy in the Soviet era. As G. pointed out, this hierarchy was not straightforwardly based on rank, because sons of those in powerful positions were given precedence over their superiors. It thus combined the rigidity typical of many large bureaucracies with a system of personal ties. This system worked in such a way as to underline continually the subordination of the individual, both to the state machine and to his superiors. There was little room for autonomy, principle or bravery in such a system – in order to prosper a man had to submit to the rules of the game. This can be seen very clearly in G.'s description of the payment system operated within the Soviet UN circuit:

> Our sense of justice and principle was constantly diminished. ... I understood that ... [protest] would achieve nothing except unpleasantness, and therefore everyone kept quiet. You hand over money – and everyone kept quiet. What does it mean 'hand over money'? All of us had UN salaries, but in the embassy no one could get more than the ambassador. The ambassadors ... received a small salary, although they had a personal chef, free food, a car, and so on – that wasn't taken into account. They received lots of representation expenses, that also wasn't taken into account. I got about $7,000 a month – I had to hand over all of [the money] ... I was left with about $1,800. We used to go to the embassy, and say, 'We've come to hand over the money.' 'Not to hand over, but to receive it,' they'd say to us. Well, somehow one professor, a doctor, came to work for the World Health Organisation. And when they said to him that he had to hand over the money, he said, 'You

know money is a trifle, and I would of course hand it over, but it's kind of very uncomfortable for me to be forced to do it. I understand that I won't be able to work here any more, but I won't hand over [the money].' He worked until his vacation, and, of course, didn't return from it. But he didn't give away the money ... and received perhaps more than I did in six and a half years of working there [laughs].

This punitive informal taxation regime obviously did not result in serious hardship for those affected, but the ritual of handing over money was humiliating – it underlined the absolute dependence of those involved. As G. noted, 'it definitely sort of put you in some sort of semi-servile position [*pol-urabskoe polozhenie*]'. The Soviets were forcibly made to feel their lack of autonomy in relation to other national representatives. This clearly had major implications for the forms of masculine identity that could be forged by members of the Soviet elite – a whole range of options, including classically 'masculine' forms of expression, were ruled out within their environment.

None the less, woven into the fabric of the *nomenklatura* system were certain codes of masculine behaviour – what was a man's due; appropriate modes of deference, and so on. Men developed ritual codes of conduct appropriate to their position and their gender. The interaction of hierarchical and masculine norms can be seen in G.'s account of the visit by an official delegation:

A big delegation came to Geneva, with a big boss at its head. They let it be known that they wanted to go out of town for a barbecue. There we had a drink and got one of them absolutely drunk. And then, as he lay there, they started sticking flowers in an inappropriate place [his anus]. Everyone thought it was funny. ... And I got involved in a quarrel with that big boss, we were literally about to grab each other by the collars. ... We quarreled about Stalin. He said, 'Stalin cared about the people. ... Everything they say about him is lies.' Anyway, we tussled with each other. The others dragged me away, and I didn't know what was going on, I didn't know who he was. And two years later I was appointed his deputy and I thought that's it, I'm done for. ... But he saw me [and] in front of everyone he embraced and kissed me. Of course, that immediately gained me respect in the eyes of the others. Yes, that generation of people have a very good quality: not taking these things personally. But not all of them, of course.

This story reveals a number of things. First, it highlights the nature of the games of humiliation which occurred within the male elite, which served to highlight the status positions of those involved (the man who was 'decorated' with flowers was a subordinate). Meanwhile, when G. tussled with the 'big boss' he was dragged away because all those around him knew that he had violated an informal code of conduct by refusing to show the appropriate deference to a superior. Second, some of these games included a ritualised homosexual element, in which social subordination was implicitly linked with male sexual passivity. The irony of the story is that G.'s insubordination brought him respect *as a man* from his superior, who signalled this with the quintessential sign of male respect in the Russian context, the manly embrace – a signal that was understood by all the status-conscious onlookers of the event. (The manly embrace, in contrast to the flower game, is a non-sexual event without overtones of subordination.) G.'s conclusion to the story, meanwhile, reveals his own unresolved feelings regarding his past. First of all, his assertion that 'that generation of people' did not take things personally is belied both by the statement that follows it, and the story itself – the boss of the story *did* take the event personally, but in a positive rather than a negative sense. G.'s stereotypical and weak defence of the mores of the Soviet era, which is at odds with the thrust of his story, highlights his ambiguous feelings towards the regime which educated and elevated, but also routinely humiliated, him.

G.'s ambivalence is well captured by his description of his gradual disenchantment with the communist regime, but also his feelings of shock regarding the fate of his superiors in the post-communist era:

> You see everything, there's already no idealism left. I was a believer you know, I had already been in the Party. ... Since 1964, I had the conscience not to throw away my membership card. One person knew more, another less. Thank God, at our level there was always the possibility to doubt. ... You know, the belief that the idols at the very top were clean went some way to compensate for the lack of belief in other things. ... All the same, by the time I left there I was no longer naïve, trusting and honest, and principled. That had been somehow washed away. ... But to go through all that, doesn't give you a feeling of loss ... you know everything, you've seen everything, nothing will surprise you. It's a good feeling. ...
>
> Finally, everyone ended up in trade or as a middleman. ... At the beginning it shocked me ... when, in the capacity of a middleman for some kind of tinned goods, the former President of Gosplan [the State Planning Agency] came to me. Nightmare! Usually from those kind of posts people went into respectable positions.

From his description at his disorientation at meeting the fallen head of Gosplan, it is clear that G. retained some residual respect for the hierarchy in which he had worked, in spite of his loss of idealism. Moreover, his description of his 'moral education' in Geneva, reveals that he was able to take from the experience other means of masculine self-identification than service within the state hierarchy. He constructed for himself a knowing, seen-it-all persona which served to compensate for the subordination and disillusionment he experienced.

The collapse of the regime for which he worked initially threw him into disarray. He was obliged to adapt not only to the new labour market, but also his identity as a man. He explained:

> Now – work. Money isn't the most important thing for me here, although of course it's important. The most important thing is the entirely different environment, which is more acceptable to me, more intelligent. ... I've sort of adapted to it [business] it also gives you some kind of feeling of satisfaction. But there was a period of despair when I thought I wasn't capable of anything. I felt horrendously uncomfortable in front of my family.

Thus, after going through a crisis, G. was able to adapt. It is precisely his survival instinct and ultimate success which now forms the basis of his new masculine identity in the public sphere: 'I made it' is now the implicit subtext of his discussions regarding his conduct in the post-communist era.

Many entrepreneurs report feeling a sense of liberation in their new position – the idea that the old state hierarchy was stifling is quite a common one. S., a former academic, now head of a building firm, explained it in the following way, 'There [in academia] they limited my freedom, opinions, conduct. I became less trusting, [more] reserved.' In place of a predictable career involving subordination in return for security, such men are now embracing the values of risk, independence and individualism. This is part of a wider rehabilitation of entrepreneurialism in contemporary Russian society – a rehabilitation which links entrepreneurship with values which are being culturally defined as masculine.[3] Such a transformation of values can be seen in the life history of Y., a businessman who operates on the edge of the law. At the time of the interview he was 34 years old. He was a former engineer-programmer. His change in profession required him to develop a new basis for his self-respect. He explained:

> I began to get to grips with life better, to understand better which stages it is necessary to go through in order to create a business. I understood what it is to do business, and not just sit somewhere or other. ... Nobody was going to bring me money on a silver platter [*na blyudechke s goluboi kaemochkoi*] on the 5th and the 25th [of every month]. It fell to me to adapt and make [it]. ...
>
> Now there is ... a place, stores where we buy goods. The interrelations [there] are absolutely normal, human. Because they are doing business and we are doing business. So I make money – and people relate to me accordingly. ... A person who is basically bad ... can't make money on a stable basis. Sooner or later he'll trip up somewhere

or other. ... They give me goods at the moment on the basis of my word ... but before that [happened] a large amount of time went by.

Y. now makes a virtue of his independence – he is no longer retained by the state; he is no longer the passive recipient of money who is merely required to 'sit somewhere or other' in return for his keep. Now he has to be active and resourceful in order to survive in a competitive world. He emphasises the challenging precariousness of his position, 'I went on holiday with my wife ... we returned and our clients had been "stolen".' He also accentuates the positive side of the business relations in which he is now engaged, claiming that only the honourable man of his word can survive in such a climate. At the same time, however, he is aware that his stress on the ethics of business is contradicted somewhat by his status as a semi-legal businessman. He later acknowledged this, saying:

Here you can't earn money honestly, it's not required. ... OK, we are not in a certain sense honest in our dealings with this state. But in a certain way this state is not honest in its dealings with us. We just deal with it like it deals with us.

Y. thus justifies his position by reference to a tit-for-tat morality, and in this way supports the idea of business as a sphere in which an ethic of honourable manhood can flourish. His key reference group is no longer the state, but the close circle of middlemen, buyers and sellers with whom he does business. Here he has continually to uphold his reputation in order to remain within the circuit.

Y.'s description of his new environment emphasises the importance of loyalty and co-operation. So, does the new world of business offer successful men an escape from the constraining hierarchy of the past? I would argue that such men are creating new hierarchies: in place of the state-defined status ladder of the past, a man's ranking is now determined within a competitive environment in which it is always necessary to be alert. This can be illustrated using the life history of K., a 36 year old, who has made his way in the post-communist world by making a career out of his old hobby – travel. K. identified himself with the culture of the *shestidesyatniki* (men of the 1960s). This group, named after the group of public figures and social thinkers, such as Nikolai Chernyshevsky, who flourished a century before in the 1860s, created small pockets of freedom for themselves, often within kitchen walls, and formed a counter-culture whose values and ideas ran against those of official Soviet ideology. One of the spaces created by the *shestidesyatniki* was a system of group tourism, in particular involving activity holidays, and it was here that K. eventually found his niche.

K. had a strict upbringing, however. His father was a railway engineer and his mother was a nursing sister. His father ensured he got a good education; he had always said to him, 'you've got to study, otherwise you'll end up there, with the workers, on the street'. K. managed to escape army service, but he found choosing a career hard. He eventually found work in a physics institute, a job which he found interesting, and also had the virtue of long vacations. At this stage, 'I began to go hiking, it was my escape [*otdushina*], my world'. He would go travelling four times a year, and developed a group of close male friends connected with this. This proved to be his salvation in the transition era:

> The new era began. ... We began to sort of get involved in commerce little by little. To make and sell things. We began to make tourist equipment. What else could we do? The thing that we found interesting. Then we understood that it was impossible to do two jobs. We were all very close, but we were working for the tourist club. Then we opened our own office, and made catamarans, raft equipment, then we opened a sewing workshop and began to make camouflaged clothes. We had high-quality goods and low prices, so we could keep our place in the market.

When K. describes the values of those who work in tourism, it is in a way which harks back to the era of the 1960s when tourism was a means of escape into a sphere of authenticity remote from the official world. His firm hired people who had travelled, 'a section of people who needed inner freedom', people who were 'easy going, with a high level of capability, endurance, and sense of purpose'.

Thus, initially the firm which K. and his associates created was the site of brotherly co-operation among rugged individualists, all of whom were concerned to preserve their autonomy. But there were dangers:

> In principle I knew that it was dangerous to invite people I was close to, friends [to work at the firm]. ... One time we had a problem with a good friend – it didn't work out. And we parted company. ... It seems to me that he simply changed. Sometimes people are different at work and on holiday. If I feel that a person loves to work, I'll forgive him a lot, because then we're on the same ground.

K. thus quickly adapted himself to the new reality of the Russian market. Old ties from his travelling past were all very well, but the future of the firm was the most important thing. And what the firm needed was hard workers. As a result, the firm moved from being a place of informality to one which was gradually formalised and professionalised. The process went further than this, however. K. himself undermined the collective management system of the firm, to replace it with a one-man management structure which put him in control. His embarrassment about having done so (in the light of all his previous comments regarding inner freedom and so on) is revealed in his deployment of the passive voice to describe the process, and his shifting use of personal pronouns:

> There was a timely and wise decision – the dividing up of pay, even for the co-founders – all of it was farmed out to me. Nobody knew what they were talking about, who was getting what. *We* decided to let one person [be responsible] and let him alone decide. *I* proposed that scheme and *everyone* agreed. [My emphasis.]

It is notable that K. only introduces himself as initiator of the transformation of the firm at the very end – and then covers himself by claiming that he had the full support of his colleagues. Although K. is still keen to pay lip-service to the collectivist values of tourism, his practice is now governed by market rationality.

This story and others like it reveal that while new entrepreneurs often express a desire to escape the rigid structures of the past in order to feel freer, in practice they are creating new hierarchies in which success as an independent player is crucial. The story of K. is a particularly interesting illustration of this process precisely because he was previously an adherent of counter-cultural values which eschewed the official Soviet world.

The private sphere: gender trouble on the road to greatness

As well as finding their place in the brave new world of business, men have to define themselves in relation to women. During the transition period, all the men who I studied had been through a crisis period while they 'found their feet' in the new society. In the case of the men examined here, this took the form of a period of financial dependence on their wives, who appeared to adapt to their new environment more rapidly. This, however, had little impact on the men's views regarding women.

The road to success of these entrepreneurs is strikingly similar in one respect: the crucial initiating or supportive role played by their wives in the first instance. A typical example is provided by the case of M., the director of a large shop:

> [Before 1992] I worked as the boss of a laboratory of a certain research institute which was part of the Ministry of the Electrical Industry. It was a high position, good money. Then after 1992, penniless, I understood for the first time what it was to feel hungry. Of course, I had many possibilities of earning extra money, and, yes, I had reserves. But they were quickly used up. All the same, I didn't have the feeling that there was no way out. It meant that it was necessary, in the light of the possibilities, to find a way of surviving. My wife was in the same situation. We finished the same higher education

institute, she was a specialist in town administration, she'd done a dissertation, she was an employee in a reasonably well-respected structure. She understood everything, everything. She was in the same situation. We had nothing to bake with. Then we understood ... that from a professional point of view we had things going for us. In actual fact, it was a question of time or luck. And then things turned out the way they should. *First*, my wife moved over into an insurance company. Her friend was working in that company already. Then, by chance, through acquaintances, I moved into a commercial structure. [My emphasis.]

What is of note here is M.'s emphasis on the fact that his wife was in the same situation as him, despite her education and position. All the same, it was she who made the first move into the brave new world of commerce.

The sequence of events was similar in the case of K., and Y. the tourist turned businessman and the entrepreneur quoted in the previous section. In the case of K., before he moved into tourism there was a point where he was receiving very low wages. At this stage his wife took the survival of the family into her own hands and began to sell *matreshki* (Russian dolls). But K. said this did not affect his standing: 'The subject didn't come up. I simply worked continuously. I was somehow going somewhere.' Y.'s situation was similar. Despite all his glorification of the challenges of the business world, it was actually his wife who initially bore the risk of moving into a new field:

> While my wife was doing business, I basically just looked around. I simply asked questions. I wasn't sure. ... It's a risk, the ability at a certain moment to take your own decision. Now there isn't a risk, just routine work, a smooth way [*nakatannyi put'*] ... I am more careful, but my wife is more impulsive ... I try not to take on contacts with the state bureaucrats – that's my wife's [job], relations with businessmen are easier for me.

Despite the fact that it was his wife who smoothed the level path which Y. is now so proudly treading, he manages to deride her decisiveness – which he transforms into the more stereotypically 'feminine' attribute of impulsiveness. He is not timid (which his wife would have surely been accused of being had she been in his position), but 'careful'. Meanwhile, though the couple are working together, their space is neatly divided up into gendered spheres – she deals with the official world of the state (which he now characterises as a sleepy backwater), while he does the man's work with the other businessmen.

Y.'s attempt to diminish his wife stems from a kind of cognitive dissonance. For, despite the fact that it was she who created the foundations for their present success, any direct admission of this would challenge his highly traditional views of gender roles. At the level of discourse, these have survived the temporary experience of dependence intact. The same is true of K. His views of the destiny of men and women were definite:

> The final destiny of women is domestic work. Man, he is on an eternal quest for creative realisation in life – like businessmen, intelligence officers, creators. But women realise their creativity through mother-hood. We are sort of like intelligence officers, but a woman gathers more, preserves [things], she is more structured, she strengthens what a man makes.

The idea of the man as the Creator (which links him with God) and the woman as the Mother is entirely traditional. It also contradicts K.'s experience which included a period during which his wife was the breadwinner. But he now views this as a temporary aberration. Y.'s position is similar. He is pleased that he and his wife are working together, as this has restored the natural balance of things: 'relations in the family are more normal now, and, let's say, dinner isn't ready, now I know why it's not ready. Because we do business together and I know what she's doing.' Interestingly, Y.'s wife also feels things are easier now that Y. is back on his feet:

> Before I had even more responsibilities, when I did business, and he sat with the children. I had to prepare the dinner and go to work, for me it was harder. Now he does the business and that suits me fine. And for him it's emotionally easier. To be now, head of the family, so to speak.

As can be seen, even when the business was in the wife's hands, the gender division of labour in the home was little changed. Y. looked after the children, but his wife still took care of the cooking. What is also clear is that she actively protects and bolsters Y.'s position; she realised that her temporary dominance was difficult for him, and was ready to relinquish her position to accommodate him. But she is also keenly aware that this is what she is doing: he is only head of the family '*so to speak*'.

This is a common position among female entrepreneurs and managers, who often help their husbands to preserve at least the appearance of traditionalism. These, for example, were the comments of a 28-year-old manager, A.:

> I am now independent from my husband. I already can't remember the last time I asked him for money. I never ask for money, because it's completely unnecessary, but he asks me for it. Of course, I don't talk about my income with him, and never tell him; well, I might some-times show him the smallest pay cheque. In principle, for me the main thing is that my husband is paid, comes home and brings in money, if

only for the food, because I have to feel from him that he is at least the father of the family [*ottsa semeistva*]. Because, as lots of people say, a man must bring home the money and a woman *ostensibly* [*yakoby*] should sit at home and do housework. Well, I could never sit at home and do housework. ... But if my husband is going to earn money and keep all of [it] to himself, then I will stop feeling the man in him, and because of that his rank in the family will diminish. And if he didn't bring home money, and sat at home, not working, then at a certain stage it would be possible to ask: 'what's the point of being with you?' The wife does the housework, the wife goes to the shops, the child goes to kindergarten, what else is there to do? The husband, he is overall the breadwinner [*kormilets*], and so let him bring the money in. [My emphasis.]

Even though A. feels that the traditional woman's role is not for her, she wants to feel that her husband is playing his allotted part: if he ceases to do so her respect for him will diminish and, eventually, it seems, she will have no further use for him. Other female managers felt similarly uncomfortable about moving ahead of their husbands. L., a 37-year-old manager of a joint venture, had also taken to hiding her new-found wealth from her husband:[4]

For a woman I get really quite good pay. Expenses such as shoes, a dress I bought for myself with my own money, I didn't go to my husband. It seems he understood that I could allow myself this. ... Suddenly this thing happened ... he began to think that I already had everything. It was already too much. Then I began to hide various purchases from him. I bought [something], hid [it], and then got it out, as if I'd already had it. He, of course, understood that it was something new but ... Look, I bought myself a new fur coat with my money, a bonus. I told him that my parents had given it to me as a present.

It would therefore seem that members of the new group of successful Russian businesspeople are making a concerted effort to maintain an 'ostensibly' traditional pattern of gender relations. And this effort is being made *by both men and women*. In some cases this results in more strain, in others less, but what is notable is the tenacity to which both men and women cling to the idea that it is the husband who should be successful. Meanwhile, the role of women is less clearly articulated. While at a rhetorical level, both men and women will invoke stereotypes regarding motherhood, apple pie and housework, in practice women do not want to give up the amount of autonomy that fulfilling these roles in a 'traditional' way would imply. Meanwhile, most men, those who have already been married for a while at least, tend to accept that in reality a full return to the home is no longer an option for women. As S., the head of the building firm, put it, 'I wouldn't be against my wife staying at home. But the time has already passed, and it's too late. Of course, from the point of view of a quiet life – there wouldn't be any problems.' Clearly, however, there would be major problems for his wife, which is why he has had to accept that it is 'too late' to confine her to the home. Having tasted life outside the home she is not going to give it up willingly.

Conclusion

In terms of their relations with women, the male entrepreneurs interviewed were of the opinion that the ideal relationship was a hierarchical one in which they were in control. All the men studied went through a period of dependence on their wives as they adjusted to the post-communist environment, but they did not see this as a serious challenge to their belief in the traditional gender order, but, rather, as a temporary trial before moving to greater things. Thus, they all emerged from the experience with their views of the 'natural differences' between men and women intact. All of the businessmen now see themselves as the undisputed leaders of their families. What should not be forgotten, however, is the crucial role of women in maintaining this system of beliefs – the men are only heads of the family '*so to speak*' because of the wives' support, and their ability to turn a blind eye to the occasions when the men's rhetoric does not match the reality.

With regard to their relationship with other men, the businessmen studied expressed a desire to escape the hierarchy of the past, to feel freer. But in practice they are creating a new hierarchy in which success as an independent player is crucial. Notably, K. who felt very attached to one of the few non-hierarchical spheres of Soviet society – tourism – had managed to take control of his firm, destroying the collective culture which had existed at the beginning. This gulf between discourse and practice serves to highlight the fragility of masculine identity – which needs to be constantly asserted, often in the face of all the evidence.

Notes

1 My analysis of masculinity has been heavily influenced by the work of Robert Connell. He argues that the concept of masculinity is 'inherently relational', in that it 'does not exist except in contrast with "femininity" ' (1995: 68). He also talks about hierarchies of masculinities, again taking a relational approach, arguing that while one form of masculinity may gain a hegemonic position at any given moment, this is always contestable (ibid.: 76).

2 I have previously worked as a researcher for a project headed by Daniel Bertaux, one of the pioneers of the life history method. For an account of his method and examples of its application see Bertaux (1981).

3 On entrepreneurialism and masculinity in contemporary Russia, see Kornilova (1997) and Chirikova (1997: 114). On the historical aspects of the issue, see Tokarenko (1996).

4 It is interesting to note that it appears to be the case that once women begin to earn money, many of them seem to behave in exactly the same way as the male breadwinners: they do not disclose the true level of their earnings and they do not pool all of their resources. They also indulge themselves, albeit in a different way to men.

References

Bertaux, D. (ed.) (1981) *Biography and Society: The Life History Approach in the Social Sciences*, Beverly Hills, London: Sage.

Chirikova, A. (1997) *Lidery Rossiiskogo predprinimatel'stva: mentalitet, smysly, tsennosti*, Moscow: IS RAN.

Connell, R. (1995) *Masculinities*, Cambridge: Polity Press.

Kornilova, T. (1997) *Diagnostika i motivatsiyagotovnosti k risku*, Moscow: IP RAN.

Tokarenko, O. (1996) 'Russkie kak predprinimateli (istoricheskie korni ustanovok i povedeniya)', *Mir Rossii*, 1: 195–207.

6 The changing representation of gender roles in the Soviet and post-Soviet press

Irina Tartakovskaya

The aim of this chapter is to analyse the changes in gender roles as presented in Russian newspapers in the Soviet and post-Soviet period. Why newspapers? I strongly support the arguments of my colleagues in this volume that the Soviet state played a significant role in the framing and constitution of gender roles. Correspondingly, the collapse of the Soviet system had an immediate impact on gender relations in Russia. In my opinion, the newspapers provide a good illustration of the nature of these processes, since during the Soviet period they presented the only absolutely official position on any social issue and were a mouthpiece for the normative, or as I prefer to call it, 'legitimate discourse' of the Soviet regime. Newspapers in post-Soviet Russia are now independent, but they still serve as a mirror of dominant gender stereotypes of various kinds. This chapter is therefore a comparison of gender representations in the Soviet and post-Soviet era.

For my research, I chose three of the most well-known and influential Soviet newspapers: *Izvestia*, *Komsomol'skaya pravda* and *Sovetskaya Rossiya*. In order to chart the changes that have occurred within Russian society, I studied issues of these papers from January and February 1984, and then looked at the same papers in the same months thirteen years later in 1997. Since the collapse of communism, all three newspapers have preserved their leading position in the Russian media: *Izvestia* has become the most influential liberal newspaper; *Komsomol'skaya pravda* has remained the most popular youth newspaper; and *Sovetskaya Rossiya* has become the largest opposition newspaper (it is the official paper of the Russian Communist Party). My research was done in two stages. First, I conducted a content analysis of the papers, noting how much attention was devoted to different gender-related issues. Second, on the basis of this preliminary analysis, I carried out a more detailed examination of the types of representation found in the papers.

Preparing citizens for a life of service: newspapers in 1984

The Soviet media was strongly unified in terms of values and all the newspapers were essentially tools in the same ideological system. Certainly

there were subtle differences in the positions of Soviet newspapers, but nevertheless their general characterisation of the role of men, women and the family was very similar. What the papers had in common was the assumption that the 'higher goal' of individual men, women and their families was to assist in the building of communism. Given that the achievement of communism was supposed to be in everyone's interest, the papers assumed a congruence between state and society: to serve one was to serve the other. And what state and society needed above all was for citizens to reproduce, work, and to live orderly, functional private lives which did not distract them from the fulfilment of state tasks.

At the same time, however, the papers had different visions of the optimal arrangement of gender roles required to promote state ends. *Izvestia* journalists generally wrote optimistically about 'normal' hard-working families with several children; in the main, they endorsed those gender roles which were considered to promote functional families. *Komsomol'skaya pravda*, on the other hand, had a slightly different vision. The accent of the paper was on the lives of women, and in particular single worker-mothers. The prominence of single female heroines in *Komsomol'skaya pravda* suggested that devotion to the state and love for the individual man was not something that could be easily combined. At the other end of the scale, many of the stories in *Sovetskaya Rossiya* seemed to point to the idea that the needs of the state could be reconciled with traditional familial relations in which the man retained his dominance. Such differences serve to highlight the various strands of Soviet gender politics, as well as revealing some of its key unresolved tensions.

Izvestia: *the family as the primary cell in communist society*

All the articles in the 1984 editions of *Izvestia* are informed by the notion that individual aspirations must be shaped in accordance with state priorities; however, this is viewed as being fully compatible with personal fulfilment. The paper does not see any conflict of loyalty between the family and the state: rather, the family is viewed as a building-block of Soviet society, and hence loving spouses and parents serve to strengthen the foundations of communism. In the paper, there is little emphasis on the idea, popular in early Bolshevik ideology, that close personal relationships are a distraction from more serious political and industrial tasks. Within the bounds of the Soviet family, love is permitted and even endorsed, although even in *Izvestia* it is not considered a private matter.

The first duty of Soviet couples was to reproduce, and this is a recurrent theme throughout articles in the paper. Having children is portrayed as the greatest happiness in that it answers both individual and social needs, as can be seen in the following announcement:

In a family of knitters from the Riga factory 'Sarma', Ausma Straum and her husband Yura recently gave birth to triplets – two boys and a girl. The birth of triplets is a great joy for the family and all the inhabitants of Riga. The Straum family babies are receiving special care and attention. Every day they visit experienced medical workers. The parents received one-off financial assistance from the state. The executive committee of the Proletarian district has provided them with a newly built flat with all amenities.

(*Izvestia*, 1, 1984)

This story highlights two very characteristic positions taken by the paper: first, that to have lots of children is a cause for celebration, and second, that it is not the private concern of the parents, but a matter for wider society, which takes part in the celebrations over the births and provides for the family. The article notably pays more attention to the actions of the authorities in response to the births than to those of the family itself. The attention devoted to the care of the state is quite deliberate. In contrast, stories about the West emphasise that the individual is left to fend for her/himself under capitalism. A typical story, for example, concerns one 'Janin Shtoker, another addition to the ranks of the unemployed. Her husband ended up in prison for theft, which he resorted to having despaired of providing for his wife and daughter in a normal way' (*Izvestia*, 2, 1984). The implication of such stories is clear – while Westerners are forced into crime simply in order to survive, the Soviet state looks after its citizens. Even unexpectedly having triplets thereby becomes 'a great joy'.[1]

With regard to relations within the family, *Izvestia* generally endorses an egalitarian domestic division of labour: as one wife, quoted approvingly by the paper, puts it, 'My husband and I never calculate who does what: whichever of us can helps the other with their load' (*Izvestia*, 9, 1984). The paper writes in the same vein regarding the upbringing of children. For example, in an article entitled, 'A literal paradise', a proud mother explains, 'I leave Vanya in charge of the home without worrying. ... He cleans the floor no worse than me, and can cook like a girl.' The phrase 'boys must receive a masculine education' does occur in the article, but within the context of the piece, it seems as if this refers only to participating in sport. Moreover, the article stresses that 'Boys ... can do everything in the home: cook dinner, knit warm clothes, help with tidying up' (*Izvestia*, 9, 1984). In the same article, a general recipe for bringing up 'good children' is deduced: 'It can be traced back to certain common features: two-parent families, with two, three, five children, working parents. And the majority have a respectable home, strengthened and warmed by the love of the mother and the father for each other, and for their grandmother and grandfather's generation.' This is *Izvestia*'s version of the ideal family of the 1980s: respectable, large, with working parents and capable, independent children. There appear to be no conflicts in such families.

It should be stressed, however, that the egalitarian emphasis of *Izvestia*'s prescriptions is openly instrumental. Women need help in the home so that they can go out to work, at the same time as being mothers to 'two, three, five' children. This instrumentality is starkly revealed in the paper's discussion of childcare. Here, the primacy of the state's demographic and industrial needs is stated outright. For example, an article stressing the need for high quality pre-school childcare, argues that kindergartens 'help to resolve not only social, but also economic, problems. Ninety-eight per cent of the women in the town work in factories, in various establishments and organisations. And so every day spent looking after a sick child translates into a straightforward loss in the volume of production, in its quality' (*Izvestia*, 30, 1984). Childcare is regarded as necessary, not so much to allow mothers the choice of working, but so that production, along with the birth rate, is maintained.

The same applies to questions of personal relationships: individuals must give priority to the needs of society (which in the Soviet ideological system corresponded to the interests of the state). This can be seen, for example, in the paper's discussion of the issue of divorce, in an article entitled 'A different life':

> Happiness in personal life – in reality it is far from a personal matter. If a mistake has occurred, if a marriage breaks down, a person shouldn't remain on his own. It is necessary, absolutely necessary, that he has a second, different life. It is a question of the interests of society.
>
> (*Izvestia*, 9, 1984)

It is not in the interests of society to have lone adults within its ranks – society is interested in reproduction and in families, which also serve to keep citizens under control. The article cites a number of letters by way of example, the message of which is that when a marriage collapses the noble person will let her partner go without undue fuss: 'I have lived with my husband for forty-three years, but if our relationship suddenly broke down, I would wish him happiness.' It is worth noting that the letters cited are exclusively from women. It is precisely from them that such self-sacrifice is expected in the name of the happiness of the former spouse, and, ultimately, in the name of society.

While 'positive' characters tailor their lives to serve the greater good, negatively portrayed characters are egotistical and overly concerned with appearances: they lack the serious devotion to state tasks which distinguishes the good citizens. This is well illustrated by a story about a dispute between a divorcing couple over the division of a flat. The ex-husband of the story is an invalid. 'The doctors diagnosed second category invalidity.

In the same year my wife divorced me,' he complained to the journalist. 'Why are you throwing away seventeen years spent together?' asked the journalist, 'was there really no love, no respect between you?' ' "Yes", Raisa [the wife] stated decisively, "he wasn't to my taste. Why did I marry? Out of stupidity. He was insistent and I gave in. ... And now what's the point of ruining my life?" ' There follows a series of heart-rending details: Raisa and her sister had beaten the husband and had made him sleep on bedding on the kitchen floor. The most striking thing is the description of the appearance of the anti-heroine, the wife: 'she stands before me in a victorious pose, stately, beautiful, fashionably dressed. At that moment a thin man with deep, sunken eyes enters the room. The charming smile disappears from my interviewee's mouth, and she sends out an evil look' (*Izvestia*, 23, 1984). In line with Soviet tradition, the key external signifier of Raisa's dubious status in this passage is that she is fashionably dressed.[2] It is noteworthy that in this case it is not implied that the invalid husband should allow his ideologically challenged wife to have 'a different life'.

It can be summised, then, that the good citizens of Soviet newspapers had two foils – Soviet villains and Western victims. While well-ordered Soviet families were portrayed as the norm, with a few negative examples thrown in for didactic purposes, the implication was that a happy family was impossible under capitalism: only under communism could family life be joyful and meaningful. This is supported by the *Izvestia* story, 'A mask for the death factory':

> In Komiso, a small, but well-known Sicilian town, located near an American missile base, the first marriage between a local girl and an American serviceman has been announced ... Komiso appears to public opinion in a completely different, unusual light, opening up a tempting future of personal happiness and material prosperity for the local population.
>
> (*Izvestia*, 7, 1984)

The author does not openly state that the marriage is one of convenience, but it is clearly seen as inappropriate, as obscuring the 'true' situation. Indeed, the suggestion is that the only way for benighted Italian citizens to achieve 'happiness and material prosperity' is through marriage to agents of an imperialist 'death factory'. Once again, this is in marked contrast to what is portrayed as the fate of Soviet citizens, where 'a literal paradise' can be achieved with a little bit of male co-operation on the domestic front.

Komsomol'skaya pravda: *married to the state*

Komsomol'skaya pravda shared many of *Izvestia*'s key assumptions regarding the duties of Soviet citizens, but it none the less took its own distinctive line. *Komsomol'skaya pravda* was a youth paper with a romantic, melodramatic tone. Whereas *Izvestia* was pragmatic and firmly grounded in the present, *Komsomol'skaya pravda* harked back to episodes of the glorious past, such as the Great Patriotic War. The fact that as late as 1984 the newspaper should devote a significant amount of space to discussing the war is at first sight perhaps slightly unusual. However, the explanation lies in *Komsomol'skaya pravda*'s status as a youth newspaper, its message being that 'your parents sacrificed themselves for the mother-land, and you should do likewise'. The fervour of the paper, and its backward-looking stance, had implications for its presentation of gender roles: did those who were truly devoted to the state have room in their lives for significant others?

The typical heroic protagonist in a *Komsomol'skaya pravda* story was female, an activist who revealed her high moral quality through her work for the state. The paper was especially fond of the heroic single worker-mother: indeed, it seems as if the patriotic devotion of these heroines is so intense that it could not be combined with love for an individual man. Of course, this was not openly articulated, but was revealed in the news-paper's choice of topics and the context in which the heroines were situated. For example, a long article was devoted to the work of a brigade of female lumberjacks during the war:

> Nobody, not the dawn nor the light, witnesses how the brigadier herself, Ul'ka, gets up. She is not even 20 yet – probably she would like to sleep too ... At the end of the shift not a cry or a wheeze, but a groan goes up. Oh, my friends, you poor things ... the thin Maria is on the verge of collapse. Their men are soldiers, the women worked in the rear for the front. ... Anastasia is a strict woman; she doesn't allow weakness. Although the sweat pours into her eyes, she still hurries everyone along.
>
> (*Komsomol'skaya pravda*, 9, 1984)

The article concludes with a romantic idealisation of the typical postwar figure of the widow, focusing on the experience of 'strict' Anastasia: 'I sat on a stump and wrung my hands. The war was over, and I had no one to wait for.' At the end of the article she is transformed, in the author's eyes, into a truly epic figure: 'I close my eyes and see: she unties her widow's scarf and it drops down onto her shoulders.' Once her scarf is untied Anastasia's headgear resembles that of the famous Soviet poster of Mother Russia: in the fitting expression coined by Barbara Heldt, she undergoes a process of 'iconisation' (1992: 160). If the ideal women in *Komso-mol'skaya pravda*'s world are akin to the archetype of Mother Russia it is clear why they are alone: men cannot approach such women; Mother Russia needs no husband.

In stories like that of Anastasia, the absence of men can be explained by special circumstances such as the Second World War, but even long after the war single women made frequent appearances, not simply in the guise of war widows, but also as positive Soviet role models such as shock workers and political activists. Lyuba, a member of the Komsomol, is a typical example:

> One day Starodubtsev [the chair of the local collective farm] noticed her, energetic and exuberant [*boevuyu i bedovuyu*]. She had been elected secretary of the Komsomol farm committee. ... Although her daughter is less than a year old, not a meeting goes by without Lyuba. The door of her flat is never locked. It's not for nothing that people fondly call Lyuba 'our deputy'.
>
> (*Komsomol'skaya pravda*, 8, 1984)

The heroine had to be completely devoted to her electorate, and to renounce entirely her privacy and her personal life: her door was never locked. Despite her selflessness, Lyuba is not treated by the author as a victim, she is happy: 'A few minutes later the platform applauded. Lyuba embraced her daughter, with tears in her eyes. From emotion and joy.' The article mentions Lyuba's daughter several times, whom she takes for walks around her native farm. 'They say to her "Why are you freezing your child?" and she jokes, "Let her get used to it." And drags the sledge to the farm.' The father of the child is never mentioned. From the context it is clear that he plays no role in the life of Lyuba and her daughter: it seems that the relationship between Lyuba and the state is so all-consuming that there is literally no room for anyone else. Her walks with her daughter are also symbolic: she is clearly being prepared for the same work and the same destiny – 'let her get used to it'.

In contrast to this self-sacrificing behaviour, the youthful villains portrayed by *Komsomol'skaya pravda* are hedonists. They have a pragmatic 'consumerist psychology', which leads them into illegal behaviour. The typical anti-hero is a young black-market dealer trying to lead a 'beautiful life'. It must be said that, judging by material presented in *Komsomol'skaya pravda*, black-market traders and those fond of the 'high life' (*khailaifisty*), in contrast to shock workers, live intense personal lives. The disapproving tone of the following comment in one article is typical: 'On that evening Irina B., a young housewife with a diploma in Soviet retailing, didn't go to drink coffee and dance in the bar. But, as always, people there were expecting her' (*Komsomol'skaya pravda*, 9, 1984). Black-market traders are used as signifiers of wrong-doing – they do not live lives which Soviet citizens would want to emulate. In terms of gender relations, their main crime is 'sexual dissipation'. The following account of the sexual practices of a black-market trader provides an example of the tone of such remarks:

He remembered something about what they, Asen and two girls, whom he had never met before, had got up to. And later they repeated that evening more than once – they changed only the partners. For the sake of [fashionable] clothes Dima spares nothing and no one. Even his bride. Poor Tanya!

(*Komsomol'skaya pravda*, 9, 1984)

Tanya is, ironically, referred to as the 'bride' of the black-market trader, when in fact they are only living together. Dima calls Tanya his wife, but the story makes it clear that only the Soviet marriage registry (ZAGS) has the authority to declare couples husband and wife. Tanya is purely incidental to the main story – Dima's economic activity – and appears in it only to draw a moral lesson. The story delivers two mutually reinforcing messages: the black-market trader's dubious moral status is underlined by the fact that he is living with a woman, unmarried, and is cheating on her with whoever happens to be available, while at the same time the unacceptability of such practices is underlined by their perpetration by an anti-Soviet element. Such distractions undermine the harmony of Soviet society. Moreover, it is clear that people with such torrid private lives would not have time to defend the Motherland, save the harvest, or to meet the plan.

Sovetskaya Rossiya: 'Where the needle goes the thread will follow'

Like *Izvestia*, *Sovetskaya Rossiya* perceived the family as a key institution in Soviet society. Indeed, it was portrayed as an almost quintessentially Soviet formation – only in the Soviet Union would the interests of society tally with those of the family. This idea was manifested in a letter to the paper which asked: 'Does President Reagan have a family – mother, wife, children, – and if he has them, how do they take the fact that their son, husband, father plans to kill all the planet at once, [and] all humanity on it?' (*Sovetskaya Rossiya*, 1, 1984). The fact that the letter hinted at the treachery of imperialist fathers and husbands was particularly telling, for *Sovetskaya Rossiya* had a distinct vision of the family: one in which the man was at its head. The families portrayed by the paper were all highly traditional – single-parent families were very rarely mentioned. The paper had a masculine tone, and it seems that its vision was tailored for a largely male audience.[3] The terms 'master' (*khozyain*), 'head of the family' and 'strong' (as an adjective applied to men) featured prominently in the newspaper's discussion of relations between the sexes.

The following example serves to highlight the well-defined terms on which men were allowed to assume a commanding position in the family. It comes from a description of a family of Second World War veterans, and begins with a harassed wife preparing dinner:

'Blow! The *pelmeni* [ravioli] is completely overcooked. What a hostess, they'll say!' And a second later she was bustling in the kitchen ... The restless hostess does most of the talking. The head of the family, Grigorii Grigor'evich, is mainly silent. Or in two or three words he confirms or clarifies what his wife has said.

In this article, the relations between men and women are clearly specified and delineated. The saying, 'where the needle goes the thread will follow' is repeated several times. The key ingredient for a happy family life is identified as being a wife who is prepared to follow her husband unquestioningly: 'without discussion Matrena Egorovna got ready for a long journey'. Although the 'thread' may be legitimately devoted to her needle, however, the real man has other priorities. As does Grigorii Grigor'evich: ' "Because of his work," Matrena Egorovna [said] with a playful wink, "he was the last in the settlement to hear about the birth of his youngest son, imagine!" ' (*Sovetskaya Rossiya*, 1, 1984). The last detail reveals that everything is in its place: for real men work in the service of the state is the primary meaning of life; the family comes second. As a shock worker quoted in the paper puts it, 'only an involved and self-confident worker can be the head and master of the family. Wives love us when we are strong, what if not work keeps us together?' (*Sovetskaya Rossiya*, 9, 1984). Thus, men only acquire the status of legitimate heads of the family under certain conditions. Their position is dependent on their devotion to work, and is not acquired by virtue of their sex alone: a man has to earn his wife's respect by being an 'involved and self-confident worker'. Meanwhile, the implication is that really strong men, such as Grigorii Grigor'evich, probably do not have much time for domestic concerns: indeed, absent fatherhood is all but endorsed by the paper.

Thus *Sovetskaya Rossiya* allows space for masculine strength and dominance within the familial realm. But the role of the wife is not to be devoted to her husband *per se*, it is to assist him in his capacity as a worker. This is revealed in the story of a different family, this time of a middle-aged couple. The head of the family is the chair of a collective farm, and his wife is faced with the question of what her role should be:

'What does a husband-leader need?', advised her experienced well-wishers, 'A strong home front! [*krepkii tyl*]. So that when the husband comes home in the middle of the night, the wife, with a towel in her hands, will lead him to the chair and brush the dirt from his collar. So that the husband can lead, without looking back towards home.' Tonya thought and pondered and increasingly rejected [the idea of] that kind of home front for her husband. Even if Vitya comes home tired and hungry, she reasoned, all the same he'll soon want to talk, perhaps to share some of his doubts and troubles. And what can a housewife talk about – about saucepans, jam and pickles? The first

time she'd keep quiet, the next, he'd brush her away and stop confid-
ing [in her].

(Sovetskaya Rossiya, 15, 1984)

Finally, Tonya goes to work as a brigadier, helping her husband not only
at home, but also on the collective farm. And then everything is put in
order. The grateful husband says, 'If it wasn't for you I wouldn't have
managed.' At the end of the article, the writer slips in a reference to
the two teenage daughters of the couple, who regularly wait for them 'on
the porch of the house until sunset, but often they fall asleep while they
wait'. How the girls spend their time during the day and what they eat is
not explained. This is not treated as a problem: on the contrary, it is
presented as another element of the family idyll.

This article has a message for both men and women. It implies that men
should accept women's work, indicating that this will lead to a more
fulfilling relationship: housewives can't relate to the world of work. At the
same time, however, it is careful to show that work is a sphere of
legitimate male dominance: Tonya the brigadier is firmly cast in the role of
assistant. For the female reader, the message is that though she should
support her husband, she too has a higher mission in the world of work.
She should be careful to contain her aspirations, however – only the
subordinate woman worker could serve a husband and the state at the
same time. This is a consistent message of the paper. Although the paper
occasionally presents female heroines, they are always in a secondary
position to men.

Fractures in the idyll

The papers from 1984 have a great deal in common, but their differences
are instructive. While all shared the idea that individuals should subordinate their private aspirations to the needs of the state, there was some
confusion surrounding the appropriate relationship between men, women
and the state. The problem was that the state was so demanding: it wanted
men to be devoted workers and soldiers, while women were required to
work, reproduce, and ensure the smooth-running of the domestic sphere.
As the concern over the birth rate and labour productivity in the late Soviet
era revealed, neither men nor women were managing to live up to these
expectations, and thus solutions, models of correct conduct, had to be
provided. None of the papers under review came up with anything very
convincing. *Komsomol'skaya pravda*'s implicit answer was for women to
dispense with men. In keeping with the romantic and rather juvenile tone
of this paper, the state was implicitly portrayed as a jealous and all-
consuming partner: the devoted comrade-heroine had no time for a
husband or lover. Nevertheless, she managed to derive some form of
'higher' happiness from her lonesome labouring – a kind of joyful,

transcendent tearfulness was her lot in life. While such ideas may have been capable of inspiring readers of the 1920s and 1930s, by 1984 this was hardly a realistic or an appealing vision of gender relations. As the desperate attempt to discredit the behaviour of characters such as Irina B. and Dima revealed, the ethic of self-sacrifice – so central to the task of building communism – was being eroded by the individualism of the younger generation.

The gender relations portrayed in *Sovetskaya Rossiya* seemed designed to appeal chiefly to men. A man was allowed to be master in his own home, but only on condition that he proved himself at work. He also had to take care to avoid becoming embroiled in such 'trivial matters' as his children, saucepans and pickles. While this may have been an attractive vision for some men, it put a heavy burden on women's shoulders. The silent but dominant man of *Sovetskaya Rossiya* needed to be looked after – he was unable to perform his role in the public sphere without the help of a supportive wife. In order for husband-leaders to flourish, women had to accept their subordinate status in the home and the labour market. They too were to be careful of the seduction of pickles and the like – they might at any time face a journey. What a wife had to do was find a way to facilitate her husband's work without losing sight of her public duties.

Izvestia was the most optimistic of the three papers: it pointed the way to a radiant future in which the worker-mother's load would be lightened by the 'helpful' son or husband. Of course, the ultimate responsibility for the home would still rest with the woman, but the 'good' man would assist her. The main tension in this vision was between the family unit and the state: it was always necessary to stress that the happiness of the model families was bound up with their relationship to the state. The catch was that it was precisely the demands of the state that rendered the achievement of private happiness so problematic.

Paradise lost: 1997

All the papers from 1997 reflect a world in which gender relations are in flux and old certainties have dissolved. Just how this is portrayed depends on the political affiliation of the paper. For *Komsomol'skaya pravda*, the new freedom is challenging and exciting. Freed from their debt to the state, men and women are able to pursue their own affairs with romantic abandon. Their lives may sometimes be stormy, but they are none the less full of interest. *Izvestia* views the retreat of the state in a more sober light. It portrays a world of gender conflict, a Hobbesian nightmare in which brute strength prevails. *Sovetskaya Rossiya*, meanwhile, is even more gloomy. Families have lost their purpose in the post-communist world, while personal happiness is all but impossible now the state has reneged on its responsibilities.

Izvestia: *women as victims*

Gender relations are not a priority for *Izvestia* in 1997, but there are usually one or two articles which relate to this topic per issue. The paper tends to portray gender relations between men and women as conflictual, and within the sex war men are the stronger party. Women are presented as helpless victims, incapable of defending themselves against masculine cruelty or violence. This is a major preoccupation: 37 per cent of the coverage dealing with women for the two months studied portrays them as victims.[4] Such stories occasionally portray women as victims of the state, but this theme is far more common in *Sovetskaya Rossiya*.

The theme of gender conflict is not limited to the discussion of individual relationships, but appears in accounts of wider social confrontations. These are often presented in a gendered form, in which men appear as bearers of brute force and women as representatives of deprived strata of the population. An example of this is provided by the article, 'Try complaining once you've been killed', in which a band of gangsters terrorised the personnel of the shop Moda ['Fashion'] and crippled the female director of the shop. The meeting of the shareholders' society is described in the following manner: 'Around the frightened women were armed people. This is your new director – they motioned towards a young man' (*Izvestia*, 20, 1997).

Even where women appear as aggressors, or murderers, the tone of the commentary tends to be sympathetic, with the events being presented as an 'objective tragedy' in which no one is really guilty. This can be seen in the story of Russia's 'first' woman killer, the milkmaid Marina, who was sentenced to seven years in prison for carrying out a contract killing. The tone of the newspaper was one of forgiveness: 'She felt very sorry for her neighbour, who had troubles with her good-for-nothing husband. He had a criminal record, he abused his wife and her old mother' (*Izvestia*, 14, 1997). Thus, Marina, by agreeing to kill her neighbour's husband for a fee, is presented almost as a defender of justice. The basis of this moral position is clearly the assumption of female helplessness: the implication is that women need to defend themselves using whatever means are available.

In contrast, 60 per cent of the articles which have a male protagonist show them in a negative light. The main characteristics of those negatively portrayed are the use of *mat* (the Russian sub-language of curses), drunkenness and hooliganism. Male murderers are usually written about in an impassive fashion, and their personal characteristics are not explored – their actions are left to speak for themselves. The only exception to this are the most extreme criminals, including murderers, who, like women, tend to be characterised as victims. Often those deemed to be 'responsible' for their degeneration are women: bad mothers, cheating girlfriends, and so on. For example:

His first desire to 'try out a virgin' arose after the first night of his marriage: his wife turned out not to be a virgin. Nearly all of the latest maniacs have recalled details of their undeserved sufferings, sometimes dating from earliest childhood. Sooner or later, against the background of sexual disenchantment [and] a distorted understanding, an exaggerated feeling of injustice is transformed into a monstrous subconscious revenge complex. Burstev was his parents' fourth child. After an unsuccessful abortion, the mother gave birth to her unwanted son prematurely. When Roma was still in nappies his older brother had already been to prison twice ... – for sexual assault.

(*Izvestia*, 11, 1997)

Articles such as this one reveal that the virgin/whore dichotomy is alive and well in post-communist Russia. 'Bad' women, like Eve, are responsible for men going astray. Meanwhile, 'good' women are treated as innocent imbeciles, destined to be perpetual victims at the hands of crafty, rapacious men.

Taken together, the articles in *Izvestia* in 1997 describe a sex war in which it is difficult to find a good man, and where women are nearly always the losers: its portrayal of gender relations is pessimistic. Women are described in a way which evokes pity for the cruel, inhuman situations in which they find themselves. And although the heroines of *Izvestia* are independent, modern, professional women, such as the artist Tat'yana Nazarenko and the singer Alla Pugacheva, the attitude towards them is ambivalent. This pessimism clearly stands in stark contrast to the idealistic views of the paper in 1984.

Komsomol'skaya pravda: *romantic and sexual liberation?*

Of the three newspapers, *Komsomol'skaya pravda* devotes the most attention to gender relations: the topic features in every issue. A great deal of this – 21 per cent – is presented in the form of articles about the lives and loves of the famous. The picture that is presented is very different from that of *Izvestia*: rather than concentrating on the opposition between the sexes, *Komsomol'skaya pravda* deals mainly with their relationships, sex and the family. Sex and eroticism are prominent in the paper: sex even turns up in stories in which it is entirely unrelated to the main theme. For example, an interview with the Cuban high-jump champion Sotomaier, which was mainly devoted to sport, had the headline, 'I really want a Russian woman' (*Komsomol'skaya pravda*, 8, 1997).

The treatment of the family in 1997 issues of *Komsomol'skaya pravda* is very different from that found in the paper in 1984. The family is portrayed as an arena of stormy encounters, where divorce and infidelity play a prominent role. Divorces are mentioned one and a half times more frequently than marriages. The tone of the paper remains romantic, although it is now less sentimental and more action-oriented. One of the more dramatic 'family' articles, for example, concerns the ritual of 'bride snatching'. Since the collapse of communism this custom has been resurrected in Tartar villages in Mordovia in central Russia. *Komsomol' skaya pravda* reports this practice in the form of an individual drama, the tone of which is ultimately light-hearted:

> The strangers waited for their victim in the car; the girl had no time to squeal, and found herself on the back seat of a car with her arms and legs bound. Local lads don't waste time on courtship. If a beauty doesn't want to get married they will take her by force.

The incident that is described here is actually a rape and kidnapping. But the author of the article sees things differently:

> 'Usually they make a fuss for half a year and then they get used to it,' smiles Ibragimych, an expert in the art of abduction. He himself 'got' a wife from Saransk [the capital of Mordovia] – where they also perform abductions. First he hid her in the village ... and then gave her a choice: either you try on your wedding dress, or you can return to your parents with shame. Ravila decided not to take the risk. And now she already doesn't complain about life: there are nice guys even among abductors.
>
> (*Komsomol'skaya pravda*, 7, 1997)

The male journalist identifies with the abductors, suggesting cynically that violence can mark the beginning of a happy family life. This is an extreme example, but milder forms of such chauvinism are characteristic of this paper.

Along with sex, which in the Soviet period was a 'prohibited form of representation',[5] gender relations are portrayed mainly in the form of romantic love. The editors of *Komsomol'skaya pravda* appear to be particularly fond of articles about, or interviews with, famous bereaved women such as, for example, Marina Vladi, Albina List'eva and Ekaterina Gordeeva. Each woman is presented as a tragic heroine whose life is now dedicated to preserving the memory of her lost man. Two of the stories serve to illustrate this point:

> The heart of the public belongs to the little figure skater, whose name always appeared alongside that of another [her partner's]. Fourteen months after the tragedy on Lake Placid, Ekaterina Gordeeva went onto the ice without Sergei Grin'kov ... She said on the evening of her new triumph: 'I wasn't alone today. I skated with Sergei.'
>
> (*Komsomol'skaya pravda*, 9, 1997)

Two years ago the life of Al'bina Nazimova was divided into two parts: 'before Vlad' and 'with him'. Now, after the death of her husband, she has entered a third phase in which it is as if she has to learn to walk again. Probably, that is why to a number of my questions Al'bina answered, 'Right now I don't know. I am still young. I'm only two years old.'

(*Komsomol'skaya pravda*, 17, 1997)

From these fragments it is clear that the representatives of 'undying love' are female: there are no similar stories about men in the paper. It is interesting that, as under communism, women are presented as capable of the highest devotion, the only difference being that the state has been replaced in their affections by individual men.

In line with this preoccupation with romance, when successful women are interviewed, the interview always serves to stress the importance of love and family for the heroine. Essentially what occurs in the pages of this newspaper is the marginalisation of women. This process, as Rhode has noted, arises from an unwillingness to recognise women as self-sufficient social actors, independent of their relationship to men (Rhode, 1995: 690). Thus, a woman in *Komsomol'skaya pravda* is always above all else a woman, and her most important characteristics are related to her romantic or sexual capacities. Correspondingly, women are presented as victims less often in the pages of *Komsomol'skaya pravda* – even in the story about bride snatching, the author manages to present the women concerned as romantic protagonists!

Men are generally described less often than women, and when they do appear they tend to be characterised by their actions. Meanwhile, of course, the state does not feature as a factor in gender relations which are seen as private relations between individuals (though individuals who may wish to share their stories with the public). Private devotion is approved of; indeed, love, sex and sexual attraction – rather than work and meetings at the collective farm – are seen as the very stuff of life.

Sovetskaya Rossiya: *grieving with the Motherland*

Gender relations are mentioned rarely in the pages of *Sovetskaya Rossiya*, which deals mainly with political topics. It is, however, the most consistent of the three newspapers inasmuch as its portrayal of gender relations has changed very little. There are only two significant shifts in its treatment of gender. First, the communist idyll has been destroyed and when the Motherland suffers, private happiness is impossible. Thus the modern women described in the pages of *Sovetskaya Rossiya* are usually dressed in black, and with their tragic appearance demonstrate that they are grieving with Russia. Meanwhile, the fact that gender relations are now mentioned very rarely is not incidental. The main site of 'gender relations' as far as

Sovetskaya Rossiya was concerned was the family. If in the past the family was a unit whose meaning was defined by the state, in an era when the state has become the ideological enemy of the Communist Party, the existence of the family loses its meaning.

As in the case of *Izvestia*, women are often presented as victims, but in this case, rather than being the victims of rapacious men, they are victims of the neglectful state which has reneged on its duties. A good example of the tone of the commentary is provided by the story of 'a woman worker at a technical college, who killed herself because of her lack of money and the impossibility of surviving' (*Sovetskaya Rossiya*, 15, 1997). The same article provides a compelling account of the collapse of the system of state provision in one of the cities of northern Russia and the consequences of this for women:

> Women wait as much as six months for the payment of maternity benefits or alimony. In the last five years not one healthy child has been born in our town. Not one! Pregnant women, those who still have the courage to have children, suffer from anaemia, blood disorders, toxicosis. Today even in the maternity hospital they feed them on watery soup, and they get no milk or meat.

In such stories women are not important in their own right, but only as a means of forwarding a critique of the existing government. This is highlighted by the conclusion of this article: 'In this way they are weaning us from the practice of having children, and killing the most important instinct – the maternal instinct, the loss of which inevitably leads to the destruction of the [Russian] people [*narod*].' Thus, the real victim identified by this piece is the Russian people. The article displays the traditional preoccupation with reproduction, although this is no longer conceptualised in terms of the needs of the state and society, but in terms of the Russian nation or people.

Meanwhile, the positive and negative role models provided by *Sovetskaya Rossiya* have also remained fairly consistent. *Sovetskaya Rossiya* has hard and fast rules. 'Bad' women are mercenary: 'A teacher of geography ... was left by his wife – "you can't make money", she said' (*Sovetskaya Rossiya*, 7, 1997). 'Good' women correspond to the traditional view of wife, mother and patriot. It is revealing that *Sovetskaya Rossiya*'s ideal Russian woman is a figure from ancient Russian history, the princess Irina, wife of the Kiev prince, Yaroslav the Wise:

> In her arteries flowed Scandinavian blood, because she was by origin a daughter of the Swedish king. However, on getting married to the prince and taking the name Irina she accepted Russia as her motherland with all her soul. The Norwegians tried to use her origin to get the princess to be a mediator between them and the Prince, but she

warned that she would defend her husband's interests. The princess raised seven sons and three daughters for Russia and all of them became zealous defenders of orthodoxy. Before her death she became a nun.

(*Sovetskaya Rossiya*, 19, 1997)

The features of the ideal woman are clearly identified: wifely loyalty, religious devotion, fertility, but above all patriotism. It is notable that the patriotism here is gendered: it is not patriotism towards her own country, but to that of her husband. Again, this article highlights the shift in emphasis away from duty to the state towards duty to the nation. In the post-communist era it is no longer possible for *Sovetskaya Rossiya* to promote loyalty to the state, but the idea of the Motherland and the Russian people endure and serve to fill the ideological void. In this sense, the gender relations described by *Sovetskaya Rossiya* still assume a triangular form in which the relationship between the sexes is subordinate to their relationship to the Motherland.

Conclusion

This study of the dynamics of gender representations in Russia has several important findings. First, the examination of the Soviet newspapers revealed the central role of the state as key actor in the Soviet gender system: relations between men and women were to be formed in accordance with the higher aim of serving the state. Meanwhile, in the contemporary situation in which the character of the state has been completely transformed – from watchful guardian, to rapacious animal – men and women have been left to their own devices, with the result that the gender system has been thrown into a state of flux.

In line with this, all three newspapers have transformed their approach. Rather than portraying orderly Soviet people who somehow manage to combine having five children with paid work, all the newspapers now depict a society replete with problems. Certainly, the colourful depiction of gender conflict in part is an attention-grabbing device designed to sell newspapers, but I believe that it also reflects social and normative changes.

Soviet newspapers reveal a sort of gallery of fantastic heroes, and particularly heroines, designed to show the working of the Soviet family – which was considered to be part of the state machine, along with trade union and Party committees, and other public institutions. The tension between 'communist' ideological values and patriarchal ones is clearly revealed by the different stances taken by the papers: were men to be helpful at home, or were women to be meek assistants at home and work? Could women serve men and the state at the same time? Was the Soviet family equipped to perform the tasks demanded of it? At the end of the Soviet era, the state had no clear answers to such questions.

In the post-Soviet period, however, the picture is even more complicated. First, there is no longer a state-imposed uniform set of norms and values. Now, not only is there no communality between newspapers, there is not even consistency in the pages of the same newspaper. The only paper which has retained a consistent ideological line is *Sovetskaya Rossiya*. The system of social practices which helped to uphold particular gender identities has collapsed, and 'alternative identities' have begun to emerge. Hence, the papers reflect conflict and confusion in gender relations, with sex acting as the main link between men and women. (Except in the case of *Sovetskaya Rossiya*, which implies that men and women should be united by the desire to serve the nation.)

None of the contemporary newspapers suggests a positive pattern of gender roles. Male dominance in the public sphere is still assumed: as has been noted elsewhere, after reading the press it is possible to come away with the impression that there are five times as many men in Russian society as women.[6] Meanwhile, however, the role men should play in the private sphere is still ill-defined. With regard to women, at best, the papers write about them with sympathy, as eternal victims. There is nothing in the papers which approaches a feminist conception of gender roles. In essence, post-Soviet newspapers exhibit a modified form of patriarchal ideology. They have moved from a state-patriarchal ideology to a liberal-patriarchal position in the case of *Izvestia*, to a hedonist-patriarchal leaning in the case of *Komsomol'skaya pravda*, with *Sovetskaya Rossiya* shifting to a more nationalist position in which gender relations are still subordinate to a greater good. None the less, what is now possible is criticism and deconstruction of these positions – something to which this article is a contribution.[7]

Notes

1 Similar stories about the grimness of life in the West can be found in the other papers. Not only did Western men have problems providing for their families, Western women were portrayed as plagued by worries. For example, an article in *Komsomol'skaya pravda* emphasised the fears of West German mothers: ' "What are West German women frightened of?", I asked a young German. "The constant lack of money, problems with apartments, and uncertainty. How will their children get on in life – that is what scares mothers" ' (*Komsomol'skaya pravda*, 9, 1984). Ironically, with the possible exception of fears over money and uncertainty, this could have been a description of the average Soviet mother's list of worries.

2 From the beginning of the communist era, fashion tended to be associated with ideological and/or moral infirmity. This can be seen clearly in Kollontai's novels, where 'items from the domestic sphere [such] as food, clothing and furniture can represent "bad" or "good" political ideas', with items such as soft carpets, chandeliers, lipstick and 'foods with a seductively bourgeois allure' belonging firmly to the 'bad' category (Ingemanson, 1989). In the post-Second World War era, such austere ideals were relaxed somewhat, to allow for what Vera Dunham has called 'the big deal' between the regime and the Soviet middle class (Dunham, [1976] 1990: 3–4), but, none the less, puritanism

remained a major feature of Soviet discourse until the end of the communist era. [SA]

3   The paper tended to portray men as inherently more valuable than women. At the level of the family, for example, one story dealt sympathetically with the plight of a family for whom 'one unpleasant fact had caused endless worry. There wasn't anyone to continue the family name. It had happened that only girls had been born' (*Sovetskaya Rossiya*, 11, 1984). The same prejudices came out in discussions of wider issues. Another article, for instance, lamented that 'today in schools there are no male teachers, and it has a strong negative affect on the state of affairs. If the problem of getting more male teachers into schools is not resolved, then no matter what measures are taken, they won't have the desired positive effect' (*Sovetskaya Rossiya*, 5, 1984).

4   The portrayal of Russian women by *Izvestia* in 1997 is very similar to the same paper's portrayal of female victims in the West in 1984.

5   For further discussion of this concept, see Schostak (1993: 89–112).

6   See Hogart (1997: 37).

7   My belief in the potency of such criticism is inspired by the work of Judith Butler (1990).

References

Butler, J. (1990) *Gender Trouble: Feminism and the Subversion of Identity*, New York: Routledge.

Dunham, V. S. ([1976] 1990) *In Stalin's Time: Middleclass Values in Soviet Fiction*, Durham and London: Duke University Press.

Heldt, B. (1992) 'Gynoglasnost: Writing the feminine', in M. Buckley (ed.), *Perestroika and Soviet Women*, Cambridge: Cambridge University Press: 160–75.

Hogart, M. (1997) 'Zhenskii vopros i stereotipy v sredstvakh massovoi informatsii', *Vy i My*, 1, 13.

Ingemanson, B. (1989) 'The political function of domestic objects in the fiction of Aleksandra Kollontai', *Slavic Review*, 48, 1: 71–82.

Rhode D. (1995) 'Media images, feminist issues', *Signs*, 20, 31: 685–710.

Schostak, J. (1993) *Dirty Marks: The Education of Self, Media and Popular Culture*, London: Pluto Press.

7 'My body, my friend?'

Provincial youth between the sexual and the gender revolutions

Elena Omel'chenko

This chapter is based on research into the phenomena and notions of modern gender relations and sexuality in Russian youth culture – both as media constructs and as individual versions, stereotypes and attitudes. Since 1997 I have been working on texts concerned with modern youth cultures and subcultures,[1] and comparing Western (mainly English) and Russian academic discourses on the changes that are taking place in youth cultures in the late 1990s.

Texts dealing with youth culture, although diverse in their quality and focus, constantly refer to the same notion: that of the 'new gender revolution'. However, only in provincial Russian life can this be seen as a 'new' or novel idea. In articles in 'new' Russian magazines,[2] the representations of social constructs of modern men and women are undergoing a fundamental shift. These changes include the means and forms of social and cultural expression of one's sex (male, female or 'mixed') and the symbols and signs which determine attitudes to sex and its socially acceptable manifestations. Russian modes of behaviour compete with Western ones; traditional ideas compete with shocking novelty.

Notwithstanding the great gulf that exists between the media portrayal of youth sexual practices and the reality of the situation, personal narratives give a no less contradictory – and no less dramatic – picture, exposing a battle 'for' or 'against' sexuality. In these narratives we see a conflict between the 'Sov'[3] vision and the new market vision, between Russian models of behaviour and Western ones, old (Soviet) norms of sex within marriage and 'new', more liberal, ideas. Thus, as in media discourse, individual histories offer a highly interesting picture of the formation of sexual identity in modern youth.

First, however, it is important to explain a little about the socio-cultural characteristics of the region of Russia of whose youth are the focus of this study. Provincial life in Ul'yanovsk is peculiar in that one single event remains as hugely significant in the post-communist era as under the old Soviet system: the fact that it is Lenin's birthplace. The ideological weight of the historical past and the pro-Soviet politics of the regional administration create a 'favourable' social climate for the survival and revival of orthodox

Soviet approaches to the upbringing of the younger generation. Economic activity in the city is weak, the level of foreign investment is low, and there are few cultural activities for the young to enjoy. Life in this region is quiet and sleepy, although less stressful, than in the country's major cities. Ul'yanovsk looks provincial not only in comparison with Moscow and St Petersburg, but even compared to Samara or Kazan'. I do not mean to imply that there is a gulf between provincial youth and their Russian and Western urban contemporaries, but it can be posited that such an 'exotic' social and cultural background as exists today in Ul'yanovsk is reflected in individual attitudes towards such a closed area of life as sexuality.

Subject, methodology and logic

The research presented here is the first stage in a study of youth identity, taking as its focus the formation of individual contexts of sexuality. The material obtained was very clear and rich, and in part this compensated for initial methodological errors. Seventeen gender-standardised interviews were carried out, as well as two control focus groups. Ten interviews were conducted with women (between the ages of 16 and 28; including schoolchildren, students and office workers) and seven interviews with men (between the ages of 16 and 25; including schoolchildren, students, postgraduate students and workers).

The course of the research itself led to the adjustment of a number of practices. First, after the initial focus group sessions it became apparent that this method would not provide the necessary material. The groups included men and women, and this hindered open conversation. Therefore, further mixed group sessions were stopped. Second, in order to carry out the gender-standardised interviews, young assistants were hired: women were interviewed by women and men by men.[4] Due to this method, I believe we received sufficiently truthful information from the respondents.[5] Third, as the interviews continued, mini-seminars were held with the interviewers in order to correct mistakes and to sharpen interviewing tools, as well as to discuss problems that had arisen.

The most interesting, although not unexpected, fact to emerge from the research study was that all the respondents greeted the invitation to talk about sexuality with enthusiasm. There was not one single refusal. On the contrary, there were requests to talk on this subject from people who had heard about our research, but who were not directly connected with the project. This highlights the lack of opportunities to discuss such an important and pressing topic for young people within Russian society.

The continuing research will be fruitful if certain methods that came to light during the first stage are observed (although it should be said that these are by no means new revelations): (1) young people must be interviewed by young people (to avoid the temptation towards moralising or edifying tones, on the one hand, and the 'pupil complex', on the other);

(2) men must be interviewed by men and women by women (to avoid ambiguity and to achieve greater openness and trust); (3) the interviews must be conducted one-to-one (to avoid, or at least reduce as much as possible, the chance of interviewees saying things 'for effect'); (4) the conversation should take place between strangers and people who do not live or work closely together (to observe anonymity); and (5) the selection of interviewers must be rigorous: they must be tolerant, gentle, not authoritarian or too forthright, and able to travel.[6]

Sex and Soviet society

Attempts to reveal the principles of how models of 'Soviet sexuality' are formed lead to the recognition that behind them lies a totalitarian interpretation of the Christian concept of the 'forbidden fruit'. Communist Party leaders had to know absolutely everything about their citizens, including details of their private life (both within and outside the family). A comment like 'that's my own business' was not seen simply as seditious, but was tantamount to direct ideological sabotage against the state. 'Personal business' could exist only in the form of a 'personal dossier': material about an individual that was collected and kept by state personnel departments and security agencies, and to which almost any Party leader or *nomenklatura* member could have access. These personal dossiers contained not only an individual's biographical history, but also personal, intimate information, as well as denunciations, anonymous letters, and complaints made by family members.

Submission to the unified will of the Soviet state was important not only for the implementation of direct policy: the state's power had to cover all spheres of life, from the public to the private. Thus, the sexual sphere, as the last refuge of individual choice and free will, remained under the most intent gaze of the ideologues of new morals and morality. Sex and sexuality, from an ideological perspective, were not only dubious and strange activities, but they were also considered shameful. The writer George Orwell's concept of 'double-think' in his book *1984* provides the best definition of this improbable congruence of sexual practices which were strictly forbidden by ideology and yet, at the same time, actually existed (and how could they not?). For 'respectable' Soviet people, the public took precedence over the private, whereas for 'non-respectable' people, all that remained was suicide, the mental asylum or cynicism – the latter, a characteristic trait of many high-ranking Party workers.

Sex and sexuality were expropriated for the benefit of the state. First and foremost it was to the state that women demonstrated their attractiveness: they sought to please it, to be beautiful for it, to be faithful to it and to raise healthy children for it. The ironic statement, 'there is no sex in the Soviet Union'[7] – with the negative connotations it now carries – arises directly from this belief in state control.

Towards a history of the 'sexless' society

> The new society can solve all problems apart from one: that of gender, the family, love, sex; and in order to make people live happily in this society all that can be done is to castrate them ... this is the extreme metaphorical expression of the absolute victory of culture, society and the state over the individual and his or her sex, personality and love.
>
> (Etkind, 1996: 134)

> Sexual attraction was dangerous to the party, and the party put it to work for itself.
>
> (Orwell, *1984*)

All revolutionary movements in the course of sweeping away the old world to make way for the new, unavoidably touch upon sexual relations. History gives many examples of attempts to liberate love and intimacy between partners from the constraints of traditional morals. The motives may have varied, but sexual decadence and permissiveness were among the first signs of the birth of the 'new world'. I. S. Kon gives a detailed picture of the development of ideological discourses on sexuality in his book, *Sexual Culture in Russia*. He marks out four stages in post-revolutionary history:

1   Up to 1930: the destruction of the traditional family and married life. The weakening of the institution of marriage, the weakening of restrictive sexual morals; legislative vagueness.
2   1930–56: The years of the triumph of totalitarianism, a strengthening of the institution of marriage and the family by means of state command-administrative methods; sexuality is suppressed, sexual culture is wiped out.
3   1956–86: Authoritarianism, a move to moral-administrative methods of supporting the family, a policy of regulating sexuality: the medicalisation and pedagogisation of sexuality.
4   From 1987 to the present: anomie and moral panic, the politicisation, vulgarisation, commercialisation and Americanisation of 'Sov' sexuality, the revival of sexual culture and the growth of sexophobia.

(Kon, 1997: 117–18)

Historical background to the origins of 'Soviet sex'

The main achievement of the revolution was that the 'people', including the young, started to treat the issue of sex and sexuality as one that had a serious bearing on the state, and were thus very receptive to the pronouncements of ideologues. These were varied, but the idea that came to dominate by the mid-1920s was that private sexual relations were a distraction from the class struggle and required regulation by the state.

Such ideas reached their apotheosis in Aron Zalkind's *The Revolution and Young People* (1924), in which he put forward his famous 'Twelve sexual precepts of the revolutionary proletariat'. A selection of his recommendations accurately reflects the Soviet regime's thinking on sex:

- There must be no early sexual life for the proletariat.
- Sexual restraint should be practised before marriage, and marriage should occur after the achievement of maturity (20–25 years of age).
- Sexual intercourse should be the consummation of deep feelings. A purely physical attraction is impermissible. ... Sexual attraction to a class enemy ... is a perversion, akin to sexual attraction to a crocodile or an orang-utan.
- The sexual act is the final link in a chain of deep experiences.
- The sexual act must not be frequently repeated.
- Sexual promiscuity should be avoided – one sexual partner is the ideal.
- The progeny must be borne in mind on each occasion of the sexual act.
- Sexual choice should be made on the basis of class and revolutionary expediency. There must be use of the weaponry of sexual conquest – coquetry, flirtation, courtship. These carry a class function, not a personal one. Class virtues, not purely physiological allurements, must be victorious.
- There must be no jealousy.
- There must be no sexual perversion.

With the possible exception of the references to class, this attitude towards sex survived up to the mid-1980s, and determined Party policy. A new construct gradually took shape: that of 'unhealthy sexual interests' – healthy ones simply could not exist. At the centre of the battle was the body. The new canon of the body demanded one that was completely prepared, perfect, self-contained, revealed from without and uncontaminated. Everything that emerges from and everything that disappears into the body was closed off, cut off. 'The standards of official and literary discourse which define this canon forbid everything connected with impregnation, pregnancy, childbirth ... everything connected with the incompleteness and imperfection of the body and its purely internal life' (Bakhtin, 1990: 335). The Soviet person had to be soulless and bodiless. The Soviet person raised to his or her social essence had no need of a body. Clothing in the Soviet unisex style hid the body, creating an asexual 'Sov' fashion.

Sexophobia was supported by homophobia. The All-Russian Central Executive Committee's Decree, according to which sodomy was a criminal offence, became law on 17 December 1934. Article 121 of the Criminal Code stipulated between five and eight years' imprisonment. An anti-pornography law, 'On Accountability for the Manufacture, Possession and Promotion of Pornographic Materials', came into force on 17 October

1935. The formulation of these laws was so vague that people could be sent to prison for the flimsiest of reasons. Both laws became excellent weapons for the repression of dissent.

There are no data available about the sexual behaviour of the Soviet people over a period of thirty-five years (from 1930 to 1965). In the late 1960s, however, sociological research slowly began to take place and specialist institutes were opened, and from 1970 onwards there was a serious shift towards the study of sexual attitudes. Some of these new tendencies were reflected world-wide; although 'over there' – in the West – the theme was open not simply for research, but for society to discuss, whereas 'over here' – in the USSR – the official versions remained as before, at the same time as real behaviour was beginning to undergo drastic changes.

Starting to talk about 'it'

The conceptual space that the notion of sexuality and its corresponding emotions occupy is not reducible to sex; that is, sexual reality is not simply individual physiological reactions and automatism. The aim of the research presented here was to discover (and in the transcriptions of the conversations, remain faithful to) the thoughts formulated by the respondents themselves. In the following sections, I attempt to reproduce the respondents' contexts of their concept of sexuality, which, unlike the results of quantitative research, is described qualitatively and without anatomical-biological bases. These parameters help us to remain within the boundaries of this space, and thus avoid the opinions of the young respondents being distorted by our own researchers' thinking and perceptions.

What is sexuality?

Women's opinions

> ... if you possess such a quality [sexuality], you can achieve the impossible.
>
> (Lyudmila, schoolgirl, age 17)

For the women respondents, sexuality is a personal quality; biological in its origin and social in its intensity and expression. Sexuality is genderless, but its manifestation in men and women is very different. The main focus of sexuality is the body, which is talked about with enthusiasm. Women's descriptions of sexuality are expansive and imaginative, and the most interesting and 'aesthetic' depictions are those in which women evaluate the sexuality of women. Sexuality is not viewed as a transient state of arousal. Sexuality is far removed from the ordinary concepts of 'beauty'; physical beauty is not as important as being atypical or 'unusual'. Sexuality is an invitation to make contact, to share, to be intimate, and in so doing, to engage in a form of spiritual intimacy.

Men's opinions

> Sex and sexuality for me are the same thing, there's no difference ... you know, a bloke and a girl sleep together.
>
> (Andrei, worker, age 21)

According to the opinions of young men, sexuality is a means to having sex: sex is a physical pleasure, and it is also for procreation. It is much more pleasurable to have sex with a sexual woman. The exhibition of sexuality is always connected with gender. In descriptions of female sexuality the clichés and stereotypes of super-models predominate. Conversations about male sexuality are extremely brief. The style of conversation tends towards the technical or functional.

Conclusions

Individual accounts of the concept of 'sexuality' are fairly contradictory and, on the whole, are almost identical with concepts of 'sexual attractiveness' or 'sex-appeal'; they remain on the level of descriptions of certain or other combinations of the external or internal qualities of men and women. Sexuality is a tool for establishing power between a man and a woman, although this power, according to our respondents, only applies to the field of gender relations. The body occupies the central place in perceptions of sexuality: for women this means an active, healthy body; for men, this means the body of a super-model. Both men and women took great interest in discussing female sexuality; or rather, the first and 'natural' association of the concept of sexuality is that of female sexuality. Sexuality is the ability to arouse, therefore it is female. A man (a 'real' man) is self-sufficient, whereas a woman must 'supplement' herself by the attention of men, by arousing them. For men the concept of sexuality is more functional, often being a synonym for sex.

Male and female sexuality: how they see each other

The analysis of respondents' narratives confirmed the well-known idea that perceptions of male and female sexuality are constructed around power relations within society. These constructs remain a 'male tool', which was explicitly and implicitly confirmed not only by the young men but by the young women too. A 'web' of secrets, taboos, prescriptions and stereotypes still surrounds many details and nuances of modern sexual practices. However, times are changing fast, and Russia's provincial youth no longer think of themselves as islanders, isolated from the rest of the world. Just like their counterparts in major Russian cities and in the West, they are striving not only to understand but also to articulate the problems which seem to them most pressing. The problem of sex and sexuality is one of those problems.

Sexuality: weakness or strength? Symbolic contexts

'Female' sexuality[8]

Some of the young women share the main belief of many of the young men: that female sexuality is a sign of women's derivative and dependent nature. With certain provisos, it is possible to be even more specific – sexuality in general (and female sexuality in particular, since it is, if not a synonym, then the first association of the concept of sexuality as a whole) is a symbol of submission. When our female respondents insist that sexuality is 'for' a man (by which they mean an actual or potential partner), then it is not a self-sufficient quality, but something which is attached to the attention of men. This is what the women had to say about female sexuality:

> When a girl is told that she's sexy, then it means she looks like she is able to arouse men ...
>
> (Veronika, student, age 21)

> Men are aroused by women's bodies. ... Everything that was attractive to men remains so: the breasts, the hips, everything connected with the essence of a woman primarily as a mother.
>
> (Irina, office worker, age 28)

> Only in his presence does my sexuality show through, I can feel it, even other men tell me this. ... In his presence I talk to people very easily, I make friends easily, I become sociable, I don't have any complexes at all.
>
> (Zhenya, office worker, age 23)

Here are the men's views on sexuality:

> ... for a woman it's a full figure, a narrow waist, I mean narrow shoulders and broad hips, and for a man the other way round. ... That's how I'd make the distinction.
>
> (Tolya, schoolboy, age 16)

> ... a girl in a see-through blouse, with no bra, her breasts, let's say not necessarily a flat-chested woman – that's one of the signs of sexuality ...
>
> (Sergei, worker, age 21)

... her figure, her legs, how she holds herself, how she walks, these are the main things ... her breasts, you know, how she stands ...

(Andrei, worker, age 21)

Sexuality is, I think, the attention we pay to a woman ... naturally, I would be much keener and would pay more intense and determined attention to a prettier sort of a woman.

(Nikolai, worker, age 20)

A woman's sexuality consists of her being how she is – because a woman can't possibly be better than a man ...

(Andrei, worker, age 21)

According to the opinions of our respondents, sexuality is ascribed to whoever is being chosen, not to who is doing the choosing, in other words, it is a sign of weakness. Sexuality, as a mechanism of self-presentation, self-promotion, is embellishment, play-acting, the portrayal even of those qualities and characteristics which are not present.

The women, like the men, are preoccupied with the reinterpretation and re-articulation of many of the notions underlying perceptions of female sexuality. Young women, albeit not particularly actively, are fighting for the right to leave the confines of submissive sexuality. It is interesting that both women and men, independently of each other, put forward the concept of a 'new' phenomenon: that of 'aggressive female sexuality', and, incidentally, both groups speak about it in a positive sense.

There is aggressive female sexuality: it immediately screens out men who aren't confident of themselves, and leaves only those who know what they want and what they can give. A look from these women is one that undresses you, an appraising look, almost like a man's look, only in the female manner, it's a piercing look, it must be straight in the eyes.

(Masha, student, age 17)

It should be stressed that it is not necessarily the case that behind this phenomenon lies a proposition to engage in direct sexual activity.

Male sexuality

The idea that the sexual quality of a person may be derivative gives rise to a vague 'discussion' among the young men. If sexuality is something which is female, then how can we talk of male sexuality? And if we can talk of such a thing, then in what terms and in what conceptual space can we evaluate this quality? The interviews confirmed the hypothesis that the concept of 'male sexuality' is now rapidly taking shape. And if at the level of the media the presentation of the constructs of male sexuality has already acquired certain acceptable forms, not only following Western models but also as a result of domestic youth cultural practices, then on the level of everyday practice it is only just beginning to emerge. Further, although a whole palette of modish patterns of male sexuality – all conforming to stereotypes – has already appeared, the question of how these can be adopted without destroying 'the image of a strong and dominant man' is still for many unanswerable. And if male (self-sufficient) sexuality is immanent to the male nature, as a quality of strength and a tool of repression and aggression, while female (questionable) sexuality demands evidence and clear manifestations, then how are we to evaluate displays of male sexuality?

This is what women said about male sexuality:

> ... it's widely held that if a bloke is a muscle-mountain, then he is sexy, but my boyfriend is shorter than me and we get along fine, we understand each other perfectly and I've got no complaints about him in bed.
>
> (Anya, schoolgirl, age 17)

> a hairy chest, a piercing gaze, one that undresses you, aggressive ... his look, and, of course, muscles as well.
>
> (Masha, student, age 17)

> I'm attracted to men who are morally stronger than me, there are men you can order about as much as you like, real wet lettuces. I don't think those people are sexy.
>
> (Anya)

> He's sure of himself, he looks you in the eye – everything tells you immediately that he's a man. All you are going to be is a weak subordinate woman.
>
> (Masha)

And this is what men had to say about their own sexuality:

> ... our appearance doesn't play a particularly big part, what matters is an attitude, a certain hardness, masculinity, basically, the normal traits which correspond to strong people, you know, there's got to be a certain power, potency.
>
> (Nikolai, worker, age 20)

> The manifestation of [female] sexuality is much more calmly accepted by society than the manifestation of male sexuality. ... A man always

runs the risk of being seen in a bad light – either as a womaniser or a homo ...

(Vladimir, postgraduate, age 25)

Changing perceptions of public demonstrations and private manifestations of sexuality

If male sexuality is self-sufficient, then why does it feel the need for public demonstration? Men's aspiration to be sexually demonstrative is roused by the growth in the popularity of public female power. The example of the huge success of the all-female pop group the Spice Girls has led to the birth of many dozens of domestic imitators, and the force of 'girl power' in the media has gained significant cultural ground. Such a social clarion call could not but help lead to the birth of a reaction in response. This 'discussion' is given particular intensity by the deep-rooted and outspoken reaction of men: that male sexuality is a sign of 'gayness'. A strong, self-assured and self-sufficient male has no need of any additional accessories and evidence. There are two barriers standing in the way of the formation of a commonplace image of male sexuality: sexuality as a symbol of weakness and submission and male sexuality as a symbol of 'irregular' sexual orientation.

A slighter, although historically more significant, role is played by another stereotype. The aspiration towards demonstrations of male sexuality is a sign of someone being a 'ladies' man'.[9] This epithet is not seen as offensive to men; on the contrary, this label was given to those men who were considered the successful and fortunate owners of a long list of 'conquests', and who enjoyed huge success among women. It would seem, then, that this type of sexuality has remained within the bounds of real masculinity acceptable to public opinion, that is, it may be termed aggressive, not arousing suspicions of weakness or submission.

The revelation of implicit (from the women) and explicit (from the men) homophobia is accompanied by (more often among the women) an ostentatious tolerance and even flirtation with bisexuality. Consequently, it could be argued that the 'promotion' of homosexual and bisexual ideas by contemporary youth magazines has been successful. The peculiar fashion for 'abnormals' has even reached the provinces. It is another matter that the reactions to this fashion are by no means straightforward, and this point is examined later in this chapter.

Conclusions

First, the analysis of their opinions of each other showed that male and female views practically coincide in terms of the fixed stereotypes expressed by each group. As young women invest men with an openly pragmatic approach to evaluating their sexuality, so young men, as though in response, demonstrate just such an approach. Second, when not examining their own sexuality through the eyes of the opposite sex, our female respondents became more subtle and imaginative. This confirms the hypothesis that perceptions of 'normal' (i.e. approved of by society) and 'abnormal' (i.e. disapproved of by society) manifestations of sexuality attached to one or the other sex only are undergoing fusion and distortion. And finally, in contradistinction to I. S. Kon's conclusion that sexuality in the public consciousness, and especially in men's own self-consciousness, is synonymous with masculinity, we can speak of the synonymity of a pair of concepts: masculinity – male sexuality, femininity – female sexuality.

Male and female sexuality: reflected views

In Tables 7.1 and 7.2, I have attempted to draw together the more significant views from the men's and women's – often vague – discussions on male and female sexuality.[10]

Table 7.1 Views on female sexuality

Key moment of discussion*	Women's views**	Men's views
Female sexuality	A means of arousing men and experiencing desire for them.	The attention a man pays to a woman.
The purpose of female sexuality	To arouse men.	To attract men's attention.
Dominant ideas	A beautiful body and self-sufficiency; pride and dynamic physicality.	Sexuality equals feminine beauty. Analogous to super-models or other stereotypical sex symbols.
Appearance and body	Sexual 'female' form: breasts, hips. Neatness, tidiness, taking care of the body. The main issue is not conventional beauty, but being out of the ordinary, even up to the point of having 'defects'. Tattoos and piercings are acceptable. PO: appearance is the determining factor, it shows the most important thing: refinement and sophistication.	A beautiful figure, not 'flat-chested': broad hips, full figure, narrow shoulders, slender legs, warm eyes, sporty build, figure-hugging clothing, a certain way of walking, suppleness. Tattoos and piercing unacceptable.

Key moment of discussion*	Women's views**	Men's views
Personal qualities	Self-confidence, freedom, complete harmony with one's own nature, knowing how to present oneself, eccentricity, being out of the ordinary.	Intellect, thriftiness, perception of one's own value, inaccessibility, knowing how to relate to people.
Behaviour	Ease of conversation, no hang ups when dealing with men. Graceful walk, suppleness, sexual 'touching' of hair. 'Activating' sexuality in the presence of men.	Constantly striving to attract men's attention. Flirtation, capriciousness.
Sexual types	1. Aggressive sexuality: actively choosing a sexual partner. 2. Non-aggressive sexuality: 'inner' female power.	1. Aggressive sexuality: provocative demonstration of sexual appearance. 2. Non-aggressive sexuality: defencelessness.
Asexual types	Feminists.	Feminists.
Phobias	1. Fear of 'not being in touch with new sexual ideas' (for example, homosexual and bisexual relations). 2. Mild homophobia.	Fear of appearing sexually inexperienced.
Symbolic meaning of sexuality	'Male' view of female sexuality: conscious submission plus hidden homophobia. PO: 1. Right of women to appraise female sexuality without reference to men: aesthetic view, distinct from aspiration towards sexual intimacy with a woman. 2. Sexuality 'for oneself': as an essential element of a woman's social status.	1. Female sexuality is a sign of submission to men's power. 2. Demonstration of a woman's sexuality 'for a man's sake' is a symbol of her weakness and derivative nature. 3. Winning a 'difficult' woman gives greater glory to the man. 4 Female sexuality is natural, given to a woman from birth, by her anatomy.

contd

Key moment of discussion*	Women's views**	Men's views
Contradictions	1. On the one hand: evaluation 'through men's eyes' (the main thing being to provoke desire in men). On the other hand: over-primitive male reactions to female sexuality ('the desire to screw her') are unacceptable.	1. The main contradiction is wanting a woman to be inaccessible, but also not unapproachable.
	2. Description of female sexuality 'through the eyes of men' – a simpler 'female' approach: more subtle and imaginative.	2. On the one hand, a woman's main aim is to attract the attention of a man; on the other hand, a woman shouldn't reveal everything, 'show all her charms', so that the process of (male) conquest is gradual and exciting.
	3. Against the background of homophobia, the desire to be 'up-to-date' with new tendencies (manifest bisexuality).	3. Ideal full figure versus sexuality of disproportion.

Notes:
* The table shows the different appraisals of the male and female respondents at different stages of the discussion on sexuality. The parameters were not selected *a priori*, but in accordance with the most significant emphases that emerged on analysis of the transcripts. I have tried to encapsulate the dominant views of the respondents on these issues. Where a more 'particular opinion' emerged, it is noted separately, marked 'PO'.
** The use of the terms 'women' and 'men' is purely arbitrary, since the age of our respondents varied from 16 to 28 years. I have decided, however, that it is possible to ignore age variations, because, at this point in the analysis, what is important are appraisals made regardless of age. The most significant differences were on sexual (gender) grounds.

Table 7.2   Views on male sexuality

Key moment of discussion*	Women's views	Men's views
Male sexuality	Strength, self-confidence, aggression, sexual skill.	Firmness of spirit, physical strength, imperiousness.
The purpose of male sexuality	To dominate women.	To demonstrate power and superiority.
Dominant ideas	Strong, piercing gaze, potent energy, ability to provoke desire to touch.	Strength, potency, absolute self-confidence.
	PO: 1. Muscles, height and hairiness.	
	2. Intellect.	

Key moment of discussion*	Women's views	Men's views
Appearance and body	Tall, hairy, piercing gaze, particular lip shape, dark eyes, firm voice, neat, tidy, arousing masculine body, nice hands, pure breeding. Absence of tattoos. PO: not a 'muscle mountain', but short: main thing is that he understands his sexual partner.	Scornful attitude towards the stereotypes of male sexuality 'through the eyes of women'. The most important thing is not a handsome appearance, but moral and physical strength.
Personal qualities	Intellect, sense of humour, knowing how to relate to people, capable of gentleness and spiritual intimacy. Inner superiority, moral strength, aggression.	Strong spirit, firmness, masculinity, potency, intellect.
Behaviour	Active, aggressive. A look that undresses a woman with the eyes. Ability to convey sexual energy.	High level of sexual activity (in the sense of activity during sex).
Sexual types	1. The aggressor: 'macho'. 2. The 'intellectual-verbal' aggressor, able to put women in a subordinate, weak position. Characteristic of evaluation of young men. 3. Partner: friend, soulmate. 4. Someone who 'looks after' (materially) his girlfriend. Characteristic of evaluation of older men. 5. The 'lost male': homosexual.	1. 'Normal' man: sexually active and experienced. 2. The 'romantic', 'brain-box' (understood that he is intelligent). 3. The 'bone-crusher', 'Arnold Schwarzenegger type' (understood that he is strong).
Asexual types	Virgin.	Homosexual.
Phobias	1. My partner being a 'little man'. 2. A 'macho-man'. 3. An 'alien' man: from subcultures (punks, hippies, etc.).	1. Open and aggressive homophobia: ability to appraise male sexuality is a sign of homosexuality. 2. Male sexuality is a sign of weakness, femininity.

contd

Key moment of discussion*	Women's views	Men's views
Symbolic meaning of sexuality	Male sexuality underlines women's subordinate position. PO: struggle against stereotypes of suppression. The main thing in a man is the ability to raise a woman socially and to be her social partner.	'Struggle' to attain male sexuality (different from female sexuality) within society without attracting negative evaluations as being a homosexual or a lady-killer.
Contradictions	1. Acceptance of aggressive verbal communication from men and the non-acceptance of obscene language. 2. 'Macho-man' and man as a friend. 3. Acceptance of suppression and struggle against suppression.	Criticism of women's perception of male sexuality (as romantic or macho), yet at the same time definition of male sexuality by reference to physical strength.

Note:
* The table shows the different appraisals of the male and female respondents at different stages of the discussion on sexuality. The parameters were not selected *a priori*, but in accordance with the most significant emphases that emerged on analysis of the transcripts. I have tried to encapsulate the dominant views of the respondents on these issues. Where a more 'particular opinion' emerged, it is noted separately, marked 'PO'.

The mosaic of new perceptions of sexuality

The changes in perceptions of gender are more noticeable in women's narratives, which confirms the hypothesis of their greater flexibility and mobility in taking on new ideas, as well as accepting new cultural and social conditions.

A central position in the mosaic of our respondents' 'ideology' of sexuality was occupied by the concept of virginity, around which discussions developed of the time and place of 'playing the virgin card', the preamble to and consequences of 'losing it' or 'keeping it'. Virginity remains a symbol of male supremacy. It is interesting to note that apart from the sole possible reading of virginity as the bride's absolute value within the framework of a patriarchal moral code, a new reading has appeared: that of virginity as an unwanted responsibility. The non-virgin will not only help her partner to avoid mistakes (an 'unexpected' pregnancy) but will also help him to understand the secrets of sexual pleasure.

He said to me recently ... 'So she isn't a virgin? Well, that's okay, it'll be easier.' I made a note of that for myself. So they're not really bothered ... love ... if they're really in love, well, they'll definitely want her to be a virgin. I asked my own boyfriend: 'What about you? ... What would you prefer?' And he said to me, to be honest, I didn't expect him to say this, 'I'd prefer you not to be a virgin.' Well, I just sat there ... I think, you know, he does love me, a little bit ... well, of course, I hid all this and just asked him 'Why?' And my jaw nearly hit the floor. 'Well,' he says, 'so as not to be responsible for it.' I just sat there ... The older they get, the more they value, you know, purity, you know ... I was reading an advert: 'Man, thirty, looking for a virgin girl.' Of course, they like being the first, but take the teenagers – what do they want with that? Of course, they won't send her packing if she's a virgin, that's easy to put right, but in general they'd rather she wasn't, so as not to be responsible for it. All the worry they'd have ... whether she's going to scream with pain or not: what do they want that for?

(Lyudmila, schoolgirl, age 17)

Male sexual activity in practice is not confined within marriage. Not just young men, but young women too consider sexual experience the main criterion of male attractiveness. Therefore, the 'male virgin' appears in the women's interviews as an undesirable sexual model:

... repressed [male] virgins don't do anything for me. ... A lot of people have a virgin complex. I've read a lot [of advertisements] in 'Speed-Info', especially from blokes: things like 'I'm twenty years old, I'm a virgin, please help me, I can't go on'. Well, of course, it's terrible, you know, it is a bit awkward ...

(Lyudmila, schoolgirl, age 17)

These harsh demands show a marked contradiction to young women's complaints to do with men's 'consumerised' attitude to them – no woman wants to become another 'notch' on her partner's bed-post. And men themselves in realising these expectations strive to achieve not just an increase in the number of victories, but victories that are worthy of their efforts: the more inaccessible the woman, the sweeter the conquest.

Women's strategies for winning a future husband are changing: the old notion of a woman who waits for 'Mr Right' is being usurped by an active search for 'not a husband, but a man'. One interesting yet paradoxical observation is that, on the one hand, the stereotype still exists that after marriage, the marital bed should be the only place for expressions of sexuality. But, on the other hand, almost all the respondents deny the possibility of sexuality continuing after marriage and starting a family. Children are seen as the main reason for the cessation of sexuality within marriage. Men and women both see the solution in activity outside marriage; although this does not mean marital infidelity, but, instead, means reaffirming one's attractiveness.

> ... she [my wife] already looks completely different, not the same bombshell, so to speak, she was, she's already mature ...
>
> (Aleksandr, student, age 20)

> Well in the first place a husband and wife's sexuality is fairly weakly expressed, as a rule, in most cases, that is, they no longer worry about it. It's just a formality ...
>
> (Tolya, schoolboy, age 16)

> ... a life full of colour disappears in marriage, when it all turns into a marital duty it loses its colour ...
>
> (Irina, office worker, age 32)

> ... it's not the same in a family ... the family cuts it down somehow. Sexuality somehow gradually disappears into nothing, and, for example, the husband won't let you look like, well, for example like I'm used to looking, sexy, let's say. He'd say, for example, put on a longer skirt, don't use so much make-up, why have you got so many buttons undone on your blouse? And gradually, by the time he's 60, he'll simply forget all about what sexuality is, and he'll never come up against it again in his life. He'll treat it as something sort of shocking, you know. Like our grandmothers do now, for example.
>
> (Lyudmila, schoolgirl, age 17)

> It's just that you get different families. You can have a family and go out on the side and be sexual.
>
> (Ol'ga, student, age 17)

> Although when your partner's not there, you can show off your sexuality, you know, give yourself a breather ...
>
> (Maya, student, age 21)

In these discussions, the grandmother is seen as the antithesis of female sexuality and as the symbol of asexual family happiness. When sexuality was understood to mean a direct invitation to have sex, the only place set aside for which was the marital bedroom, and the purpose of sex was to have children, then accordingly women who had lost their child-bearing capabilities (i.e. grandmothers) were seen to have lost their sexual attractiveness too.

Conclusions

The idea of 'virginity', one of the central concepts of the ideology of sexuality, has become imbued with new readings. In contrast to the belief that virginity is something to be treasured, some young people are of the opinion that it is an onerous and superfluous thing. An experienced sexual partner (both male and female) is seen as being more desirable, and sexual experience is becoming the main criterion of female as well as male attractiveness. Male and female sexual activity is no longer linked directly to sex within marriage; and what is important is not only the number of partners but also the 'quality' of conquests of sexual partners. The abatement of sexuality within marriage is 'helped' by activity outside marriage: activity which is no longer defined simply by the clear-cut notions of 'fidelity' or 'infidelity'.

Finally, men's and women's sexual strategies are beginning to change. Some women, no longer content to wait, have begun to search actively (and even aggressively) for potential husbands; conversely, for men, as well as the strategy of the active male hunt, the strategy of waiting for a sexually experienced partner has also emerged.

Parents and children: sexuality, a forbidden area or a frank conversation?

Sexuality is no longer perceived to be a secretive topic for conversation, and is treated by young people in a much more light-hearted way in comparison to the solemn tone struck by much of the media. Many respondents said that they discussed sexual issues openly and directly with people of their own age group (and most often of their own sex), and there were almost no areas which were taboo or secret. But conversation with parents is more difficult, and has to stay within the framework of the 'permitted' sexual code as laid down by each individual family.

> We've started to talk more openly about it. ... Before, sexuality was seen as something, I don't know, something shameful, forbidden. But now people talk freely about it, and being sexual is not a failing but a virtue.
>
> (Anya, schoolgirl, age 17)

> ... before we used to have this strict censorship, everything was cut, everything that had the slightest hint of sexuality. God forbid you'd have somebody raising their skirt, in a film or something, showing their legs – all that would be cut straight out, but now it's more re-laxed. It's [the] Western influence again.
>
> (Masha, student, age 17)

Many respondents (especially young women) talked about a gulf between them and their parents. Their parents would not initiate a conversation about sex or sexuality. The children themselves try to explain this by the fact that their parents were brought up in an era of strict secrecy, when the subject of sex was seen as indecent and forbidden:

> Parents don't want their children to know more ... to be able to talk freely about this with them, because the parents always seem to hide their own intimate relations ...
>
> (Anya, schoolgirl, age 17)

> Intimate relations between parents is something private, between two people. In our family it's not acceptable to think about what is sexuality. This is something that's left over from the period of stagnation.
>
> (Lyudmila, schoolgirl, age 17)

> Sex within marriage was understood purely as a sort of ... duty ... well, as a part of family life, marriage, that is ... before marriage all intimate relations were judged ... it was simply regarded as a marital duty, that they had to. ... Everything else ... outside marriage was simply called depravity.
>
> (Zhenya, office worker, age 23)

> ... at home, no way, in my home, no way, it's like a forbidden subject, it's not acceptable, it's a closed subject, basically it's something shameful, not like you see on TV. It's connected with ... how our parents were brought up ... with Soviet schooling ... where of course these ... things were regarded as something dirty, shameful and naturally weren't talked about. I think that even ... of course I feel embarrassed saying it ... I think that even in bed my parents ... are unable to express in words what they are ... doing, and aren't able to express what they want.
>
> (Irina, office worker, age 28)

For these reasons young people try to avoid discussing sex with their parents: 'That's the way we've all been brought up, to hide it from our parents.' According to the respondents, parents are simply unable to understand how someone at their age could be having sex. 'Parents are naïve, because they don't believe their daughter has a sex life, they think she's a little girl' (Anya).

It is probable that in the conceptual space of parents' understanding of 'at their age', the biological and social ages of the child are being confused, that is, parents are bewildered, not only by how people can be having sex at such a young age, but by how people can be having sex outside marriage. The parents are from a different generation and don't understand the demands of today's youth. Masha was surprised when she found out that her mother did not have sexual relations with men until she was 22: 'And I thought ... until she was 22, how could she? Is that how people lived?'

The fact that sex and all its manifestations are not discussed within the family does not mean that the children are not having sex; nor does it mean that their parents do not know: just that they prefer not to know.

> My parents were brought up in a family where, you know, 'there's no sex in Russia'. Well, they would never in their lives imagine that a young girl, that their daughter could sit here and calmly discuss sexuality in Russia. And if my father even suspected it, I don't know what would happen: shouting and screaming and a row with my boyfriend. He'd really be in trouble, big time ...
>
> (Veronika, student, age 21)

One female student described her strategy for playing along with her parents' expectations: 'well, even so ... how old am I? Seventeen and a half ... that's still the way we've been brought up: to hide it from our parents. I'm not going to go and say: "Mum, I've lost my virginity." ... I think that lies are better than the truth' (Ol'ga, student, age 17).

Despite the recurrent theme of families isolating their children from the subject of sex, and from sex in general, there are a small number of alternative family models. Several of the respondents said that in 'good' families, ones in which the parents show their feelings for one another, they can openly express their sexuality – and this gives the children great pleasure:

> They always loved that sort of thing, they still do, and it's a really good family. ... Sexuality is one facet of good relations between people, friendship, support. ... Their children have their own values, because they've grown up during *perestroika*. Children's attitudes to sexuality usually boils down to their treating their bodies as playthings, they don't usually discuss the subject with their parents. But I do discuss it. ... My parents talk about it lots and lots. They explained everything to me very clearly and even now they're always telling risqué jokes ...
>
> (Ol'ga, student, age 20)

Conclusions

Between young people, sexuality is not considered a forbidden or shameful topic. However, conversation on this subject with parents is determined by an accepted unspoken code of sexuality within each family. As a rule, children play along with parents' scenarios, helping them to maintain their own model of 'normal' sexuality. Parents, too, are often willing to play along with their children's efforts, not wanting to know the 'truth'.

Studying sexuality is fashionable

On an everyday level of consciousness, the concepts of 'sexual culture' and 'aesthetics of sexuality' have begun to take shape, a process which bears witness to the effectiveness of the mass of material in the media and literature exploiting this now economically profitable theme. Without exception, all the young people sought not only to demonstrate their high level of knowledge, but also to underline the fact that to be sexually illiterate is to be out of date: a knowledge of sexual trends and ideas is akin to knowing about new pop groups and music trends. In conversation, there was a recurring theme that many fashionable ideas do not simply 'appear' in the press, but are actually posited as models and examples to be imitated: sexual technique and sexual culture must be studied in order to keep up with the times and be sexually knowledgeable:

> ... the opinion today is that people should strive for that like they strive to get a good figure or a good education: they should also strive to be sexually attractive, that's more or less the attitude. In order to keep your status, your inner confidence, maybe some people just do it out of a love of aesthetics.
>
> (Ol'ga, student, age 20)

The changing interpretation of the semantic space of the word 'partner' is also of interest. This word is acquiring shades of a normatively significant social concept, connected to the presence or absence of sexual culture. One respondent, in an attempt to explain what 'partner' meant, sought help in the contradistinction of 'over here' (in Russia) and 'over there' (in the West): 'over there everyone tries to treat each other as partners. With mutual understanding and respect, even when they get divorced over there they stay friends'; whereas 'over here' things are seen as different: 'if people get divorced, then it's serious, for ever and for good. They were friends, now they're enemies for the rest of their lives.' This respondent linked the birth of a partnership culture to the positive influence of religion on children's upbringing, and to the fact that Western culture has taken shape over a longer period of time:

> Whereas over here everything's quick, hurried, one thing after another; the period they went through in a few decades, say, has happened in two or three years over here. Things are moving at a greater tempo and speed, headlong, so to speak, and that culture as such hasn't yet taken shape, the culture of good relations in sex.
>
> (Aleksandr, student, age 20)

None the less, he is optimistic, believing that there is a fairly large percentage of people who do want to be sexually literate, 'who want to acquire a certain knowledge of their partner's psychology as well as their anatomy. ... And I think society is beginning to realise that it isn't hereditary. ... That is, it's a product of upbringing. You have to cultivate sexuality within yourself' (Aleksandr).

Sexual culture is often linked with the shift from the individual (or private) expression to the public one. And opinions vary about the consequences of the legalisation of 'public' sexuality. Some young people think that this change will result in a degradation of Russia's sexual culture. While for Aleksandr the new culture is connected with the development of relationships between partners along Western and more 'educated' lines, things look rather different for Andrei: 'Before it used to be only at home, but now it's wherever you like, wherever you are, in the street, on the tram. Sex has now become completely uncultured' (Andrei, worker, age 21).

As soon as an understanding of sexual culture appeared, and along with it a system of knowledge and techniques, people were required to observe the rules. Here is one interesting example of a functional explanation of the importance of sexual changes (changes in sexuality):

> ... of course, it's much more difficult to maintain relations if they are already built on sex, if you don't observe the rules. That is, if you buy a car, then you've got to observe the highway code; if you have a special person and have a sexual relationship with them, then you've got to build your relationship properly, so that it doesn't lead to any harmful consequences.
>
> (Vladimir, postgraduate, age 25)

Conclusions

To be sexually educated and knowledgeable is considered fashionable in youth circles. In this respect, the media has played a major role in sexual enlightenment, often, according to the respondents, insistently positing role models borrowed from Western mass culture. The concepts of 'sexual culture' 'the culture of sex' and 'the aesthetics of sex' were used fairly frequently by our respondents, although exact interpretations varied widely. For some, they are synonyms of enlightenment, knowledge, literacy, while for others they are synonyms of degeneracy and debauchery.

The West's role in 'obtrusive and insistent' sexual education

The influence of the West is closely linked with the collapse of the USSR and the changes in the political system that have since taken place. This influence, to an incredible degree, has had both positive and negative aspects. On the one hand, all the respondents understand that without the 'interference' of Western culture, such a rapid process of sexual emancipation, education and enlightenment would not have been possible. On the other hand, the flow of information from the West brings with it something else (something 'dirty'), which is easy and profitable to sell on the new, sexually illiterate, Russian market:

> The reason the sexual revolution is happening is because over here ... all the information was banned. And then, I suppose with *glasnost'*, they let it [sexuality] out, and naturally it all came to the surface. Even all these, you know, minorities, for example, not minorities, but ... and of course that's the way it is over here, if they allow something, then it starts to take over completely and they start promoting it. ... Well, gradually, after a short time it takes root in your normal way of looking at things, you start to treat absolutely everything as normal.
>
> (Nikolai, worker, age 20)

Notwithstanding the youth of our respondents and their cultural and temporal distance from the Soviet era, they frequently spoke of direct ideological sabotage by the West in general, and by America in particular, which continues to be associated (at least within the framework of this study) with a heartless, mean-spirited, cruel world, as distinct from Russian, 'homespun' emotion, purity, sincerity and spirituality. Western sexual mores are seen as a deliberate ideological attack on Russia. 'They really push Western stereotypes, they place them at the top, and all this has come through to us' (Masha, student, age 21).

Therefore, it is considered very important that the state continues to monitor ideas of sexuality and to regulate foreign influences. A perception has taken shape of a 'homespun' Russian (meaning 'Soviet') sexuality: one which is pure and emotional, as distinct from the debauched and calculating Western sexuality. The most powerful channel of this ideological 'sabotage' is the mass media, and one of the most significant symbols of Western influence is the open and fairly insistent promotion of homosexuality.

This Western 'sabotage' can also be seen with regard to female sexuality, where, according to our respondents, the mass media's main theme is the presentation of women as sexual objects: 'Dress like this and this, and the men will be chasing after you' (Ol'ga, student, age 20). Young people are influenced by these examples because, according to the respondents, they are uncritical and ready to swallow everything that comes from 'over there':

> Young people today are passive: they don't want anything, they accept sexuality because they watch Western films. They see that you can, even that you have to, behave like that.
>
> (Lyudmila, schoolgirl, age 17)

Young people didn't use to talk about sex ... Now our young people are sexually literate. All they're talking about everywhere ... is that you've got to educate yourself sexually, especially condoms and that ... safe sex. ... And I just want to shout out: what are you playing at? Even in America the tide is already turning. More and more young women are remaining virgins. But over here that's all they can talk about.

(Masha, student, age 17)

Conclusions

Opinions about the West's influence on sexual education are contradictory, and can be summed up as: 'the bad influence of the good West'. There is a fairly widespread view that the West has carried out direct ideological sabotage, with the help of sexual education, which undermines Russian 'homespun' notions of sexuality. The main weapons in this war are the promotion of aggressive female sexuality and the sexual objectification of women. This propaganda has been possible due to the passivity and uncritical nature of Russian youth.

Nostalgia for social order

In a very similar way to their parents (only in different terms), young people display a nostalgia for social order and state censorship on questions of morality, ethics and sexuality. On the surface, this nostalgia is an unusual development, since the 'children of *perestroika*' have no obvious source from which to draw their ideas. Combined with this nostalgia is a strong desire for a model of 'correct sexuality', with the condition that this model should be a Russian one. There are fairly high expectations that explanations should come 'from above' (from the state) about what constitutes 'normal' sexual behaviour and what is debauched behaviour. The respondents feel that the political changes have affected, not sexuality and expressions of sexuality as such, but the system of control. This strange nostalgia for strict state policy on matters of sexuality was apparent in respondents of both sexes:

The whole country, the society is in a state of complete anarchy. There's no order. And although it is a fact of Russian life, I don't think people should use swear words. There should be censorship ... In Russia, in the pursuit, as they say, of profit, so to speak, in Russia now if you look at a profitable time-slot, most of the programmes and topics come from the West. And a catastrophic lack of direct attention is paid to the real problems of society, which are connected to sex and sexuality. Just where people need help, to explain everything, there's nothing.

(Aleksandr, student, age 20)

It is seen as important to address real sexual enlightenment: there is a need 'to explain to people what's what':

> There are, well, different people, so to speak, of a homosexual persuasion, so to speak, and then again, with lesbian tendencies. And if in the top universities and colleges students ... so to speak, have a good attitude to that, you know, approach things sensibly ... the middle class, you know, those with an average education – there it's still the law of the street, wherever you look, even in the capitals. Most children, whose parents don't really bring them up, they're just in a complete mess, in the big capital cities, in St Petersburg and Moscow. It's all linked to drugs, it all goes on in the cellars, in drunkenness, you're not going to find real love there.
>
> (Nikolai, worker, age 20)

It is not surprising that the overt promotion of homosexuality is seen as the main ideological weapon of the West. Most of our respondents were convinced that homosexuals were not born in Russia but had come to Russia from the West. The view is that Russian men are simply not capable of such behaviour.

> It's the influence of the West again, you get all sorts of people like homosexuals. I think it's the direct influence of the West, before, for example, I think, there simply weren't men like that in our country.
>
> (Lyudmila, schoolgirl, age 17)

Conclusions

All the respondents spoke in favour of state regulation with regard to what constitutes appropriate and inappropriate sexuality. In their opinion, models and patterns of behaviour need to be presented in order to educate people. At present, these models come from the West, whereas Russia needs its own models; ones which would take account of the specific nature of the Russian character and spirit, and its tradition of warmth and emotion. The most striking example of a Western model is, according to our respondents, homosexuality, which they do not believe occurs naturally in Russian society.

'Open' conversation about homosexuality

Conversation on the topic of homosexuality gave rise to many arguments and discussions. Heterosexuality, although still the sacred norm, is none the less becoming more of a grey area. Even so, same-sex relations remain for the majority of people a mysterious and scandalous thing; the life of so-called 'sexual minorities', and their peculiarly constructed relationships, their feelings, their appearance in public – their 'parallel existence' in society – is a subject of curiosity and fear. This fear is often connected with challenging beliefs in what is unshakeable and absolute, the loss of which threatens to destroy a person's world-view.

The sexual dichotomy, which in the opinion of the majority is a natural given, is defined by the fundamental conditions of sexual morals before, during and beyond marriage and the family. Female innocence, pre-marital courting and its rituals, the creation of a family, sex within marriage and the birth of children, bringing up children and observing their changes, remaining faithful, the symbolism of sexuality before and within marriage – all these points of reference are overturned by homosexual practices and thus are subject to doubt and criticism. According to one female respondent, 'homosexuals are lost males and females, over whom neither a man nor a woman will be able to exert their customary power'.

The respondents were clear in their demands for a simple definition of sexuality: either you are a man, or you are a woman. 'Unnaturals', as they are termed, are in a difficult spot: many of the respondents deny them not only acceptance, but even the right to have contact with 'normal' people. The young men are more categorical in their evaluation of 'non-traditional' male sexual orientations; they are more able to tolerate 'non-traditional' female (i.e. lesbian and bisexual) tendencies, but will not tolerate homosexuality:

I wouldn't like to see any 'gays', sexual minorities, as they call them. All that's unhealthy. If someone likes that sort of thing, then he should have an operation done.

(Aleksandr, worker, age 20)

But these queers, I sort of, sort of despise them, to be honest. You go and do what you want. I mean, if from the very first day, since you were 2 [years old] or something, you know who you should be, then be that, but then they start giving it this and giving it that.... That ___ for example [a famous designer and make-up artist] – he's obviously a queer, fuck that. No, I don't like it. Either be a woman or ... not...

(Nikolai, worker, age 20)

... talk to a homo – not on your life. Well, maybe if I met one on the street I could, but with real contempt. But to sit down and share a bottle and some bread and cucumbers, you know ... nah ... Not likely.

(Sergei, worker, age 21)

According to the respondents, sexuality is linked to the sex of a person 'by an iron chain': 'if someone wants to show their sexuality, then let them just show what sex they are' (Anatolii, schoolboy, age 16). This iron chain is formed by the limits, acceptable to public morality (that is, 'public opinion'), of one's own sexuality and the permissible reaction to the sexuality of someone else. As one man expresses it:

> What's sexuality for? To acquire a certain image ... glory. Well, not glory, that is in the first place it's so that among the other sex, among those who according to certain moral standards of society have the right to react to sexuality. That is, I mean, to put it simply, a bloke tries to attract the attention of women and vice versa. That is, it's aimed at women.

(Vladimir, postgraduate, age 25)

The comment was made fairly frequently that homosexuality was an illness which had to be cured. In one session, a young man even resorted to obscenities in an attempt to explain his attitude to homosexuals. This was not simply an expression of disgust, but a state of incomprehension:

> Masturbators, homos, queers. Fuck, where did they think up their names? Anyway, I think everyone in life should do what's normal ... everyone. What you need to do according to nature, then do it. But this lot fuck each other with their cocks, God knows what else they do....

(Nikolai, worker, age 20)

Homosexuals – gays and lesbians – are seen as a direct threat to patriarchal power relations because, for 'straights', they are outside the system: 'a homosexual is a person over whom I will never be able to hold any power ... a homosexual is a lost partner' (Irina, office worker, age 28).

On the one hand, all the respondents (particularly the young women) tried to seem enlightened and demonstrate a tolerant attitude to homosexuality and bisexuality. On the other hand, they distanced themselves from non-heterosexual relationships, at times appearing almost too zealous in their protests (God forbid anyone should think they too were ...). Therefore, although acknowledging the 'right' of people to have a different sexuality from their own, the young women made special reservations on this account (the public stigma is still strong) – sexuality is, of course, directed at the opposite sex: 'I can say that a woman is sexy without any ulterior motive. A bloke might ask me what I think of his girlfriend, and I'd say yes, she's sexy, without meaning that I want to sleep with her' (Anna, schoolgirl, age 16).

Some views, although not very frequent, were encouraging. Although here, too, slight adjustments – nods in the direction of 'public morals' – were unavoidable:

I think that any sexual behaviour is acceptable if the participants agree to it ... Therefore I don't agree with bestiality: a goat can't agree.

(Ol'ga, student, age 20)

A person has the right to sleep with whoever they want. I don't mean it doesn't make any difference. But they've got their reasons, it's their life. They can do what they like if it doesn't harm anyone.

(Masha, student, age 17)

Conclusions: new socio-cultural accents in the attempt to understand sexuality

Despite the fairly harsh evaluations of non-traditional sexual orientations, significant shifts are discernible in people's attitudes. However, for the present time at least, these are contradictory – which testify to new socio-cultural accents in the attempt to understand sexuality.

First, purely biological grounds, if they are acknowledged, in the opinion of many are simply the basic 'material' of personal sexual identities. Therein lies the reason for the change in the system of certain basic stereotypes, the most 'sacred' perceptions of anatomical and biological givens as determining sexual orientation. Consequently, the space allowed for medical evidence of the necessity to cure forcibly these 'pathologies' is shrinking. No less significant in the opinion of our respondents are social environment, trends of fashion, new information and trans-gender cultural borrowing.

Second, perceptions of permissible displays of male attractiveness are spreading beyond the bounds of the value space of 'gay'–'not gay', and together with this the 'gay'–'not gay' dichotomy itself is dissipating in the extremely varied mosaic of transient conditions, perceptions and relations. And although our (male) respondents held that gender definition (one's own attitude to one's sex) is the most important factor in sexual relations, our female respondents no longer see this as being so significant. The women's evaluations were more tolerant and less categorical: whereas the men demanded socio-cultural isolation for homosexuals, the women demonstrated an indulgent pity for the difficult life-scenarios of 'unnaturals', and talked of their 'asexuality'.

For both men and women, the main failing of homosexuality lies not in the inability of same-sex unions to bear children, but the fact that personal power and control is lost. Consequently, we can see a change here too: the main thing is not the encroachment on the norms of sex within the family, leading to the birth of children, but in the redistribution of power and authority within the sphere of personal relations. As Kon has argued (1988: 450), heterosexism and heterocentrism will be weakened when people begin to relate in a more free and tolerant way to their own sexuality. This is a long and difficult process, but none the less it is already under way. The foundation of tolerance is not sympathy (one can feel sympathy for the weak, the sick and the oppressed) but indifference (I don't care who you sleep with and in what manner) and respect for each person's right to individuality and self-realisation.

Meanwhile, perceptions of public standards of female and male beauty and sexuality are rapidly changing. The argument is not just about life-styles, clothing, and experimentation with the body form (male and female bodybuilding, slimming, make-up, hair-colouring, piercing and tattoos), but it is about the permissible limits of the use of public sexuality in order to achieve non-sexual aims. In the future it will be very interesting to analyse the changes in these perceptions, both within sexual relations (in the homosexual as well the heterosexual sphere) and in the professional arena: for example, in companies' personnel policy and in the personal careers of both men and women. It is interesting to note that in the Russian situation of the universal male 'boss', the issue of using sexuality as a career tool has traditionally only been examined with regard to women. However, young people are beginning to speak not only of new possibilities for men (two variations: the boss being a woman, or the boss being a man, but a homosexual), but also of new possibilities for women (the boss being a woman, but a lesbian).

> Well, if a girl wants to build her career on her sexuality, then accord-ingly her boss will have to be either a young man, or if the boss is a woman she will have to be a lesbian. Don't you agree? I mean, sex is supposed to bring people together. And by virtue of that their relations are going to be different.
>
> (Sergei, worker, age 21)

The prospect of Sergei's fantasy being realised opens up the possibility of a whole new era of gender relations in Russia.

Notes

1 I am presently preparing a course on 'Youth cultures and subcultures' in the series 'Specialised courses in sociological education' (with financial support from the EU TEMPUS/TACIS programme, project JEP 08517–94).
2 Previously, I carried out comparative research of sexual discourse in three magazines: *OM*, *Ptyuch* and *Rovesnik*. See Omel'chenko (1999).
3 The Russian word *Sovkovyi* has been translated here and elsewhere as 'Sov'. *Sovkovyi* is a colloquial word which essentially means 'Soviet', but carries negative connotations because of semantic links with *sovok*, meaning dustpan or shovel, and implies something which is poor quality or second-rate.
4 This proved effective. None the less the issue is still unresolved as to how truthful were the young men when talking to men, and the young women when talking to women, about issues of 'non-traditional' orientations. We may have confirmed the same 'normal' orientations in carrying out discussions with same-sex groups.
5 I am grateful to the following for their help in carrying out the discussions: G. Sabirova, I. Fliagina, E. Smirova, D. Filatov and D. Belozerov.

6 We did not carry out any analysis of ethnic diversity. We plan to rectify this evident failing in our ongoing research, this stage of which took the form of a pilot project. The Ul'yanovsk region is a multi-ethnic one, and in order to achieve more accurate results with regard to the analysis of individual sexual identities according to ethnic and religious specifics (the difference between Muslim and Orthodox traditions), this needs to be taken into account. In the future this list will therefore be augmented by a need to maintain ethnic homogeneity between interviewers and respondents.

7 This phrase came into widespread use after the consternation it caused when it was said by a Russian woman, in response to being pressed about sexual issues during a live TV link-up in the early days of *glasnost'* between a group of Russian women in a Moscow studio and a group of American women in the US.

8 Here we are reproducing the formulation given by the respondents. Their formulation was of 'male and female sexuality', although of course it would be more correct to speak of the sexuality of men and the sexuality of women.

9 In ordinary Russian speech this term was applied to a man who constantly changed (female) sexual partners, both before and during marriage. The women 'flocked', so to speak, to these men. It does not imply that these men were physically attractive, but rather had what is known as 'sex-appeal' and could consider themselves local sex symbols.

10 This approach helps to make clear the differences and similarities in how the respondents see each other, although it must be pointed out that it is helpful because both groups of people were talking of different people, although bearing in mind their own examples.

References

Bakhtin, M. (1990) *Tvorchestvo Fransua Rable i narodnaya kul'tura sredneve-kov'ya i Renessansa*, Moscow: Khudozhestvennaya literatura.

Etkind, A. (1996) *Sodom i Psikheya: Ocherki intellektual'noi istorii Sepebryanogo veka*, Moscow: Its-Garant.

Kon, I. S. (1988) *Lunnyi svet na zare*, Moscow: Olimp.

—— (1997) *Seksual'naya kul'tura v Rossii*, Moscow: O.G.I.

Omel'chenko, L. (1999) 'Ot pola k genderu? Opyt analiza seks-diskursov molodezhnykh rossiiskikh zhurnalov', in I. Aristarkhova (ed.), *Zhenshchina ne sushchestvuet: Sovremennye issledovaniya polovogo razlichiya*, Syktyvkar: Syktyvkar University Press: 77–115.

Zalkind, A. (1924) *Revolyutsiya i molodezh'*, Leningrad.

Index

abortion: in post-Soviet era 42; in Soviet era 9, 14, 32–3, 33–4, 39
Afghanistan: contemporary gender politics 25n
Agricultural Workers (Kapusto, Yu.) 15–16
Akiner, S. 4
All-Russian Central Executive Committee: legislation on sodomy 141
Anthias, Floya 3, 4
Aristarkhova, Irina 5, 7, 13, 74–5

Bakhtin, M. 141
Batrak 77
Bebel, August 72
birth control: advocation of by Soviet state 32; inadequacy of Soviet provision of contraception 39; post-Soviet attention paid to contraception 42; *see also* abortion
birth rate: fall in post-Soviet era 22, 43–4; rise in Stalin era 32–3
black-market traders: as portrayed in Soviet press 124–5
the body: and concepts of sexuality expressed by post-communist youth 142, 143, 148; and sexuality in the Soviet state 141; woman's control over 40
Bolsheviks: anxiety regarding sexual issues 6–7; contradictions in approach to gender 14–16; early legislation on marriage and family 7–8; exploitation of women 3–4, 5; imposition of new culture in Central Asia 4; plans for child care and education 10–11; problematization of family 5; *see also* communism; Soviet state

Bragrazyan, G. 16
breadwinners (*kormilets*): men in Soviet era 18, 61, 65, 88, 91–4; men's loss of status as 96–9, 103; traditional idea of men as 91–2, 102, 115; women in post-Second World War era 17, 55, 61–6, 92; women in post-Soviet era 55, 66–9, 96–9; women in Stalin era 55, 56–61, 66, 69
bride-snatching: press stories of 131
Bukharin, Nikolai Ivanovich 4
business environment: men adapting to in post-Soviet era 109–10, 111–12; supporting role of wives 112–15

castration: symbolism of 23–4n, 103, 140
censorship: of sexuality 155; young people's nostalgia for 161
Central Asia see Soviet Central Asia
chauvinism: *Komsoml'skaya Pravda* (1997 issues) 131
Chechnya: mothers' campaign to stop the war 44–5
Chernyshevsky, Nikolai 110
child colonies: idea of 10, 31, 73
childbirth: as portrayed in Soviet press 119–20; press debate in post-Soviet era 41; and the Soviet state 35, 119; *see also* reproduction
children: Bolshevik idea of rearing as public matter 35–8, 39; crimes against and cruelty towards 38, 45; development of state nurseries 39; early Soviet legislation 7, 73; importance of grandparents in Soviet era 81; post-Soviet change in state's attitude 19; post-Soviet idea of father's role 42–3; press discussions on orphans and abandoned children